IS THERE A NUTMEG IN THE HOUSE?

Elizabeth David published eight books during her lifetime, from the evocative *Book of Mediterranean Food*, published in ration-bound 1950, to the masterly *English Bread and Yeast Cookery* of 1977 – both books being immensely influential in very different ways. In 1984 she published *An Omelette and a Glass of Wine*, which was the direct forerunner of this book: in it she allowed herself to look back on three decades of popular and successful journalism. Her last eleven years were taken up with the ever-expanding and never-finished project which, after her death in 1992, emerged as the scholarly social history of ice and ices, *Harvest of the Cold Months*.

The subject of two very different biographies and a major television programme, Elizabeth David continues to fascinate both her long-time devotees and also a younger generation discovering a *grand dame* of the past who speaks a language and conveys a message they feel completely at home with. Her writings testify to an inevitable gift of making her many passions, be they loves or hates, come alive.

Jill Norman, who created the Penguin cookery list and went on to publish and eventually write equally distinguished work, was Elizabeth David's editor and friend for over a quarter of a century, and is now the Literary Trustee of the Estate. She saw *Harvest of the Cold Months* through to posthumous publication, then persuaded many of Elizabeth's friends and enthusiasts to contribute notes on their favourite pieces for the anthology *South Wind Through the Kitchen*, and has here completed this last of the projects left unfinished on Elizabeth's death.

Jill Norman is an author in her own right, her most recent book being *The New Penguin Cookery Book*.

Elizabeth David

Is there a Nutmeg in the House?

compiled by Jill Norman

PENGUIN BOOKS

PENGUIN BOOKS

Published by the Penguin Group
Penguin Books Ltd, 80 Strand, London WC2R 0RL, England
Penguin Putnam Inc., 375 Hudson Street, New York, New York 10014, USA
Penguin Books Australia Ltd, 250 Camberwell Road, Camberwell, Victoria 3124, Australia
Penguin Books Canada Ltd, 10 Alcorn Avenue, Toronto, Ontario, Canada M4V 3B2
Penguin Books India (P) Ltd, 11 Community Centre, Panchsheel Park, New Delhi – 110 017, India
Penguin Books (NZ) Ltd, Cnr Rosedale and Airborne Roads, Albany, Auckland, New Zealand
Penguin Books (South Africa) (Pty) Ltd, 24 Sturdee Avenue, Rosebank 2196, South Africa

Penguin Books Ltd, Registered Offices: 80 Strand, London WC2R 0RL, England

www.penguin.com

Penguin Books Ltd, Registered Offices: 80 Strand, London WC2R 0RL, England

www.penguin.com

First published by Michael Joseph 2000
Published in Penguin Books 2001

5

Set in Linotype Sabon
Printed in England by Clays Ltd, St Ives plc

Contents

Introduction

In the early eighties, Elizabeth and I spent many very agreeable hours selecting the articles which appeared in her first anthology, *An Omelette and a Glass of Wine*, published in 1984. The kitchen in her house in Halsey Street may have been crammed with utensils of all sorts, but bookcases and shelves took up every wall in the other rooms and corridors overflowing with her substantial library of cookery, history, travel and reference books, and numerous files and folders of assorted papers. Out came the dusty files of articles written for the *Spectator*, *Vogue*, *House & Garden*, *Wine & Food* or for a wine merchant's catalogue. Most of this material was new to me: I had not seen the articles when they were first published and knew only from references in Elizabeth's books that some chapters were based on early journalism.

Our routine was to take a number of files each, select the pieces each found most stimulating, most expressive of the pleasures of good food, and likely still to appeal to readers, and then compare notes. It was one of the most enjoyable editorial tasks I have ever undertaken. The articles were a pleasure to read, and Elizabeth's reminiscences about the research and writing of many of them often kept us talking until late at night.

In the end we had too much material, and decided to put some pieces aside for a later volume. This, at last, is that volume: during the last years of her life, most of Elizabeth's energy went into gathering material for *Harvest of the Cold Months* which was finished after her death and published in 1994. By that time mountains of miscellaneous papers had been transferred from Halsey Street to our house, and only much patient sorting by my husband, Paul Breman, made it possible to assess their contents and select further material for this new collection. The articles Elizabeth and I put to one side sixteen years ago are here, but others were published later: scholarly and historical essays appeared in *Petits Propos Culinaires* and Mark Boxer persuaded Elizabeth to do a monthly column for the *Tatler* in the mid-eighties. Here she was free to write on anything that engaged her at the time: the potato as aphrodisiac, useless kitchen equipment like garlic presses, the travesties wrought by British chefs and caterers in the name of pizza or quiche, the story behind the Oxo cube. Often the basis of a piece would be a review of a recently published book.

Elizabeth always read widely in early cookery books in English, French and Italian and enjoyed trying out their recipes. Many of those which she adapted from well-known English writers have appeared in her English books, but here we have her versions of *Relishes of the Renaissance* from one of her favourite works, the *Opera dell'Arte del Cucinare* of 1570 by Bartolomeo Scappi, cook to Pope Pius V; notes on the ices recorded by Emy in *L'Art de Bien Faire les Glaces d'Office* in 1768; some simple vegetable dishes from Bartolomeo Stefani's *L'Arte de Ben Cucinare* (1662); and more articles about other writers – William Verral, master of the White Hart Inn at Lewes; John Nott, author of a dictionary of receipts of the late Stuart period; the enigmatic Countess of Kent to whom is attributed *A True Gentlewoman's Delight*; and the ebullient chef Alexis Soyer, nineteenth-century self-publicist who would have made some of today's television cooks look like mere amateurs.

In 1965 Elizabeth opened her kitchen shop and during the next few years published privately some booklets of recipes which were sold through the shop. *Syllabubs and Fruit Fools* and *English Potted Meats and Fish Pastes* were published in *An Omelette and a Glass of Wine*; parts of others are reprinted here.

During the twenty-five years I worked with Elizabeth she was constantly experimenting and trying out new dishes, sometimes for a book, sometimes because a food she or one of her friends particularly liked was in season, or because there was a dish she wanted to explore more thoroughly. When she was satisfied with the recipe and it was typed in its final form, it was her custom to give copies, usually signed and dated, to friends. Many subsequently appeared in her later books, but others which did not are included here. The folders from her house yielded many unpublished recipes, and occasionally accompanying articles. During the preparation of *Harvest of the Cold Months*, Elizabeth assembled a file of ice cream and water ice recipes. In the end, her curiosity about the use of ice took over, and the ice cream collection was not used. It appears here for the first time.

With very few exceptions, none of the material in *Is there a Nutmeg in the House?* has appeared in book form before. The notable exceptions are the essays on yogurt making, mayonnaise and poached eggs which she contributed to a little book called *Masterclass*, published in 1982 and long out of print.

Elizabeth's recipes were written as a text to be read, not as is currently the norm, a list of ingredients in the order to be used followed by a list of instructions. Usually the ingredients and quantities were given in the first paragraph, with the most important ones, and those for which you would need to go shopping rather than look in the cupboard or refrigerator, first. A short, straightforward recipe might simply begin with a combination of ingredients and instructions: 'Soak ½ lb of beans overnight. Drain them, put them in the jar with a half onion, a piece of celery, a clove or two of garlic, two or three leaves of fresh sage . . .' (Fagioli alla fagiolara toscana, page 75). No metric measurements were included in recipes written before the 1970s. When working on *English Bread and Yeast Cookery* Elizabeth decided that both metric and imperial measures should be used and her recipes have a paragraph of imperial quantities followed by one of equivalent metric quantities. For the metric measures the quantity was given after the ingredient. This follows the style of Eliza Acton in *Modern Cookery for Private Families*. Miss Acton wrote her paragraphs of ingredients and quantities at the end of her recipes after explaining the method. In recipes written in the late 1970s and 1980s or those translated and adapted from other sources Elizabeth adopted the same procedure. The recipes from that period included here have been edited to put the ingredients before the method for the sake of consistency.

I have tried to give approximate dates of writing for unpublished pieces and recipes, based on recollections of what Elizabeth was working on at different periods, on the style of writing, on whether or not she included metric measurements, and even on the appearance of the typescript (which often gave a clue to who had typed it).

Now that all our food is purchased in metric quantities I have given metric measures first in the recipes, and since we buy in quantities of 500 g or 1 kg, for ease of shopping I have used these measurements as the basis for conversion rather than the more usual (and accurate) 450 g to 1 lb. For the recipes in this book, the extra few grams is unlikely to make any difference to the success of the dish.

ACKNOWLEDGEMENTS

I am very grateful to Jack Andrews, Gerald Asher, April and Jim Boyes, George Elliot, Johnny Grey, Rosi Hanson and John Ruden who gave me ideas and encouragement, sent me cuttings of old newspaper recipes and copies of letters, notes and recipes they had received from Elizabeth. Jack Andrews also gave me copies of papers from the Estate of the late Lesley O'Malley. Elizabeth's nephew Johnny Grey also gave permission to use the plan and photographs for Elizabeth David's 'dream' kitchen.

Special thanks to Paul Breman for help with the organisation and selection, for typing almost unreadable photocopies of old newspaper cuttings and compiling the index, and to Jenny Dereham for her constant support and helpful suggestions and for her thorough and painstaking editing of a messy and complicated typescript.

Unless otherwise indicated, the drawings are by Marie Alix for *107 Recettes ou Curiosités Culinaires*, edited by Paul Poiret, published by Henri Jouquières et Cie, Paris, 1928.

Jill Norman, June 2000

Kitchens and their Cooks

The old brick-floored kitchen of the Sussex manor-house where I grew up with my three sisters is not a place I look back on with nostalgia. The cook and the kitchen staff had a hard enough time without small children running in and out getting under their feet, so if we were unwelcome there, that was understandable. Every day there were four separate sets of meals to prepare. For the dining-room, there was breakfast, lunch, tea and dinner. For the nursery, lunch and supper (breakfast and tea were made by Nanny and the nursery-maid); for the schoolroom, lunch, tea and a supper tray for the governess; for the servants' hall, breakfast, lunch, tea and supper. Everything was cooked on a coal-burning range, vegetables were prepared in the scullery, and throughout the day a massive black iron kettle was kept with water on the simmer for the cups of tea to be administered to any outdoor staff, such as the gardener bringing fruit and vegetables, or a stable boy who might drop in. There would also be a succession of van drivers delivering groceries and household stores from the town seven miles away, the baker and the butcher bringing bread and meat from the village three miles down the road, the postman with parcels, a telegraph boy with telegrams from the village post office. All would be offered tea, biscuits, bread and cheese, cake.

How, I wonder now, did anything at all in the way of formal meals get cooked in that kitchen, busy as it was all morning and afternoon with non-cooking activities? The answer, I think, is that, picturesque though it may all sound, most of the food which emerged from it was really very basic. We ate a lot of mutton and beef plainly cooked, with plain vegetables. The boiled potatoes were usually put through a device called a ricer so that they came up to the nursery in dry, flaky mounds. Vegetable marrows were yellow, boiled and watery. There were green turnip tops, spinach, Jerusalem artichokes, parsnips. I hated them all. Puddings weren't much better. Junket was slippery and slimy, jam roly-poly greasy, something called ground rice pudding dry and stodgy, tapioca the most revolting of all, invented apparently solely to torment children. The obligatory mugs of milk at breakfast and tea time were a penance, although hardly one to be blamed on the cook or any of the kitchen staff.

Presumably my mother, in league with Nanny, decreed those mugs of hated milk, and also chose to ignore the odious puddings and vegetables dished up for her daughters. Yet, as each of us in turn grew old enough to be promoted to grown-up tea, we discovered a rather different world. True to English country house usage at the time, tea at five o'clock was presided over by my mother sitting at the head of a long table, the silver hot water urn set over a spirit lamp and the silver teapot in front of her. There was a jug of milk, of course, but that was for visitors, because once we were out of the nursery my mother, who was nothing if not inconsistent, considered that it was wrong to put milk, not to mention sugar, into her fine China tea. Lemon, yes, but nothing else. I can't answer for my sisters, but I at least was more than thankful for release from the odious tea-time milk. Five o'clock food was nice too.

I don't remember anything spectacular, but there was always a spread of simple wholesome things, like thin bread and butter, scones, home-made jelly – crab apple, quince, or blackberry – cucumber sandwiches, a sponge cake. For special visitors there was usually a cake with a delicious orange-flavoured icing, one which must have been a house speciality, passed on from cook to cook. At any rate, I have memories of it all through my childhood and school holidays.

Today it is still a source of wonderment to me that anyone contrived to cook such faultless and delicate cakes in the oven of that old coal range, and for that matter how a cook could with one hand, so to speak, produce the abominable vegetables and repulsive puddings of our nursery days and with the other the refined cakes and beautiful jams and jellies. Looking back, I suppose that the simple explanation is that our nursery food must have been left to the kitchen maid, while the cook herself made the preserves and the cakes.

The orange cake wasn't the only good one I remember. There was a cherry cake and a chocolate cake – my mother was all her life a great chocolate fancier – and on one unhappily memorable occasion the family's golden retriever found his way into the larder and was discovered gobbling down the remnants of what had been an entire chocolate cake, fresh from the oven. Who had left the larder door open? Recriminations and arguments raged for days, the younger children were, as always, suspected, and the kitchen regions were more strictly than ever out of bounds to us.

Frankly, then, the kitchen of my childhood and the food it produced left few glowing memories. Another matter altogether is the illicit cooking that went on in the nursery. A sort of sticky fudge, which we called 'stuff' – it now sounds like some addictive drug – was one of Nanny's specialities. She cooked it over the nursery fire and gave it to us in spoonfuls out of saucers or soap dishes. Then there were mushrooms, gathered in a field close to the house – as children we knew very well where to look for the best ones – and carried back to the nursery for breakfast. Nanny cooked them in the good, thick cream which we had in abundance, and no mushrooms since have ever tasted quite so magical. In high summer there was the best treat of all, big fat red gooseberries, redcurrants and raspberries from the garden which Nanny used to throw into a saucepan with sugar, heat quickly over the nursery fire, and give to us then and there. This hot fruit salad somehow embodied the very essence of summer, and as everyone knows, the summers of childhood are longer and sunnier than those of later life.

When I was eighteen I left home and joined the Oxford Repertory Company as a student, sweeping the stage, making the tea (somebody had to show me how), occasionally taking small parts, understudying the bigger ones, and scouring the town for unlikely props such as the famous hatbox in Emlyn Williams' *Night Must Fall* (it contains a severed head, or so the audience is led to believe). I lived in digs in various parts of Oxford, including the Banbury Road, Beaumont Street, and I forget where else, but in the two years I stayed there it was scarcely possible to cook. Anyway, digs seldom included anything you could rightly call a kitchen.

I suppose I was over twenty when I moved to London to work in the Open Air Theatre in Regent's Park. After a spell in an aunt's house in Chester Gate I rented rooms – not a real flat – in a big house on Primrose Hill. I had an immensely large living-room with huge, high windows, a rather cramped bedroom, a bathroom, and a kitchen improvised out of what was really a landing. There I installed a gas cooker, one of those old food safes with perforated metal sides which nowadays you see only in junk shops, and eventually a biggish refrigerator, bought with a generous twenty-first birthday cheque from an uncle. What a funny way to spend all that money, friends said. I thought then, and I think now, that it was a perfectly rational way to spend it. I couldn't see that a refrigerator was anything but a necessity, even if the immediate use I put it to wasn't very laudable. Ready-cooked food was what I filled it with, although as things turned out, not for long.

It was opening an account at Selfridges that went to my head. I had only to pick up the telephone for roast chickens, smoked salmon, butter, fruit, cheese, cream, eggs, coffee to be delivered next day. It wasn't until the monthly accounts seemed to be adding up to much more than I could afford that it dawned on me that having a roast chicken always handy in the fridge was a rather extravagant way of entertaining friends. And that anyway, bought food, although an improvement on the horrors of nursery and school meals, and the post-rehearsal high teas with tinned fruit salad at the Cadena Café in Oxford, was not exactly comparable with the fine cooking I had recently sampled in the Paris household I'd lived in for nearly two years while at the Sorbonne. (This food I described in *French Provincial Cooking*, published in 1960, so I will not repeat the description here.)

There had also been the six months with an aristocratic Munich family who employed an Austrian cook, where I had encountered many delicious and unfamiliar things such as sweet buttery bread for Sunday breakfast, a marvellous chocolate confection called *Mohr im Hemd* or moor in a nightshirt, a rich chocolate and almond cake covered in thick, soft white cream, venison with a mysterious wild red berry sauce, apricot and plum dumplings like tiny, very superior doughnuts ... Would I ever be able to cook such things for myself?

At about that time I saw in Selfridges (a store which played a big part in my youth) a towering pile of copies of a book called *Recipes of All Nations* by a Countess Morphy. It was a thick book, priced at 2s 6d, or 3s 6d for a version with a thumb index. Bound in shiny covers in a choice of colours, yellow, pale blue or red, the book seemed amazing value for money. One day I carried a copy home with me on the bus and began reading it. It was fascinating – it still is – but Countess Morphy, whose 'all nations' did indeed extend across the five continents, threw little light on such matters as quantities, timing, temperatures and other technical details. Still, with the help of Mrs Hilda Leyel's *The*

Gentle Art of Cookery, given to me by my mother, I began to teach myself to cook nice food. Mrs Leyel's book, it has to be said, was appealing in its imaginative approach to cooking, but almost as notably deficient in technical instruction as Countess Morphy's. Had I known how huge was the gap between the urge to cook and the instruction necessary to achieve satisfactory results, perhaps I wouldn't have embarked on so perilous a course of action. As things were, I blundered on, not much daunted by mistakes.

As demonstrated by Nanny's surreptitious nursery cooking, what you can cook on a stove in a passage or on a staircase landing, or over a gas ring or small open fire, is fairly surprising. Granted, the will to do it, plus a spirit of enterprise and a little imagination, are necessary elements in learning to cook. You have to have a healthy appetite, too, and not worry too much over the failures or shortcomings of your kitchen and its equipment.

During the war years in Egypt, when I ran a reference library for the British Ministry of Information, I lived in a ground floor flat located in a car park for the vehicles used by one of the secret service organisations whose offices, in a nearby building, were known to every cab driver in Cairo as The Secret House. My cook, a Sudanese called Suleiman, performed minor miracles with two Primus stoves and an oven which was little more than a tin box perched on top of them. His soufflés were never less than successful, and with the aid of a portable charcoal grill carried across the road to the Nile bank opposite (the kitchen was so small it didn't even have a window, and if he had used charcoal he'd have been asphyxiated), he produced perfectly good lamb kebabs. The rice pilaff I named after him and the recipe for it which I published in my first book in 1950, became part of quite a few people's lives at that time. When something was lacking in my kitchen, which was just about every time anyone came to dinner, Suleiman would borrow it from some grander establishment. All Cairo cooks did likewise. Thus a dinner guest was quite likely to recognise his own plates, cutlery or serving dishes on my table. Nobody commented on this familiar custom.

In Cairo and Alexandria, ice was easy to come by – although I never thought, in those days, to ask where it came from, I now know that there were flourishing ice factories in Egypt – and so from an old hand-cranked churn on loan for the evening, Suleiman would produce delectable ice-creams. At that time, Groppi's, the famous Cairo café, was well known for its ices, although those at Baudrot's in Alexandria were even better, and many of the hospitable local families employed cooks who made fine ices, so there was plenty of competition. All the same, it would have been hard to beat Suleiman's home-made *mish-mish* or apricot ice-cream. The only drawback was the cranking of the churn, which made so much noise that it tended to bring dinner-table conversation to a standstill.

My Cairo kitchen, absurdly inadequate though it was, is one I remember with some affection. I couldn't now contemplate cooking in such a hole in the wall, nor indeed did I then, except on rare occasions when I took it into my head to show Suliman how to cook something I had learned in France or Greece before the war, but all the same some memorable food came out of that kitchen, including one year even a Christmas pudding. This pudding Suleiman, too hastily briefed by me, very understandably supposed was a main course to be served after the soup, and bore it in flaming according to my instructions. Crestfallen, he took it away, but brought it back again at the appropriate moment, in undiminished style, once more drenched in rum and distinctly more alcoholic than was quite orthodox.

After the war, when I returned to a drastically rationed and chilly England, my first kitchen was in a furnished flat in Kensington. It was one of those in which the table was also the cover of the bath. There was a gas cooker, a very small Electrolux fridge – a blessing which I certainly appreciated, given that such things were then in very short supply – and a sink. There wasn't much room for equipment, but I didn't have much because most of my belongings, including my big, old fridge, had been destroyed in a store which had been hit by a bomb. Still, with such ingredients as I could find, rationed and unrationed, I cooked a lot. In those days there weren't many London restaurants one wanted to go to or indeed could afford, and I was thankful to have learned a little about cooking foods such as lentils and beans which weren't either rationed or totally unobtainable. Rice, alas, was one of the latter commodities, and was not to return for another year. Lemons were still scarce, but after a long absence tomatoes re-appeared, and the Italian shops in Soho began to sell real spaghetti and olive oil. Butter, eggs and milk remained on ration for many years, but there was bootleg cream and butter from Ireland, and eggs from a farm in Wales. We all learned to make the best of what we could get.

As for that squalid kitchen/bathroom arrangement, it did at least keep clutter at bay. If you have to clear your kitchen table every morning before you can have a bath, you do tend to put things back in their proper places. I hate clutter in the kitchen. Not that that means I don't live with it. There are some people, and I have to recognise that I'm one of them, who if they had a kitchen the size of the Albert Hall would still contrive to be surrounded by clutter. But as long as I have plenty of cupboards, spacious wooden draining-boards, a deep, roomy sink – porcelain, none of your tinny stainless steel – and a wooden, not a plastic, plate rack which takes serving dishes as well as plates and cups and saucers, oh, and of course a large fridge (actually I have two), I suppose I don't have any excuse for clutter. I am not advising anyone to follow my example. It's not a good one.

Smallbone of Devizes' catalogue, Summer 1989

Elizabeth David's 'Dream' Kitchen

So frequently do dream kitchens figure in the popular newspaper competitions, in the pages of shiny magazines and in department store advertising that one almost begins to believe women really do spend half their days dreaming about laminated work-tops, louvered cupboard doors and sheaves of gladioli standing on top of the dishwasher. Why of all rooms in the house does the kitchen have to be a dream? Is it because in the past kitchens have mostly been so underprivileged, so dingy and inconvenient? We don't, for example, hear much of dream drawing-rooms, dream bedrooms, dream garages, dream boxrooms (I could do with a couple of those). No. It's a dream kitchen or nothing. My own kitchen is rather more of a nightmare than a dream, but I'm stuck with it. However, I'll stretch a point and make it a good dream for a change. Here goes.

This fantasy kitchen will be large, very light, very airy, calm and warm. There will be the minimum of paraphernalia in sight.

It will start off and will remain rigorously orderly. That takes care of just a few desirable attributes my present kitchen doesn't have. Naturally there'll be, as now, a few of those implements in constant use – ladles, a sieve or two, whisks, tasting spoons – hanging by the cooker, essential knives accessible in a rack, and wooden spoons in a jar. But half a dozen would be enough, not thirty-five as there are now. Cookery writers are particularly vulnerable to the acquisition of unnecessary clutter. I'd love to rid myself of it.

The sink will be a double one, with a solid wooden draining-board on each side. It will be (in fact, is) set 760 mm (30 in) from the ground, about 152 mm (6 in) higher than usual. I'm tall, and I didn't want to be prematurely bent double as a result of leaning over a knee-high sink. Along the wall above the sink I envisage a continuous wooden plate rack designed to hold serving dishes as well as plates, cups and other crockery in normal use. This saves a great deal of space, and much time spent getting out and putting away. Talking of space, suspended from the ceiling would be a wooden rack or slatted shelves – such as farmhouses and even quite small cottages in parts of Wales and the Midland counties used to have for storing bread or drying out oatcakes. Here would be the parking place for papers, notebooks, magazines – all the things that usually get piled on chairs when the table has to be cleared. The table itself is, of course, crucial. It's for writing at and for meals, as well as for kitchen tasks, so it has to have comfortable leg room. This time round I'd like it to be oval, one massive piece of scrubbable wood, on a central pedestal. Like the sink, it has to be a little higher than the average.

Outside the kitchen is my refrigerator and there it will stay. I keep it at the lowest temperature, about 4°C (40°F). I'm still amazed at the way so-called model kitchens have refrigerators next to the cooking stove. This seems to me almost as mad as having a wine rack above it. Then, failing a separate larder – in a crammed London house that's carrying optimism a bit too far – there would be a second and fairly large refrigerator to be used for the cool storage of a variety of commodities such as coffee beans, spices, butter, cheese and eggs, which benefit from a constant temperature of say 10°C (50°F).

All the colours in the dream kitchen would be much as they

Perspective of the 'dream' kitchen

are now, but fresher and cleaner – cool silver, grey-blue, aluminium, with the various browns of earthenware pots and a lot of white provided by the perfectly plain china. I recoil from coloured tiles and beflowered surfaces and I don't want a lot of things coloured avocado and tangerine. I'll just settle for the avocados and tangerines in a bowl on the dresser. In other words, if the food and the cooking pots don't provide enough visual interest and create their own changing patterns in a kitchen, then there's something wrong. And too much equipment is if anything worse than too little. I don't a bit covet the exotic gear dangling from hooks, the riot of clanking ironmongery, the armouries of knives, or the serried rank of sauté pans and all other carefully chosen symbols of culinary activity I see in so many photographs of chic kitchens. Pseuds corners, I'm afraid, many of them.

When it comes to the cooker I don't think I need anything very fancy. My cooking is mostly on a small scale and of the kind for intimate friends, so I'm happy enough with an ordinary four-burner gas stove. Its oven has to be a good size, though, and it has to have a drop-down door. Given the space I'd have a second, quite separate oven just for bread, and perhaps some sort of temperature-controlled cupboard for proving the dough. On the whole though it's probably best for cookery writers to use the same kind of domestic equipment as the majority of their readers. It doesn't do to get too far away from the problems of everyday household cooking or take the easy way out with expensive gadgetry.

What it all amounts to is that for me – and I stress this is purely personal, because my requirements as a writing cook are rather different from those of one who cooks mainly for a succession of guests or for the daily meals of a big family – the perfect kitchen would really be more like a painter's studio furnished with cooking equipment than anything conventionally accepted as a kitchen.

Article contributed to *The Kitchen Book* by Terence Conran,
Mitchell Beazley, 1977

When Terence Conran initially asked to photograph the kitchen at Halsey Street for *The Kitchen Book* Elizabeth refused, explaining that her nephew, Johnny Grey, was designing some new furniture for the kitchen. They came up with the idea that she should write a piece for the book on her 'dream' kitchen. Elizabeth asked Johnny to design it with her and he drew up the plan (page 9). The kitchen she describes is in fact a larger and more orderly version of her original kitchen (upper photograph, facing); the plan shows many of the features of Elizabeth's kitchen – the French armoire, the English dressers, the wooden plate rack next to the sink and the Cannon cooker. She also had a chaise longue in front of the French windows leading on to a small courtyard and a small round window in the opposite wall.

In the early 1980s the basement was converted into a kitchen, designed in the spirit of this plan (lower photograph, facing) and the second fridge was placed just beyond the kitchen door. The original kitchen remained as it was, but was used less. JN

How Publishers like to have their Cake and Eat it

His glance at the typescript I had put on his desk was one of distaste, not in the least disguised.

'It looks rather long.'

'Does it? I suppose there was more material than I expected.'

'You've certainly taken your time about it.'

'Er, well, yes.'

Captain Eric Harvey, MC, director of the publishing firm of Macdonalds, lumbered across to his filing cabinet, extracted a folder, re-inserted himself behind his desk, scrutinised the document now before him.

'Good gracious. I see Mr Lehmann contracted to pay you an advance of three hundred pounds. Is that right?'

'Yes.'

'Three hundred pounds. THREE HUNDRED POUNDS? For a *cookery* book?'

'Well, yes.'

'No wonder Mr Lehmann's business wasn't making a profit.' The brave Captain sighed a surly sigh. 'Well, all I can say is I hope we get our money back.'

The John Lehmann contract which Captain Harvey affected to find so outrageous had been signed in the autumn of 1951. Early in 1952 I left for Italy to research for what was to be my third book, *Italian Food*. It was by now late in 1953. Half-way into the book – that is to say both the cooking and the writing of it – I had heard from John Lehmann that after a dispute with the directors of Purnell's, the printers who were the majority shareholders in his publishing firm and owners also of Macdonalds, he had decided to close down his business. His authors, or those of them thought worth taking over – I learned later that I had only one fellow victim, the American writer Paul Bowles – found themselves in the hands of the unknown Macdonalds. I was to discover, step by ugly step, that what had happened to me as a writer was a most unenviable fate.

Even with hindsight there was little I could have done. To abandon the book on which I had already spent a year and a half and done much very difficult work, return the hundred pounds which was all I had so far received of that prodigal advance, and cancel my contract would perhaps have been a feasibility. A publisher has no means of forcing an author to deliver a book which that author has decided he will not finish. But the publisher can threaten action for breach of contract and/or seek to prevent the author selling that book to any other publisher. In any case my two earlier books were now beyond retrieval from Macdonalds' grasp. I could not know what that was to mean to my own and their future. Although I then had no agent I was aware that the contracts John Lehmann had given me were the standard ones of the period and, except that no provision was then made for paperback or book club rights, are not so very different today. The clause providing for the transfer of an author's contracts and rights to a publisher who takes over the business of the one with whom that author has originally contracted is generally accepted. It should not be. Authors learn too late that they and their books are part of the fixtures and fittings which go with the house. Their new owners may be uncongenial as well as ill-qualified to deal with their work. Not all authors now under contract to the Heinemann group will be overjoyed, I suspect, to find themselves the property of Paul Hamlyn and Octopus.

As quickly became clear to me, I had been spoiled by my initial contacts with the publishing world. The author–publisher relationship between John Lehmann and myself had been friendly, fruitful, civilised. He had produced my first two books in an attractive format, with good paper, pleasing design and binding and with striking dust jackets and illustrations by John Minton. He had set high standards. Had he remained in publishing I hope and believe I would still be on his list. Authors are not widely known for what the advertising business calls brand loyalty. All the same it does exist. Patrick Leigh Fermor, for example, has remained all his writing life with John Murray whatever the blandishments of other publishers. As is well known, Nancy Mitford would never have strayed from Hamish Hamilton. These are not isolated examples of abiding loyalty on the part of success-ful writers to their original publishers.

Those publishers who might more properly be termed account-ants or printing tycoons fail to take into account the ties which bind an author to a publisher who has not only taken a gamble with his first book – and Heaven knows if the publication of

Mediterranean Food in the conditions prevailing in the England of 1950 was a gamble – and brought it off to a modest extent, but who has also fostered his frail talent, shored up his tottery confidence, encouraged him to produce more and better work, treated his failings with tolerant understanding. That first publisher is likely to remain the yardstick by whom all subsequent ones are measured. So an author who has cause to feel that he and his work have been somehow sold up river will sooner or later turn on his new master and take action to effect his escape. It is unlikely that he will get much further than freeing himself from the option clause in his last contract. If he has any sense of self-preservation he will never again sign a contract which includes one.

In as po-faced an understatement as you could come across in a day's reading, Anthony Blond in *The Book Book* remarks that some publishers have always been less perfect than others. During the past thirty-odd years it has been my lot to have personal dealings with, let me put it this way, more than one of the less perfect practitioners of the trade. Macdonalds, if not quite at the top of the list, remains highish on it.

Let us return now to gallant Captain Harvey who we have left recoiling from the sight of my typescript and fearful that his company might not recoup the three hundred pounds so recklessly allowed for in my contract. Not to waste more space on ancient history, yes, Macdonalds did get its money back on *Italian Food*. The firm is still gathering in, via the Penguin paperback, plus those of my two earlier books, that harvest which it did not sow. Paperback royalties, it should be explained, are customarily shared 50/50 between author and original publishers or, as contracts have it, 'their successors and assigns'. Those publishers will retain their share of the paperback royalties long after they have relinquished the hardback rights. Nowadays Macdonalds is controlled by another bonny fighting man, Captain Robert Maxwell, and the last time I had any direct communication with a member of the firm was when in 1982 its accountant reluctantly – well, how else would it have been – agreed to pay me interest on three years', repeat three years', back royalties which I had at last succeeded in extracting from him.

No. I am sorry. I have no counsel to offer inexperienced writers on how to avoid falling into the hands of a bad publisher. Anthony Blond believes an agent is the answer. To me it seems that unsatisfactory publishers are one of the built-in hazards, and those are not few, of the condition of authorship. The trouble is, one writer's good publisher may well be another's bogeyman.

What Bernard Shaw thought of publishers is fairly common knowledge. He held they were rascals, to a man. 'The one service they have done me is to teach me to do without them,' he wrote ninety years ago. If we don't all feel quite as strongly as that, it *is* sometimes difficult not to agree with the wondrous Amanda McKittrick Ross who, fifteen years after GBS, expressed herself in more picturesque but no less forceful words. 'I don't believe in publishers who wish to butter their bannocks on both sides while they'll hardly allow an author to smell treacle. I consider they are too grabby altogether and like Methodists they love to keep the Sabbath and everything else they can lay their hands on.'

Tatler, October 1985

Scoff Gaffe

Ann Barr and Paul Levy, begetters of *The Official Foodie Handbook* (Ebury Press) are too young perhaps to remember that during the last war Greece was tragically occupied by the Germans. Still, if they'd checked with some responsible adviser they needn't have committed the whopping gaffe of asserting that during the war years there was a British Ministry of Information in Greece and that I worked in it. For that matter, if they'd asked, I could have told them that I was not at any time 'the Librarian at Alexandria'. Has there even been a Library there since the famous one was burned in AD 270? Anyway, it was in Cairo that I ran the modest wartime Reference Library established by the Ministry of Information Middle East. There *is* quite a distinction to be made between Alexandria and Cairo. And while we're about it, whoever thought up the bit about my being married to a Lt-Colonel in the Bengal Lancers must have been seeing too much of Hollywood's Raj and Gary Cooper riding off in full-dress uniform, immaculate with turban and sash, to defend the North West Frontier.

Readers may well ask: what's all this got to do with the Foodies? Well, Levy and Barr, having a crack at establishing the appearance of familiarity with the careers and backgrounds of living writers and professional chefs bearing well-known names, have compiled a list they call the Foodies' Who's Who. I take it they didn't want to ask the persons concerned. It's time-consuming to obtain facts. Why bother when you can invent? So in the only really funny phrase in the whole of their facetious guide to food snobbery they disclaim responsibility for 'any variance of fact from that recorded in good faith'. Variance of fact? Good faith? I'd like to hear a legal definition of a fact variant. And, in the context, of good faith. Oh well, 1984 was the year of Newspeak. Have a nice variant for 1985.

Sorry I had to mention myself. Over now to Paul Levy and the Dorchester dinner last October for the launch of *Foodie*. 'I am a chronicler,' confided Levy to Joe Hyam, editor of the trade weekly *Caterer and Hotelkeeper*, 'the Boswell rather than the Dr Johnson of the Foodies.' Well, Dr Johnson he ain't. But Boswell? Hang on there. 'An eighteenth-century parasite . . . passionately interested in himself . . . used others as his mirrors . . . an opportunist and a snobbish opportunist at that.' Sorry Mr Levy. That's how Sean Day Lewis described Boswell in November last when the BBC presented a programme called *Boswell's London Journal*. It does indeed seem to me that in *Foodie* there's more than a little of the mirror image of Paul Levy, whose aspirations, if not his achievements, appear all ways Foodie. As for Miss Barr's editorial snobberies, I'm sure she would agree that they are nothing if not opportunist. After all, as deputy editor of *Harpers & Queen* it's her business to sell her archi-snob magazine. *Foodie* is a sales ploy. In conception quite a clever one, but her foodist Boswell lacks both the detachment and the style requisite to carry it through. The fond mirror reflections keep getting in the way.

Leaving aside the detachment deficiency, have a look at the style. Here comes the Magimix, page 30. 'Suddenly, in the early seventies, the whole monstrous heap of meunière was seen to have been fertilising the soil for new plants of every kind.' Ouch. Our Boswell, describing the old-fashioned puréeing, whisking and mincing demanded by the nouvelle cuisine, is of the opinion that it was only the advent of the food processor that enabled home cooks to adapt the style from the restaurants. But without food processors there wouldn't have been nouvelle cuisine in the first place, or at any rate not the one we've got, and anyway food processors of one kind and another were around long before the household Magimix explosion. Now skip two paragraphs and proceed to page 31. 'Suddenly the whole monstrous heap of business lunches was seen to have been fertilising a dead idea.'

Oh help. Change the needle. Cram that heaving heap of compost back into the processor. All right, the word processor if you like, and re-extrude it as a great big beautiful crunchy puff for, you've guessed, *Harpers & Queen*. The magazine, its advertising people say, is read by more *men* – oh, them – than '*Vogue, House & Garden, Punch*, and the colour supplements'. Chuck it, psoodies. Back with you to your Bombay Brasserie tiffins and your Dorchester foodscapes laid out on white octagonal plates – the shape helps the chefs align the foie gras parfait with the tomato-skin rosebuds, you know – lay down your editorial pens, go reactivate your gelato chefs and your pasta mastas, and in between bouts of wild-mushroom spotting and headhunting in Foodieland you might every now and again spare time for a glance at Dean Swift's furiously ironic *Modest Proposal* concerning the feeding of the half-starved Irish peasantry of his day.

The point is that an examination of the fads and foibles of a consumer-crazed society, its preoccupation with the glamour-invested personalities of the classy professional chefs and their food and the emergence of the restaurant as a theatre-substitute could well make an entertaining little study, even a useful one. The *Foodie Handbook* is not such a study. For one thing, what the subject really calls for is the worldly wit of a James Thurber combined with the bite of a Jonathan Swift; for another the authors of *Foodie* are, for their different reasons, too self-enmeshed to create valid social comment. To be sure they are skilful enough in the arts of toadying to their public and providing it with a little giggle at itself, but the meaning of satire in its true sense eludes them. Their truly awful brand of teasy jocularity isn't any kind of substitute.

Tatler, February 1985

The Oxo Story

A book celebrating seventy-five years – yes, really – of Oxo cubes is to be published by Collins at the end of November. Its short title, predictably enough, is *Taking Stock*. The book offers plenty of reproductions of period Oxo advertising, effectively dating from 1910, when the cube was introduced, through two wars and up till recent years. There is a selection of recipes for dishes with names like 'Pork 'n' Peaches' and 'Oxo Parsnips'. There's more about Oxo Katie than this reader wants to know. There's a commentary written in a dottily blithe PR style: 'Oxo has always been a part of history' . . . 'Immortalised for ever was the red Oxo van, scaled to Dinky Toy size to sell for 3d' . . . 'The second world war was battled through and won.' In 1953, 'the Queen sat on her throne and the Union Jack flew over Everest.' Oh, and the little red Oxo cube, we find, was right up there alongside the triumphant mountaineers and the red, white and blue waving over the eternal snows.

Critical assessment of the value of meat extracts and cubes wasn't to be expected from *Taking Stock*. After all, the book is a publicity exercise. That and other aspects of the subject are not without general interest though, so here goes.

When the first proprietary brand of beef extract was launched in Europe in 1865 the price of meat was high. Refrigerated ships in which cheap surplus beef and mutton from Australia, New Zealand and the Americas could be exported to meat-hungry Europe became a reality only in the 1880s; so when Liebig's *Extractum Carnis*, as its creator called it, appeared accompanied by claims that one pound of the extract contained the concentrated essence of 40 pounds of meat – the figure varies over the years – the impression made was deep and lasting. As the late Sir Jack Drummond put it in his great work *The Englishman's Food*, first published in 1939, it was not then generally appreciated, even in medical circles, that clear soups were devoid of body-forming qualities. The beef tea produced by adding water to Liebig's extract made an agreeable hot or cold drink but it couldn't be regarded as a foodstuff in the ordinary sense. Such broths were more in the nature of nerve stimulants, the experts agreed. That thousands upon thousands of people still today persist in the belief that meat extracts provide – again in Drummond's phrase – 'the essential nutritive principles of meat in highly concentrated form' is a tribute to the power of skilled and sustained advertising combined with the boundless capacity of the human race to believe what it wants to believe.

Baron Justus von Liebig, a world-famous German professor of chemistry ennobled in 1845 in recognition of his contribution to the science of nutrition, was a man of deeply serious purpose. He was well aware that the constituents of his condensed meat broth could not alone contribute to the formation of tissue, but did not on that account dismiss it as worthless. He believed that its stimulant action on appetite could prove beneficial, and was convinced that the nitrogenous elements and the mineral salts extracted from the meats must have some nutritive value. He was not entirely mistaken. In 1944, ninety-seven years after he had published a description of his extract, it was established that certain quantities of riboflavin and nicotinic acid are present in meat extracts, and that if supplemented with other proteins such as those contained in wheaten bread, could be regarded as helpful for nutritional purposes. Not much more than that, however, and not on their own. Liebig had made a faulty deduction, oddly so for a man trained in the discipline of scientific analysis. He was basing his belief mainly on the example of that trusty old warhorse, the French peasant, who lived a healthy life on a diet consisting primarily of broth, potatoes and bread. The key component of course was the bread, and the potatoes were a help. But on a diet of thin meat broth alone, the toiling peasant wouldn't have survived for long.

At the time of Liebig's launch in Britain the extract's promoters had little difficulty in gaining favourable publicity. Whatever the scientific opinion concerning its value, the product took off. Before long Florence Nightingale declared her faith in its medicinal benefits. In 1871, when Henry Stanley set out for darkest Africa in search of Livingstone, supplies of Liebig went with him. Charles Elmé Francatelli, one of the most respected chefs in Britain, gave the product his blessing. He didn't refer to any supposed nutritional value it might have, but provided a testimonial guaranteed to appeal to cooks everywhere. 'The very soul of Cookery is the Stockpot,' he proclaimed solemnly, 'and the finest Stockpot is Liebig's Extract of Meat.'

What more could Liebig's advertisers ask for? Francatelli, billed at the time he wrote his testimonial as 'chef de cuisine to the late Emperor of the French', died in 1876, three years after his ex-Imperial Majesty. Twenty years on, the Liebig Company was still quoting the great chef's pronouncement. Bedevilled as it was by the stockpot-worship of the period, and ever keen to dodge its tyranny, the world of middle-class professional household cooks surely greeted Francatelli's liberating licence to forget their cauldrons of simmering meat and bones and merely dip their spoons into the Liebig jar with a collective cheer.

The reappearance in December 1895 of Francatelli's magisterial dictum, prominently incorporated into a full-page advertisement for Liebig's Extract which appeared in *The Epicure*

LIEBIG COMPANY'S
PRACTICAL COOKERY BOOK

magazine for that month, was probably not unconnected with the publication the previous year of a Liebig cookery book in which every recipe except those for sweet dishes called for the inclusion of a small amount of the extract. It was now Liebig's policy to promote its product as an aid to middle-class domestic cookery. There was no emphasis in their little book – a pretty one, and today a collectors' item – on the nutritional virtues of the extract; the quantities advocated in the recipes were extremely restrained, reckoned mainly in quarter and half teaspoons, and the book was sent free to all who applied for it to the company's offices. An introduction revealed something of the scale of the Liebig operation. The vast works established on the banks of the Uruguay dealt with the processing of 1,500 head of cattle a day for seven months in the year and employed over 1,000 hands.

The publication of the Liebig cookery book was a shrewd move in what had become something of a meat extract war. As the recognised and much-bemedalled founders of a new branch of industry, the Liebig Company had attracted many imitators. Among several upstart extracts was one called Vimbos, manufactured by the Scottish Fluid Beef Company of Edinburgh. Advertisements for the product claimed a superior percentage of stimulating and flesh-forming content, plus 'heat-producing fatty bodies and bone-forming mineral matter'. Proclaiming Vimbos the Prince of Fluid Beefs, its advertisements featured an ox squatting in a cup, its front hooves dangling forlornly over the edge. Armour & Co of Chicago produced a meat extract named Vigoral, marketed in solid concentrated form, each pound of it containing, so its producers claimed, the essence of 45 pounds of lean fresh beef, which made Liebig's 40 pounds of beef to the pound of essence look rather meagre.

By the mid 1880s, Bovril was also flourishing. Bovril's special claim was that it combined the stimulative properties of a meat extract with the nutritive constituents of meat. To achieve this end, so much desired by Baron Liebig (he had died in 1873 and was succeeded as head of the company by his son Baron H. von Liebig) the albumen and fibrine from fresh beef were desiccated, reduced to powder and added to the basic beef extract. It was beef on beef. As sustenance for polar explorers and warriors fighting Britain's endless colonial wars, Bovril was already becoming a formidable rival to Liebig's Extract.

Another serious competitor for Liebig's sales was a Swiss Maggi product which was launched in the 1890s. This was a concentrated consommé, ingeniously marketed in capsules, costing only 2d each and containing enough concentrate to make three-quarters of a pint of 'perfect clear soup, strong and appetising', its admirers maintained. There were also those who held that Maggi's thirty-three varieties of French vegetable soups in tablets were equally invaluable, even indispensable.

Keeping up with its competitors in the field of advertising and publicity was one of the Liebig Company's brilliant successes. The little cookery book was supplemented in many appealing ways with decorative souvenirs, most notably with sets of cards to be exchanged for wrappers from the jars. A seemingly inexhaustible series of brightly litho-printed cards featured an immense variety of subjects ranging from episodes in the history of ancient Rome to the contemporary seaside and its bathing machines, scenes from Shakespeare's plays to decisive battles, popular operas, famous love stories, harlequinades. The familiar Liebig jar appeared of course on every card, and on the reverse side of each was a recipe. Wherever Liebig's Extract was sold the cards were printed in the appropriate language – German, Italian, French, Russian, Dutch, English. Long before the advent of the cigarette card, Liebig's pictorial cards had become collectors' pieces.

Towards the end of the century, at a time when all other European countries fully recognised and protected Liebig's right to the exclusive use of the name, Britain was the exception. Prior to the passing of the 1875 Trade Marks Act, unscrupulous imitators had been permitted by the British courts to appropriate the name, the design of the jars, the labels, the wrapping, of Liebig's product. The directors of the British end of the Liebig Company at last decided that enough was enough. A drastic change of name was sought. The one they came up with – and no bad one – was Oxo. In June 1900 it was registered as a British trade mark, protected in all European countries. A new name for the new century.

For Oxo a new jar was devised, in a shape reminiscent – not entirely by coincidence, it may be supposed – of the already familiar Bovril bottle. Suggestions thrown out in the early advertising copy to the effect that a drink of Oxo was appropriate to any number of daily occasions could hardly have been more innocent. They included such non-events as before shopping and after shopping; after motoring; in foggy weather; in wet weather; when depressed; in long intervals between meals; when too busy for ordinary meals. Then came the harder sell, not exactly guileless. 'Oxo makes children grow into strong men and women' was surely a reckless claim. There was also talk of 'the energising, nourishing force of the best beef' entering the bloodstream 'in the shortest possible time', references to 'the rapid and continuous nourishment of prime lean beef' and to 'the highly nutritious properties of Oxo extract'. People believed the claims, and somehow, along with those made by Bovril, they entered the national consciousness.

When the first Oxo cubes – as distinct from the extract – appeared, selling them can have presented no problem at all. They were so cheap that almost anybody could afford them. Baron Liebig would have been pleased. Whether he'd have been so pleased to read the list of ingredients contained in the cubes of 1985 is a matter for conjecture. But it's as well to mention that out of the two so-called flavour enhancers listed, 621 is the suspect MSG, and the second, 635, turns out to be a combination of substances called purines, prohibited from foods intended for young children. Gout sufferers and rheumatics generally should also avoid them. In Britain that means the great majority of the population.

Tatler, November 1985

Taking Stock

Nearly all Englishwomen get panicky when a recipe calls for stock. Every time the word occurs in the cookery copy for a magazine or newspaper, sure as fate there'll be a sub. on the 'blower' asking, can she add 'a bouillon cube will do'? I don't think this feeling that stock is a worrying subject is primarily a hangover from rationing. It existed, I fancy, long before the 1939 war, perhaps even before 1914. One can't help wondering how much the cookery books of the late Victorian and Edwardian eras are to blame.

The instructions in some of these books were enough to put off the most intrepid cook. The 1891 edition of Mrs Beeton's *Household Management* (Mrs Beeton herself had died in 1865, and the instructions are emphatically not her own) told the cook that 'everything in the way of meat, bones, gravies and flavourings that would otherwise be wasted' should go into the stock-pot. 'Shank-bone of mutton, gravy left over when the half-eaten leg was moved to another dish, trimmings of beefsteak that went into a pie, remains of gravies, bacon rinds and bones, poultry giblets, bones of roast meat, scraps of vegetables . . . such a pot in most houses should always be on the fire.'

Heavens, what a muddy, greasy, unattractive and quite often sour and injurious brew must have emerged from that ever-simmering tub.

There were, of course, also excellent recipes in the books for first and second stocks and broths made out of fresh ingredients, although, always with large households in mind, given in very large quantities. But somehow it was that stock-pot-cum-dustbin theory which stuck. So that gradually people have come to believe that unless they have large quantities of left-over meat and chicken carcasses, bones and scraps, it's no use setting about making stock. It's a good excuse too. And a shilling spent on a superior sort of bouillon cube with a continental name will, with one blow, both expunge the guilt and conceal the ignorance upon which the manufacturers and advertisers of these things are relying.

Well, *will* a bouillon cube 'do'?

Ninety-nine times out of a hundred it will do nothing. Not, that is, if what you are hoping for is the extra stimulative value which an extract of meat is supposed to give to a soup or stew; the advantage of the extra flavour, such as it is, seems to me very doubtful.

If it is colouring you are after, then you will get it; salt, too; plus that curious prickly after-taste which appears to be character-istic of every foodstuff in which monosodium glutamate figures. All harmless enough no doubt. And as a matter of fact I think many meat-soup substitutes are more acceptable taken straight, at times when warm liquid rather than food is what one needs, than when used in cooking.

However, in the now remote days when nearly all basic ingredi-ents were short, I used to use these cubes for soups, and other dishes which traditionally required stock. I even recommended some such product in a book. Too hastily. I soon found that every dish into which liquid made from a cube had entered had the same monotonous background flavour. (This would, of course, equally apply to pot-liquor, as the fluid from the stock-pot was called.) Pretty soon, I found, as no doubt many have found before and since, that the best way out of the difficulty was to use plain water instead of the missing stock, and to make up for the flavour

thus lacking – and, incidentally, adding nutritive value and vita-
mins – with a little of the then very precious butter, olive oil, or
milk, an egg or some wine in the case of soups; extra cheese for
rice dishes, a larger than usual allowance of flavouring vegetables
and herbs, plus wine again, for stews.

As far as vegetable soups were concerned, the policy paid off
handsomely. The taste of vegetable purées unaltered by
extraneous flavouring is much truer, cleaner, fresher; they become
dishes of considerable delicacy; and how much more satisfactory
than that feeble clear soup with a julienne of vegetables floating
on the surface.

So all those quarts of stock advocated in the pre-1914 cookery
books had never been necessary as far as flavour or consistency
was concerned. And with all the meat consumed in middle-class
households at that period, such infinitesimal extra nutritive and
stimulative elements as might be contained in a light stock were
not needed either. But still, some use had to be made of the
quantities of surplus materials in the larders of well-to-do households, and some occupation contrived for the kitchenmaids.
Everyone was satisfied that these 'good nourishing soups' made
with stock-pot liquor also implied thrifty housekeeping.

There are, obviously, exceptions in which stock, clear and true
in flavour, does help to give a little body to a vegetable soup and

also brings out the taste of the main ingredient. Mushrooms are one example of such a vegetable and tomatoes another. The cooking process with these vegetables involves the evaporation of some of the large amount of water they contain and its replacement with a broth. These are good vegetables to use for soups when fresh chicken or meat stock is in the larder. But that doesn't preclude the making of a delicious and no less valuable mushroom or tomato soup with olive oil and cheese, or butter and milk, instead of stock.

Braised and stewed meat, poultry and game form another category of dishes which often call either for meat stock for the moistening at the beginning of the cooking or, in French recipes for concentrated meat glaze, for strengthening the body and flavour of the sauce in the final stages of cooking – the moment when in English cookery the liquid, of which there is commonly rather too much, is thickened with flour and coloured with that unique commodity called gravy browning. If the dish has been properly cooked to start with, neither of these operations is essential or even desirable.

In the case of beef and lamb dishes the meat itself should be sufficiently fat and juicy to supply the necessary body and flavour to the sauce – always supposing that the appropriate flavouring vegetables are included and the meat not drowned. In those made from white meats inclined to be dry or insipid, such as veal or modern battery poultry, a little clear veal or beef broth is undoubtedly a help as regards body, flavour and appearance of the finished dish. If broth or stock is lacking and cannot be made especially (although really it is very little trouble to make a small quantity) and if there is no wine available to help the flavour, then I still prefer water to either cubes or meat extracts, genuine or so called. This goes for the most expensive ones to be bought at luxury grocers as much as for the cheap and widely advertised brands. One and all seem to me to give a flavour both false and ineradicable. But this point is mainly one of taste, and perhaps of habit.

What does seem certain is that any nutritional and beneficial elements contained in the concentrated meat tablets and extracts as experimented with by cooks and chemists since the early eighteenth century and commercially developed in the 1860s from the formula evolved by Baron Liebig in no way justify the faith still so widely placed in them. Dieticians have been saying this for decades, but the superstition persists.

Finally, I know that many people who feel as I do about the pointlessness of cubes and extracts set their faith in jellied stock made from bones and water and cooked by pressure to extract the maximum gelatine. Such stock *can*, in conjunction with fresh meat, be used as a working basis for various culinary purposes. But the fact that the stock jells does not mean that it has any extra virtue from a nutritive point of view.

I think that once one has understood these points and realised that for many dishes there are sound alternatives to, and in some cases improvements on, stock then at least one common kitchen problem becomes automatically solved. Whether a bouillon cube 'will do' is no longer a question one troubles to ask.

The Spectator, 16 September 1960

The Making of Broths and Stocks

The making of broths and stocks and consommés is to me one of the most interesting and satisfactory of all cooking processes. Although it may seem to involve something of a performance, especially when you are doing it for the first two or three times, the results – a broth hot and clear and pure flavoured from the beef and vegetables which have gone into it, a consommé softly jellied, sparkling, subtle and restorative, a nice piece of boiled beef to make into a salad or that most friendly of left-over dishes, the French miroton – are immensely rewarding.

Nobody I think can really call themselves an informed or even useful cook until they understand how a true stock and genuine consommé are constituted. There is another point, and a very relevant one. Anybody who has once learnt the correct way to do these things will never again resort to the awful haphazard way so deep rooted in English cookery lore of flinging any old remains – gravy, sauces, bones, stale left-over vegetables, bits of bacon rind and cabbage – into that much misused and misunderstood receptacle, the stock-pot. Not that I mean to imply that ingredients which would make a perfectly good stock for all sorts of purposes should be wasted. Far from it. But when you know how to set about making a stock or broth from specially bought fresh ingredients then you will also know how to make one from what you may have in hand. You will have a sound idea of which of these things are useful and which should be rejected, which ones will add savour and nourishment to your broth, which will cloud it, introduce a false flavour or unfit it for the purpose for which it is intended. Successful improvisation and the truly economical use of by-products and left-overs comes easiest when you already know the basic methods and quantities.

One other aspect. The cost. Looked at in the light of specially bought ingredients and lengthy cooking it is expensive to make broths and jellies. But when you treat the meat, chicken, calf's foot and so on which may have gone into the broth, as separate and specially made dishes then you can reckon you have got your broth or your consommé for practically nothing. So it is worth knowing how to use these ingredients to the best possible advantage.

SIMPLE BEEF BROTH

Ingredients are a 1 kg (2 lb) piece of forequarter flank of beef with bone, a small piece of knuckle bone of veal with its meat, approximately 500 g (1 lb) in weight altogether, 1 large onion, 1 large tomato, 3–4 whole carrots, a bunch of herbs consisting of a bay leaf, a sprig of thyme, 2 or 3 sprigs of parsley and the white part of 2 leeks, all tied together, 1 tablespoon of salt, 2.4 litres (4 pints) of water.

Put the beef and veal (if you can't get veal knuckle substitute a piece of shin of beef) into a tall pot of about 4.5-litre (1-gallon) capacity and cover it over with the water. Bring extremely slowly to a bare simmering point. At this stage, grey-looking scum begins to rise to the surface. Skim this off with a perforated spoon. This operation has to be repeated several times during the next 20–30 minutes, and it is important that this should be done, otherwise the finished broth will not be clear or a good colour. When the scum begins to be white and foamy instead of grey and muddy, stop skimming and put in the scraped carrots, the bunch of herbs, the tomato cut in half, the salt and the whole onion, washed and freed of any grit but not peeled. The skin helps to give a good colour to the broth. Add 150 ml (¼ pint) more water to replace that which has been lost with the scum. Put the lid on the pot and turn the heat very low, so that throughout the cooking process, which takes just about 4 hours, the broth should never for an instant come to a full boil. So from time to time, lift the lid, check that all is well and if necessary regulate the heat.

When the 4 hours are up, remove the beef, veal and vegetables to a dish.

Put a colander over a deep receptacle, and inside the colander a dampened cheese cloth or double muslin. Through this strain your broth. You will have close on 2.2 litres (4 pints) of pale straw-coloured broth, quite clear except for a few 'eyes' of fat and tasting of fresh meat and vegetables. It can be served at once exactly as it is, as a clear soup, or you can chop up the vegetables and add them, you can thicken it by cooking rice in it, or you can leave it until next day. Then remove the fat, heat it up and let it simmer a little time so that it reduces and concentrates in flavour. (But don't overdo this or it'll be too salt.) Or you can use it as stock for sauces.

This is the simplest possible version of beef broth: to the French it is Pot-au-Feu. Mistakes to guard against are (a) putting in too much salt; (b) adding anything such as potatoes or cabbage which cloud the broth; (c) including any too powerful ingredient such as strong herbs like rosemary or sage, bacon rinds, ham, lemon peel and so on; and (d) adding any artificial colouring matter or gravy browning which will falsify the taste. Two or three pea pods dried in the oven do, however, help as far as the colour goes. Of course, at a later stage, you can turn the broth into any soup you please, but unless you have planned precisely what you are going to use the broth for it is best not to add any flavourings in the form of wine, garlic and so on to start with.

For dishes to be made with the beef from the broth, *see* recipes for beef salad, boeuf miroton and boeuf à la mode in *French Provincial Cooking*, *French Country Cooking* and *Summer Cooking*.

TOMATO CONSOMMÉ

This is simple, cheap and delicate.

Ingredients are a small parsnip, cut into 4 pieces, 2 carrots, sliced, a clove of garlic, 2 sticks of celery, a generous sprig of fresh tarragon or approximately a teaspoon of good, dried tarragon leaves, a few saffron threads, one 400-g (14-oz) can of Italian or Spanish peeled tomatoes or 750 g (1½ lb) of very ripe and juicy, fresh Mediterranean tomatoes, 900 ml (1½ pints) of water, 600 ml

(1 pint) of chicken stock, seasonings of salt and sugar. For clarifying the consommé, 3 egg whites. For the final flavouring, 1 teaspoon of Madeira.

Put all the ingredients except the chicken stock, egg whites and Madeira into a capacious saucepan. If you are using fresh tomatoes – but don't bother unless it is the height of the season and you have really sweet and wonderfully ripe ones – chop them roughly, skins and all. Season only very moderately, say one teaspoon each of salt and sugar to start with. You can always add more later. Add the water. Simmer in the open pan for about 40 minutes. Line a colander with a dampened doubled muslin cloth and strain the broth. Don't press the vegetables, just let the thin liquid run through.

Return the broth to the rinsed pan. Add the chicken stock. Bring to simmering point. Beat the egg whites for a couple of minutes. As soon as they start to froth pour them into the simmering broth. Cover the pan. Simmer very gently, until the whites have solidified and formed a crust, and are thoroughly cooked. By this time all the particles and impurities in the broth will have risen to the top and will be adhering to the crust. Leave to cool a little. Filter through a piece of dampened muslin placed in a colander, over a deep soup tureen or bowl. The consommé should be as clear as glass and a beautiful amber colour.

When you heat the consommé for serving – and not before – add the teaspoon of Madeira, and a little more seasoning if necessary. Serve in big cups. There should be enough for 5 helpings.

Notes

1. An unorthodox, but uncommonly successful way of clarifying the consommé is to transfer the saucepan, covered, to a low oven as soon as you have added the egg whites. You can leave it for an hour or more. The first time I saw someone doing this – it was a Moroccan cook with whom I worked briefly in Marrakesh – I was aghast. And when I saw how well the system worked, amazed. It has to be remembered that unless your egg whites are cooked into a solid crust, your consommé will never be truly clear and clean. The oven method is a good way of achieving this aim without over-reduction of the consommé and attendant loss of its delicate flavours.

2. Alternatives to chicken stock are beef, veal or pork stock. Or for a fish broth, a concentrated fish fumet. A non-alternative,

I'll repeat that, a non-alternative is a bouillon cube. Water is a preferable one.

3. Please don't be tempted to double the prescribed dose of Madeira. (You won't taste anything but the wine.) If you have no Madeira, use white vermouth, or manzanilla or any decent sherry.

4. To serve with the consommé it is a good idea to have some little croûtons or slices of good bread, sprinkled with olive oil, spread with grated Gruyère or Parmesan and baked in the oven.

Unpublished, pre-1975

WATERCRESS SOUP

This is a cheap, quick and wonderfully refreshing soup for the times when you have 1 litre or a bit more (a couple of pints) of good clear chicken or meat broth in the larder.

Other ingredients are 2 bunches of watercress, 1 tablespoon of butter, 3 of grated Parmesan, the yolks of 2 eggs.

Rinse the watercress and put it, stalks and all, in a saucepan with the butter. Let it simmer a few minutes until it has melted. It will reduce down like spinach. Now remove the watercress with a draining spoon, leaving the liquid in the pan. Chop the watercress as finely as possible. Return to the pan, add the broth and, when hot, stir in the cheese.

Have the beaten yolks ready in a bowl. Mix a little of the hot soup with the eggs, stir, then pour the mixture back into the saucepan and heat up again, stirring all the time. Don't let the soup boil, or the eggs will curdle.

The soup should be no thicker than cream.

Unpublished, pre-1975

PASTENAK AND CRESS CREAM

This is a lovely soup, a welcome change from the routine water-cress and potato soup. Pastenak is the medieval English word for parsnip, a corruption of the Latin *pastinaca*. In Italy, parsnips are still *pastinache*, a prettier name than parsnip, to me forever associated with a character created by the immortal Beachcomber.

Ingredients for the soup – a French one in origin – are 500 g (1 lb) of youthful parsnips (there should be six; don't buy large horny old roots. They are both wasteful and disagreeable in flavour), 600 ml (1 pint) of thin clear chicken stock, 1 little punnet of mustard-and-cress, 1 level teaspoon of rice starch (*crème de riz*) or fine ground rice, or potato starch (*fécule*), or arrowroot, salt, 60–90 ml (2–3 fl oz) of cream. To serve with the soup, a bowl of little croûtons fried in clarified butter.

Scrub the parsnips. With a small sharp knife or a potato parer prise out the hard little pieces of core from the crowns.

Put the parsnips in a saucepan with cold water just to cover. No salt at this stage. Boil them until they are soft – about 25 minutes. Remove them with a perforated spoon and leave them on a dish to cool. Keep the cooking water remaining in the saucepan. There will be about 300 ml (½ pint), a valuable addition to the soup.

When the parsnips are cool enough to handle, the skins can be rubbed off, although personally I don't find this necessary. In the process of sieving, or puréeing in a blender or food processor, all skin will be smoothly incorporated. Advice often given to discard the central cores of parsnips is presumably intended to apply only to the above-mentioned ancient and horny roots, the cores being so woody that I doubt if even the sharp-bladed food processors of these days could chew them up. The cores of parsnips in their prime, however, are soft as bone marrow, and have a sweet flavour and buttery texture, which are important to this soup.

Having, then, sieved the parsnips through a stainless steel wire sieve or whirled them in a blender, turn the resulting purée into a clean saucepan, stir in the reserved cooking water and the stock, adding a seasoning of salt – 2 or 3 level teaspoons should be enough, but taste as you go.

Put the teaspoon of whichever starch you are using in a small bowl, ladle in a little of the warmed soup, stir to a smooth paste, return this to the saucepan and stir well until the starch has done its work of binding the vegetable matter and the liquid content to a smooth but slightly thickened cream.

When the soup is hot cut off the leafy tops of the cress with scissors, chop them small, stir them into the soup. Finally add the cream.

Have the croûtons already fried in clarified butter and drained on kitchen paper. Serve them separately in a warmed bowl.

There will be enough soup for five big cups.

Notes

1. If the soup is made the day before you intend to eat it, it will thicken again on the second reheating, so have a little extra stock or milk ready to thin it down again. The soup shouldn't be thicker than pouring cream.

2. Watercress is an alternative to ordinary cress, but in this soup the latter is preferable.

3. Rice starch, *crème de riz*, is also labelled ground rice, although it is much finer than the slightly gritty product we used to know under that name. Rice starch and potato starch, *fécule de pommes de terre* in French, are both useful for binding soups and, occasionally, a custard or other sweet sauce. Both are used in very small quantities, so a packet lasts for years.

Unpublished, *c.*1980

SPICED LENTIL SOUP

An interesting soup, oriental in flavour, very easy to make, cheap and a comforting standby on which many variations can be made.

Basic ingredients are 125 g (4 oz) of ordinary red lentils and 2 celery stalks. Others, which can be varied, are 1 small onion, 2 large or 4 small cloves of garlic, 2 teaspoons of cumin seed (either whole or ground), 1 teaspoon of ground cinnamon, olive oil or butter, water or stock, lemon juice, parsley or dried mint, salt.

In a soup pot, saucepan or casserole of not less than 3-litre (5-pint) capacity, warm about 6 tablespoons of clarified butter, ghee, or light olive oil or 45 g (1½ oz) of butter. In this melt the chopped onion. Stir in the spices. Let them warm thoroughly before adding the crushed garlic cloves and then the lentils – it is not necessary to soak them – and the celery, cleaned and cut into 5-cm (2-in) chunks.

Let the lentils soak up the oil or butter before pouring over them 1.5 litres (2½ pints) of water or stock, which could be made from lamb, veal, pork, beef, chicken, turkey or duck. No salt at this stage. Cover the pot and let the lentils cook steadily, but not at a gallop, for 30 minutes. Now throw in 2 teaspoons of salt or to taste and cook for another 15 minutes.

By this time the lentils should be completely soft. It will be a matter of moments to sieve them through the mouli or purée them in the blender. I prefer the former method.

Return the soup to a clean saucepan, and when it is reheated, taste for seasoning – it may need a little extra ground cumin and perhaps a sprinkling of cayenne pepper – stir in a tablespoon or two of chopped parsley, or a little dried mint. Lastly, a good squeeze of lemon juice.

SPICED LENTIL SOUP (2)

As above, but instead of cinnamon and cumin use 1 teaspoon of the garam masala mixture given on page 97, and 1 teaspoon of whole cumin seeds. (The cardamom in the garam masala mixture makes the whole difference to the flavour.) For those who do not mind a rough soup, it is not even necessary to sieve the lentils or whizz them in a blender. Just beat them to a purée with a wooden spoon or a whisk. In this case, it is best to cook the lentils with 900 ml (1½ pints) water only and to add broth when they are cooked and reduced to a purée.

Unpublished, 1973

BARLEY CREAM SOUP AND BARLEY SALAD

A dual-purpose recipe which produces a soothing, untaxing soup and an excellently original salad, all in one cooking operation, seems to provide an answer, and a sound one, to the question of how best to utilise the stock made from turkey or chicken carcases.

Into about 2.4 litres (4 pints) of turkey stock put 125–180 g (4–6 oz) pearl barley, and some flavouring vegetables such as carrots, an onion, celery and a halved grilled tomato or two (for colour). Cook extremely slowly, in a covered pot, in the oven if you like, for at least 2 hours. Strain off the liquid and sieve a little of the barley and the carrots and celery into it – just enough to make a thin cream soup, to which, when you heat it up, you add a little fresh cream, lemon juice and a few drops of sherry or Madeira.

The rest of the barley cooked in the soup is strained off, turned into a bowl, and while still warm, seasoned with salt, pepper and nutmeg, dressed with 3 or 4 tablespoons of olive oil and one of lemon juice or tarragon vinegar. Into the salad mix a few cubes of green or yellow honeydew melon (in the summer use cucumber) and, if you like, a few orange segments.

The idea for this salad stems from a Boulestin recipe which, on a first reading, sounded freakish. Boiled barley and oranges. . . Boulestin, however, is a writer in whose taste one has faith, no matter how odd his recipes may occasionally sound. He gives, in this instance, no quantities and no method. Last year I tried out the idea, cooking the barley as explained above. I served the salad with cold tongue and chicken. It was most delicate and attractive – better, I thought, than the well-known rice salad made on similar lines.

Wine & Food, Winter 1964

TUSCAN BEAN SOUP

Put 250 g (½ lb) of the white haricots known as cannellini beans, or of pink borlotti beans, to soak in cold water. Leave them overnight.

Next day put the drained beans into a *fagiolara* (a flask-shaped Tuscan earthenware bean jar – *see* above) or into a tall soup marmite or stock-pot. Cover them with approximately 1.8 litres

(3 pints) of fresh cold water. Add 3 or 4 bay leaves, a teaspoon of dried savory or basil leaves (Tuscan cooks use sage. I find it too overpowering), 3 tablespoons of fruity olive oil.

Cook the beans, covered, over moderate heat for about 2 hours. Add a tablespoon of salt and continue cooking for another 20 to 30 minutes, until the beans are quite soft.

Now sieve half the beans only, with about half the liquid, through the mouli-légumes (or purée them in the electric blender, but not for long enough to get an unattractive electric-mixer-foam on the top); mix the purée with the rest of the beans, add a good fistful of parsley, coarsely chopped with a clove or two of garlic, and reheat the soup. Before serving, stir in a ladleful of fruity olive oil and the juice of a lemon.

In each soup plate or bowl have ready a slice of coarse country bread – or the nearest you can get to such a commodity – rubbed with garlic and sprinkled with olive oil.

This amount of beans should make enough soup for four.

Dried Herbs, Aromatics and Condiments, 1967

LEILAH'S YOGURT SOUP

Yogurt soup is well known in all Middle Eastern countries. Every region – probably every family – has a slightly different version. This one came to me from a Turkish source. Quantities given should make 4 ample helpings.

For 750 ml (1½ pints) of clear chicken stock, the other ingredients are 30 g (1 oz) of butter, 2 level tablespoons of flour, 1 whole egg, the juice of half a lemon, salt, cinnamon, cumin and dried mint, 300 ml (½ pint) of yogurt.

In a heavy saucepan melt the butter. Add the flour. Stir over gentle heat until the mixture is smooth. Add, gradually, the warmed stock, and cook until all trace of the floury taste has disappeared. Should the mixture turn lumpy, sieve it and return it to the rinsed-out saucepan. Let it get really hot.

Whisk together the egg and lemon juice. Add a little of the hot soup, whisk again, then incorporate this into the soup. Now add the yogurt. Keep the pan over the lowest possible heat – it must not boil – add salt if necessary, and a sprinkling of powdered cinnamon and cumin. Whisk once more. Lastly stir in the dried mint – about a tablespoon.

A good method of keeping egg-thickened soups hot without boiling is to transfer the saucepan, once the soup has reached the necessary temperature, to one of those electric hot plates made especially for keeping coffee hot without boiling. It takes up little space and is invaluable for keeping sauces as well as soups hot for a short time.

Unpublished, April 1973

Yogurt

You don't need electrical gadgets and you don't need 'special' cultures to make yogurt. You don't need padded boxes or those incredibly complicated do-it-yourself incubator tea-cosy things that people used to advocate. I'd never have been capable of making one, so I'm thankful that insulated food jars have taken their place. I have those in the house anyway for ice and picnic food, and I have a beautiful old dairy thermometer with its own wooden case. And I have a very large, old and thick saucepan to boil the milk in. So I've never bought any special equipment, and I'd find it a bore to use an electrical machine for yogurt, as well as a nuisance to have to house it.

The most effective insulated jars are the kind made by Thermos, called 'the super food flask', but Insulex also make very satisfactory ones. Both brands are stocked by department stores and plenty of other shops. Junket thermometers can be bought in kitchen shops, and it's a measure of the present popularity of yogurt that the correct temperature is now marked on them. Brannan's have also brought out a cheap yogurt thermometer.

I'd advise beginners to start with just one or two half-litre/ pint-size jars and buy more as needed.

Personally, I use rich, creamy Jersey milk for my yogurt, but many people prefer skim milk. It's a question of whether or not you're on a low-fat diet.

Bring the milk to a bare simmering point, very slowly, stirring from time to time. The object is to reduce the milk somewhat, quite an important part of yogurt-making. Ideally, the milk should reduce to a little under three quarters of the original amount, but the yogurt still works if you don't have the patience or time to watch the milk that long. When you've let it boil up once, take the milk off the heat, stir it, put in the thermometer and leave it until it registers 54°C/130°F or the temperature marked for yogurt on thermometers. Have your jars ready, and some existing yogurt, preferably Loseley or Chambourcy if you're starting from scratch.

Pour the milk into the insulated jars. Quickly – and very thoroughly – stir in a good big tablespoon of the yogurt for each 600 ml (1 pint) of milk used. Clap on the lids of the jars. That's it. In about four to six hours the yogurt will be set. (You don't have to put the jars in a warm place, airing cupboard or any such.)

I nearly always make my yogurt in the evening and leave the jars on the kitchen table until the morning, when I transfer them to the fridge. Yogurt doesn't like to be disturbed when it's newly made. I don't know why but it does seem to be so. Anyway it's a pity to break the lovely creamy crust which forms on the top when you use rich milk.

The basic points to remember about yogurt are that it doesn't work if the milk is too hot or too cold. It shouldn't be hotter than 54°C/130°F or cooler than 46°C/115°F. I think if you know about yeast you also soon understand about yogurt. And of course if you make it regularly, you use your own as the starter. Before long you find you're making yogurt very superior to anything you can buy.

I believe there are many people who think you can't make good yogurt with pasteurised milk. This really is not true. Although I will say that one year when, on a number of occasions, I managed to buy Loseley untreated Jersey milk its yogurt-making performance was spectacular. So was its flavour. Loseley don't use it for their yogurt, though. In the first place, they say the public prefers skim-milk yogurt, and in the second, making it on a commercial scale with untreated milk isn't feasible. Stray and unbeneficial bacteria could wreck a whole batch, and many shops wouldn't stock it anyway. But anyone who has access to a supply of untreated milk should try making yogurt with it.

I should add that if I were going to buy new equipment for yogurt-making I'd invest in a catering-size teflon-lined saucepan. And one more point: when it doesn't suit my timetable to wait around while the boiled milk cools to the appropriate temperature I do the boiling in advance. When it comes to making the yogurt it only takes two or three minutes to warm the milk to the right degree.

Notes

1. Yogurt made from reduced milk sets much firmer than when the milk used has been simply boiled up and left to cool.

2. Many recipes I have seen recently give temperatures too low for good yogurt-making, and also specify as little as a teaspoon of starter yogurt for 600 ml (1 pint) of milk. I find that's not nearly enough.

3. When your yogurt begins to turn out rather thin and watery, it is time to start afresh with a new carton of commercial yogurt. I find this necessary only about once every three months. Advice to buy a fresh carton of commercial yogurt every time you make your own is sometimes given by home economists on the grounds that if you use your own yogurt contamination may occur. So long as you keep your yogurt covered and use meticulously clean spoons and flasks when making each batch, in any case, an essential of all dairy work, this advice may safely be ignored.

Masterclass, 1982

Summer Greenery

Between the fake luxury of the lavishly upholstered avocado (the development by the Israelis of a stoneless avocado shaped like a little fat sausage is going to spoil all the fun) and the chilly squalor of the slice of emulsified pâté perched on a lettuce leaf, what is there for the hors d'oeuvre course during our English summer months? No prizes. There is – apart from delicious English specialities like dressed fresh crab, Scottish smoked salmon and potted smoked haddock – a whole world of beautiful and delicate luxuries, true luxuries, such as fresh purple sprouting broccoli, fine French beans, asparagus, cooked and served almost before they have become cold, with a perfectly simple olive oil and lemon juice dressing. Above all, there are, less expensive than any of these delicacies, English-grown courgettes, the only truly new vegetable successfully produced in this country since the great tomato transplant of the turn of the century.

It is from Greece and the countries of the Eastern Mediterranean that Western Europe has learned how to appreciate this delicious and versatile miniature vegetable marrow. It was, curiously enough, in the island of Malta during the mid-thirties that I first became aware of the existence of the courgette. Locally grown, I fancy, on the island of Gozo, the courgettes were the smallest I have ever seen, no longer than a little finger. They were almost invariably cooked whole, unpeeled, and finished in a cheese-flavoured cream sauce. An excellent dish and one which for years I attempted to achieve at home, using courgettes far too big to be cooked whole. Nowadays I think that there are far better ways of eating the courgette. The Italians, the Egyptians, the Greeks, the southern French, all have first-class recipes. I could, but shall probably not, write a whole book about courgettes. At the moment I shall confine myself to three recipes which all in their different ways make appealing and fresh first-course dishes. (I cannot bring myself to use the terms appetiser or starter. The first is meaningless in the context, the second makes me think of a man on a racecourse with a stop-watch in his hand.)

The courgette dishes are all, I think, best served as suggested in the recipes rather than as part of a mixed hors d'oeuvre. They do not combine happily with pâtés or with crudités such as fennel, radishes, and the sweet pepper salad given further on in this article.

More positive suggestions are: a sliced hard-boiled egg or two to make up part of a mixed courgette salad; and it is worth knowing that fresh prawns – on a separate dish – make a first-class combination with courgettes.

For the rest, the vital points are the split-second timing of the boiling of vegetables to be served as salads; the importance of seasoning, when and what; the reminders that seventy-five per cent of the delicacy of most such salads is lost once they have spent so much as one hour under refrigeration and that they do not in any case keep very long, and should therefore be cooked in small quantities and quickly eaten; finally, that elegant presentation is one of the first considerations. Inviting appearance does create appetite. If a dish, any dish, is enticing enough to arouse appetite, then I would think it reasonable that it should be called an appetiser, no matter at what stage of the meal it is offered.

COURGETTES IN SALAD

Choose the smallest courgettes you can find. Allow 500 g (1 lb) for 4 people. Other ingredients are salt, water, olive oil, lemon juice or mild wine vinegar, parsley.

To prepare the courgettes for cooking, cut a small slice off each end. Wash the courgettes and, with a potato parer, pare off any rough or blemished strips of skin, so that the outside of the vegetable looks striped, pale and dark green.

Cut each courgette into about 4-cm (1½-in) lengths. Put them into an enamel-lined or flameproof porcelain saucepan. Cover them with cold water. Add 1 dessertspoon of salt. Bring the water to the boil, cover the pan, simmer for approximately 20 minutes. Test the courgettes with a skewer. (A kebab skewer, its point protected with a cork, is a working implement I find indispensable.) They should be tender but not mushy. Immediately they are cooked drain them in a colander.

Have ready a well-seasoned dressing made with fine olive oil and wine vinegar. In this, mix the courgettes while they are still warm. Arrange them in a shallow white salad bowl and scatter a little very finely chopped parsley over them before serving.

Freshly cooked beetroot, French beans, whole small peeled tomatoes and possibly flowerets of cauliflowers dressed in the same manner as the courgettes can be arranged to alternate, in small neat clumps (not mixed higgledy-piggledy), with the courgettes.

In the days of the British Protectorate in Egypt, a vegetable salad prepared in this fashion was a familiar dish on the tables of English and Anglo-Egyptian families and in the British clubs of Cairo, Alexandria and Port Said. Well prepared and with a good dressing, the cold vegetables make a delicate and refreshing salad to be eaten either as a first course or after a roast of meat or chicken. Great care should be taken not to overcook the courgettes or they will be waterlogged and no more interesting than nursery cabbage.

N.B. It should go without saying that since the size and the thickness of courgettes vary a good deal, the cooking time may also need a little adjustment.

COURGETTES WITH LEMON SAUCE

Simmer very small whole courgettes (500 g/1 lb) for 4 people), topped, tailed and washed but not peeled – or use larger courgettes, sliced as for the recipe above – in a heavy enamel-lined saucepan or small casserole with 4 tablespoons of olive oil, plus enough water just to cover the courgettes. Cooking time will be about 30 minutes or until the courgettes can be pierced easily with a fork but still retain a certain crispness and bite. Sprinkle them with salt and powdered cinnamon. Drain off the liquid, reserving it. Transfer the courgettes to a dish.

Mix a teaspoonful of arrowroot, rice flour, cornflour or potato flour with a tablespoon of cold water. Add about 150 ml (¼ pint) of the cooking liquid left from the courgettes. Reheat gently until the sauce has thickened slightly and looks translucent and gelatinous. Add the juice of a lemon and seasonings. Pour over the courgettes. Serve cold, sprinkled with parsley. This is one of the rare courgette dishes which is not spoiled by a short spell in the refrigerator.

N.B. It is essential that the initial cooking of all dishes to be served cold in the Greek manner be done in olive oil, never in butter.

The following recipe does not sound very much like a cold first course vegetable dish. Anyone who can be patient enough to read through it will see that it is indeed a vegetable dish – plus eggs – to be eaten cold.

TIAN OR GRATIN OF COURGETTES, TOMATOES AND EGGS

This is one version – entirely my own and a much simplified one – of a Provençal country dish called a *tian*. The *tian* takes its name from the round earthenware gratin dish used for its cooking; and the ingredients which go into it are variable and very much dependent upon individual taste as well as upon family and local tradition. Green vegetables and eggs are the constants. Tomatoes are almost inevitable, rice or potatoes are quite frequently included. And the *tian* is, like the Spanish omelette or tortilla and the Italian frittata, very often eaten cold as a picnic dish, or as a first – or only – course for the summer midday meal.

Please do not be daunted by the length of the recipe which follows. Once this dish has been mastered – and it is not at all difficult – you find that you have learned at least three dishes as well as a new way of preparing and cooking courgettes.

The ingredients of my *tian* are: 500 g (1 lb) of courgettes, 750 g (1½ lb) of tomatoes (in England use 500 g (1 lb) of fresh tomatoes and make up the quantity with Italian tinned whole peeled tomatoes and their juice), 1 small onion, 2 cloves of garlic, fresh basil when in season, and in the winter dried French marjoram or tarragon, 4 large eggs, a handful (i.e. about 3 tablespoons) of grated Parmesan or Gruyère cheese, a handful of coarsely chopped parsley, salt, freshly milled pepper, nutmeg. For cooking the courgettes and tomatoes, a mixture of butter and olive oil.

The quantities given should be enough for 4 people but the proportions are deliberately somewhat vague because the *tian* is essentially a dish to be made from the ingredients you have available. If, for instance, you have 250 g (½ lb) only of courgettes, make up the bulk with 4 tablespoons of cooked rice, or the same bulk in diced cooked potatoes.

To prepare the courgettes, wash them and pare off any parts of the skins which are blemished, leaving them otherwise unpeeled. Slice them lengthways into four, then cut them into 1-cm (½-in) chunks. Put them at once into a heavy frying pan or enamelled cast-iron skillet or gratin dish, sprinkle them with salt, and set them *without fat of any kind* over a very low flame. Watch them carefully, and when the juices, brought out by the salt, start to seep out, turn the courgettes with a spatula, and drop into the pan 30 g (1 oz) or so of butter, then a tablespoon or two of olive oil. Cover the pan, and leave the courgettes over a low heat to soften.

While the courgettes are cooking prepare the tomatoes. Pour boiling water over them, skin them, chop them roughly. Peel and chop the onion. Heat a very little butter or olive oil in an earthenware *poêlon* or whatever utensil you habitually use for making a tomato fondue or sauce. First melt the chopped onion without letting it brown. Then put in the tomatoes, season them, add the peeled and crushed garlic. Cook, uncovered, over low heat until a good deal of the moisture is evaporated. Now add the tinned tomatoes. These, and their juices, give colour, body and the necessary sweetness to the sauce. Sprinkle in the herb of your choice, let the tomato mixture cook until it is beginning to reduce and thicken.

Now amalgamate the courgettes and the tomato mixture. Turn them into a buttered or oiled earthenware gratin dish. For the quantities given, use one of approximately 18 cm (7 in) diameter and 5 cm (2 in) depth.

Put the gratin dish, covered with a plate if it has no lid of its own, in a moderate oven (170°C/325°F/gas mark 3) for about half an hour, until the courgettes are quite tender.

To finish the *tian*, beat the eggs very well with the cheese, add plenty of seasonings (don't forget the nutmeg) and the coarsely chopped parsley.

Amalgamate the eggs and the vegetable mixture, increase the heat of the oven to 180–190°C/350–375°F/gas mark 4 or 5, and leave the *tian* to cook until the eggs are set, risen in the dish, and beginning to turn golden on the top. The time varies between 15 and 25 minutes depending on various factors such as the depth of the dish, the comparative density of the vegetable mixture, the freshness of the eggs and so on.

When the *tian* is to be eaten cold, leave it to cool in its dish before inverting it on to a serving dish or plate. It should turn out into a very beautiful looking cake, well-risen and moist. For serving cut it in wedges. Inside, there will be a mosaic of pale green and creamy yellow, flecked with the darker green of the parsley and the red-gold of the tomatoes.

To transport a *tian* on a picnic, it can be left in its cooking dish, or turned out on to a serving plate. Whichever way you choose, cover the *tian* with greaseproof paper and another plate, then tie the whole arrangement in a clean white cloth, knotted Dick Whittington fashion.

FRENCH BEAN SALAD

Fine French beans, bootlace thin, which need only topping and tailing, not stringing, make the most exquisite salad, and one which contrasts well with the courgettes in a mixed salad as described above.

Allow 125 g (4 oz) beans per person. Cook them for not more than 7 minutes in boiling salted water. Drain them, and while still warm, mix them in a bowl with olive oil, lemon juice and more salt if necessary. Do not be tempted to add anything else. It is the simplicity of the seasoning and the fresh flavour of the beans which make the dish.

This salad is at its best made immediately before the meal. It does not keep well.

SWEET GREEN PEPPER SALAD

The first time I tasted a sweet pepper salad made in the way described below was in an hotel at Orange, on the road south to Provence.

The spread of crudités brought to the table on an hors d'oeuvre tray looked, even in a part of the country where the hors d'oeuvres are always fresh and shining, especially appetising. There were the usual salads, tomato, cucumber, grated raw carrots, olives green and black, anchovies, and this salad of green peppers cut so finely that when we first saw them we thought they were shredded French beans. There is nothing in the least complicated about preparing it, but if it's to be made in any quantity it does take a little time.

For part of a mixed hors d'oeuvre for 3 or 4 people you need one large green sweet pepper, weighing about 200–250 g (7–8 oz), plus a small quantity of onion, salt, sugar, olive oil, vinegar, lemon juice, parsley.

Cut the stalk end from the pepper and discard all seeds and core. Rinse very thoroughly. Cut the pepper across into strips about 3.5 cm (1½ in) wide. Slice each of these strips into the thinnest possible little slivers, scarcely longer than a match. Put them into a bowl. Add a very little thinly sliced onion – no more than a teaspoonful. Season rather generously with salt, add a pinch of sugar, then 3 tablespoons of olive oil, one of wine vinegar, a squeeze of lemon juice, and a sprinkling of parsley. And, if possible, make the salad an hour or so in advance. Sweet peppers are all the better for being marinated in their dressing a little while before they are to be eaten.

Greek white cheese or feta is nearly always eaten as a meze or first course and goes uncommonly well with raw vegetables such as fennel, the shredded peppers described above, radishes, and with new broad beans. The latter are simply put on the table, as they are, in the pod, on a big dish. Sea salt and good coarse bread should be part of this primitive summer feast.

Wine & Food, June/July 1969

Leaf Salads

Anyone who has visited Venice in the spring and in the early autumn will remember the ravishing and original salads offered in the Venetian restaurants, and the tremendous display of salad leaves and greenstuff to be seen on the stalls in the Rialto market.

Many of these salad stuffs are quite unfamiliar to English eyes. There are three or four varieties of chicory leaves, none of these resembling what we know by that name. One of the northern Italian *cicoria* varieties is the rose-red plant known as *cicoria rossa* of Treviso, another is pink and white and frilly and comes from Castelfranco (both these regions are in the Veneto), yet another has green, elongated leaves and is known as *cicoria spadona* or sword-leaved chicory, a fourth is a lettuce-like plant and, just to help, all these chicories are also called *radicchio*; this is not to be confused with radish or *ravanelli*, of which the leaves are also eaten in salad.

Some of the salad plants, notably the beautiful rose-red chicory, has more decorative value than taste; the green ones are mild and slightly bitter; another, more interesting, salad leaf is *rugeta* or in Venice, *rucola* (nearly all Venetian food names whether fish, fungi or vegetable, differ from those of the rest of Italy), which has a peppery little leaf once familiar in England as rocket, in France as *roquette*, in Greece it is *rocca*, and in Germany *senfkohl* which means mustard herb; then there is corn salad or lamb's lettuce (in Venetian, *gallinelle*, in French, *mâche*), and little bright green serrated leaves which the market women call *salatina*.

In the market, all these salad furnishings are offered for sale in separate boxes, each variety lightly piled up, shining and clean, ready for weighing out. (In Italy salads are bought by the kilo, not by the piece.) There will also be boxes of crisp fennel, violet-leaved artichokes and intensely green courgettes, their bright marigold-coloured flowers still intact.

In the restaurants, the true Venetian restaurants that is, rather than the hotel dining-rooms where you may well have to put up with English-type lettuce and tomato dressed with over-refined olive oil, you will see big bowls of mixed leaves arranged like full-blown peonies for a table decoration, infinitely fresh and appetising. (It is an interesting point that while few Italians are capable of making a graceful flower arrangement, their foodstuffs are invariably displayed with most subtle artistry.) When you order a salad, a waiter will bring one of these bowls to your table so that you can make your choice. Your salad will be mixed for you; the dressing will be of fruity olive oil which has character (it is rare in northern Italy to find poor olive oil) and, in the Veneto, a very good pale rosé wine vinegar. In short you will get a civilised salad which is a treat to the eye as well as a stimulus to the palate and a refreshment to the spirit.

In the early summer of 1969 the salads of Venice made such an impact on one of my sisters – it was her first visit to Venice – that we went to the market and bought seeds of all the local salad plants we could find.

Some of these plants, notably the rocket (its Latin name is *Eruca sativa*; it used to be common in English gardens) did remarkably well that summer in my sister's little cottage garden, near Petersfield; in another garden in the Isle of Wight it grew like a weed, far into the autumn. Sorrel and corn salad, single-leaved parsley, and pink chicory were all forthcoming from these gardens, and so it was that during the warm summer and the long miraculous autumn of that year we all feasted on fresh and spring-like salads almost every day of our lives. English radishes were uncommonly crisp and good, English broad beans scented the greengrocers' shops like a beanfield, mange-tout peas were so delicate and sweet that to eat them raw was like tasting some extraordinary new kind of sorbet – and there were those heartening salads, not it is true at all like Venetian salads but delicious in their own way, and original. (In Venice, we could not have eaten them all summer through. It is too hot. The leafy little salads vanish by the end of May, to reappear only in the autumn.)

GARDEN SALAD

A cos or Webb's lettuce, sorrel leaves, rocket, corn salad, single-leaf parsley (also called, variously, French, Italian, or Greek parsley), chives or green onion tops, and any fresh green salad herbs you may fancy, or have growing in your garden.

With stainless steel kitchen scissors cut the washed and dried lettuce leaves into strips or ribbons. Also cut up a few young sorrel leaves (if they are very small, leave them whole). Mix in a shallow bowl or large soup plate with a handful of corn salad leaves, chives, and French parsley cut with scissors.

Mix the salad at the table with a fruity olive oil and mild wine vinegar dressing to which you have added a very small pinch of sugar as well as salt. With the peppery flavour of the rocket you will not need to add extra pepper.

Proportions of the different salad greens are dictated by individual taste and by what chances to be available. For example, instead of rocket, you could use a few nasturtium leaves which also have a rather peppery tang. Very small tender beetroots, freshly boiled, skinned, sliced and seasoned with dressing while still tepid, make a delicious addition to this salad. *Add them to the greenery only at the last minute.*

Fresh crisp radishes, sliced into little rounds, make another nice addition.

A salad such as this one, based on seasonal leaves and green herbs, should be mixed in a spontaneous easy manner. If it is made into a great production overloaded with urban furbelows such as avocado slices, orange segments, slices of sweet pepper and so on, the rural character is sacrificed.

Unpublished, 1969

A fine example of how much our food has changed in thirty years – at least in part because of Elizabeth David's evocative writing. Now, most of the ingredients she describes are readily available and although these days some salad greens are bland and tasteless, the chicories, rocket and cresses retain their bite, corn salad its gentler flavour. What still remains hard to buy is the mixed small leaves sold as *salatina* in Italy, *mesclun* in France.

JN

Crudités

This year our English spring was cold, wild and windblown. The garden salad greens and herbs were late coming on the market. So it was well into May before I saw home-grown romaine lettuces at my local greengrocery store. On the same day there were the first new broad beans, imported from southern France, and in another shop a box of mini-size fennel offered at half the price of the big ones and worth twice as much. (Only horses could get their teeth into those great over-swollen things, large as coconuts and about as tough.) With a bunch of watercress and a lemon, sea salt and Tuscan olive oil, I had all the makings of a fresh summer salad for a couple of guests.

To be exact, it wasn't a salad that I made, it was a dish of crudités, in the true sense of the term, not meaning just another variant of salade nicoise, nor an incompatible assortment of hors d'oeuvre, cooked and uncooked, in season and out of it. A saucer of Maldon salt was at each place, so was a little boat of olive oil, unmixed, unseasoned with anything whatsoever.

Well, that innocent plateful of what I suppose would be dismissed by many people as rabbit food – lucky rabbits, sensible rabbits – gave us intense enjoyment. The salad ingredients I had found in the shops were, it is true, pretty basic. All the same, they were good enough in their own right to add up to just the kind of small luxury which reminds me very forcibly that salads aren't made to rules and recipes. The perfect salad is as elusive as the perfect omelette. It happens when you have the ingredients and not too many of them, in the right condition, the opportunity to eat them quickly, the confidence to leave them unadorned.

A big production – counting this, adding that, measuring the other – doesn't work nearly as well as a light hand assembling a few fresh green leaves in a bowl. The more swiftly a salad is put together and the sooner it is eaten the better. I don't see how it's feasible to make rules about dressings any more than it is for the salads they're to go with. Too much depends upon the kind of oil you have, and the quality of the vinegar, and whether or not you care for garlic, and what the content of the salad may be. I am certain about a couple of points though. One is that if you have fine first pressing Italian or Provence olive oil, to savage it with acid and sugar and pepper and mustard is a terrible thing. It seems to me equally thoughtless to mix it up into a dressing to store in the refrigerator. It takes less time to mix a fresh dressing than to let an icy cold one come back to room temperature.

Williams-Sonoma booklet, 1975

PARSLEY SALAD

Mix together in a dish a large bunch of chopped parsley, a fresh onion well minced and the pulp of a large lemon cut in small pieces, sprinkle the juice of a lemon on this mixture and add a pinch of salt.

ORANGE SALAD

Peel a few oranges and cut them in large pieces, taking out the pips, adding a few spoonfuls of orange flower water, stir, then sprinkle lightly with powdered cinnamon. Is very soothing.

SALAD OF COS LETTUCE

A fine cos lettuce, finely chopped, sprinkled with the juice of two oranges, a pinch of salt and a good deal of pepper. A curious and very refreshing mixture.

Three unpublished recipes, 1960s

ANGEVIN SALAD

This is a lovely salad to serve after a roast turkey or capon.

Hearts of 2 lettuces or of 2 curly endives or Batavian endives, 250 g (½ lb) Gruyère or Emmenthal cheese, olive oil and wine vinegar for the dressing.

The salad must be fresh and crisp. Wash and dry it well ahead

of time. With it in the bowl mix the Gruyère or Emmenthal (the latter is the one with the large holes, whereas the real Gruyère has very small ones) cut into tiny cubes. Add the dressing, made from 6 tablespoonsful of olive oil to a teaspoonful or two at most of vinegar, at the last minute.

Instead of olive oil, the light walnut oil of Touraine can be used for the dressing. Combined with the cheese it makes a beautiful and interesting mixture.

Dried Herbs, Aromatics and Condiments, 1967

Garlic Presses are Utterly Useless

According to the British restaurant guides, dining at John Tovey's Miller Howe Hotel on Lake Windermere is an experience akin to sitting through the whole Ring cycle in one session. Perhaps, but in Tovey's latest book, *Feast of Vegetables*, there is little sign of excess or eccentricity. His recipes are basically conventional, the novelty, and it is a useful one, lying in the seasonings. Carrots may be spiced with coriander or caraway seed, or green ginger. Orange juice and rind go into grated beetroot. Marsala and toasted almond flakes give courgettes a new look and a new taste. Chicory or Belgian endives are braised in orange juice, the grated peel added. A celeriac soup is again flavoured with orange juice and the grated rind. A celeriac, courgette and potato mixture is cooked in a frying pan into a flat cake – a useful recipe for non-meat eaters. Another in the same category is for individual moulds of cooked carrots and turnips, whizzed to a purée with hazelnuts, egg yolks, cream and seasonings of onion salt (something I can myself at all times do without) and ground ginger. Whisked egg whites are folded in, the mixture is transferred to buttered ramekins lined with lettuce leaves, baked in a water bath in a hottish oven, and turned out for serving. All oven temperatures are given in Fahrenheit, centigrade and gas marks, and timing is always carefully worked out, in many cases with three alternatives, according to whether you want your vegetables crisp – Mr Tovey steers clear of the idiotic term crispy – firm or soft.

It is when we get to the subject of garlic that I really warm to Mr Tovey. What he has to say about its preparation is alone worth the price of his book. The passage should be reproduced in large type, framed and sold in gift shops for the enlightenment of gadget-minded cooks the length and breadth of the land. In the manner of those pious thoughts which once adorned the walls of cottage parlours, proclaiming that God is Love, or Drink is the Pick-me-up which lets you Down, Mr Tovey's text is concise and to the point. Readers, heed him *please*: 'I give full marks to the purveyors of garlic presses for being utterly useless objects.'

I'd go further than that. I regard garlic presses as both ridiculous and pathetic, their effect being precisely the reverse of what people who buy them believe will be the case. Squeezing the juice out of garlic doesn't reduce its potency, it concentrates it and intensifies the smell. I have often wondered how it is that people who have once used one of these diabolical instruments don't notice this and forthwith throw the thing into the dustbin. Perhaps they do but won't admit it.

Now here's John Tovey again. The consistency you're looking for when adding garlic to a dish is 'mushy and paste-like'. Agreed. It is quickly achieved by crushing a peeled clove lightly with the back edge of a really heavy knife blade. Press a scrap of salt into the squashed garlic. That's all. Quicker, surely than getting the garlic press out of the drawer, let alone using it and cleaning it. As a one-time kitchen-shop owner who in the past has frequently, and usually vainly, attempted to dissuade a customer from buying a garlic press, I am of course aware that advice not to buy a gadget which someone has resolved to waste their money on is usually resented as bossy, ignorant, and interfering. At least now I am not alone.

Now a word of dissent. If there's one thing about expensive restaurant cooking which to my mind spoils vegetable soups, it's the often unnecessary and undesirable use of chicken or meat-based stock as a foundation. John Tovey uses just one basic chicken or turkey and vegetable stock for every one of his soups, from asparagus, courgette, fennel, Jerusalem artichoke, to parsnip, sweetcorn, tomato, turnip. I suppose that passes in a hotel restaurant where you're feeding different people every day, but in household cooking such a practice soon results in deathly monotony. That's one, just one, of the reasons stock cubes are so awful. They give the same underlying false flavour to every soup. It can't be sufficiently emphasised that many vegetable soups are best without any stock at all. It's not a question of lazy cooking.

Donkeys years ago I learned from Boulestin not to diminish and distort the indefinably strange and alluring flavour of Jerusalem artichoke purée with stock. A year or two ago, when Raymond Blanc was still at the Quat' Saisons in Oxford, I had there a creamy pumpkin soup which I'd be happy to eat every other day. He told me he used a very light vegetable stock as a base for his delectable creation. The information seems worth passing on.

Tatler, February 1986

Tians

Among the very simplest and easiest of summer dishes are those mixtures of vegetables and eggs baked in an open earthenware casserole or gratin dish called in the Provençal language a *tian*. From the earthenware tian, the dish itself takes its name. Not that there is any one specific formula for a tian; there are as many variations as there are of a salade niçoise, the idea being that you use a certain proportion of freshly cooked green vegetables – spinach, spinach beet or chard (the kind the French call *blettes*) – bulking them out, if you like, with potatoes or rice and mixing them all up with eggs beaten as for an omelette. The proportions depend to a certain extent upon what you have available, the size of your dish, the number of people you have to feed. Seasonings and extra flavourings may be onions, garlic, anchovies, capers. Grated cheese – usually Gruyère, Parmesan or Dutch – and plenty of chopped parsley and other fresh green herbs are fairly constant ingredients. Sometimes a richly aromatic tomato sauce goes into the mixture. A *tian*, as you see, is a wonderfully flexible dish, not the least of its beauties being that it is equally good hot or cold; it is indeed a traditional picnic dish of the country people around Arles, Avignon and Aix-en-Provence. Every family has a different recipe. Some are just simple mixtures of vegetables and cheese with a top layer of breadcrumbs and without any eggs at all, although these I think are best eaten hot. My own favourites are made with courgettes, potatoes and eggs, or with spinach, potatoes and eggs.

TIAN OF COURGETTES

250 g (8 oz) of courgettes, 250–350 g (8–12 oz) potatoes boiled in their skins, 2 heaped tablespoons each of parsley and grated cheese, a few spinach or sorrel leaves if you happen to have them, a small clove of garlic, seasonings of salt, nutmeg and freshly milled black pepper, 5 or 6 eggs, approximately 4 tablespoons of olive oil.

For these quantities you need an earthenware dish of 20 cm diameter and 5 cm deep (8 in × 2 in). A *tian* made with the quantities given should be enough for 4–6 people.

First peel the cooked potatoes. Cut them into cubes, put them into the earthenware dish with 2 tablespoons of olive oil, the chopped garlic and seasonings of salt and pepper. Let them warm in the uncovered dish in a low oven, 150°C/300°F/gas mark 2, while you prepare and cook the courgettes. The best way to do this is simply to wash them, trim off the ends, and leave them unpeeled except for any blemished parts. Instead of slicing them, grate them coarsely on a stainless steel grater. Put them straight into a sauté pan or wide frying pan with a couple of tablespoons of olive oil (or butter if you prefer), sprinkle them with salt, cook them gently for 5 minutes, with a cover on the pan.

Now break the eggs into a large bowl. Beat them until frothy. Add the chopped parsley and any other fresh greenery you may have – this could include watercress and lettuce as well as spinach or sorrel, uncooked and simply cut up with scissors – the cheese, salt, pepper, nutmeg, then the warm courgettes. Last of all, but gently to avoid breaking them, stir in the potatoes. Tip the whole mixture into the dish, sprinkle the top with a little oil, return it, uncovered, to the oven, now heated to 190°C/375°F/gas mark 5.

Leave the *tian* to bake for 25–30 minutes until it is well and evenly risen. The top should be a fine and appetising golden-brown. For serving hot, leave it in the dish, and simply cut it into wedges, like a cake. If you intend to serve it cold, leave it to cool before turning it out on to a serving plate. If it is for a picnic leave it in the cooking dish, put a plate on top and envelop it in a cloth knotted at the top.

Although the *tian* is a rather rough and ready dish, it is not without certain subtleties of texture and taste. And when you cut into it, it is beautiful, marbled with the green herbs, the squares of white potato, the yellow eggs. Typically Mediterranean, it is another among those many admirable inventions for which we have to thank generations of peasant farmers and cooks making the best of the resources provided by their own kitchen gardens and farmyards.

Notes

When mixing the *tian* ingredients, it's preferable that the vegetables be hot when they are mixed with the beaten eggs, and it is important that as soon as the mixture is ready it be poured into the cooking dish and transferred immediately to the oven. If it is kept waiting in the dish, the eggs tend to rise to the top, so you get a dish in two layers, instead of one integrated and nicely-marbled cake.

TIAN WITH TOMATOES AND COURGETTES*

For this variation the prepared courgettes are mixed with a thickish and well-seasoned sauce made from 500 g (1 lb) of skinned and chopped tomatoes (or half and half fresh and tinned) cooked in olive oil with a clove or two of garlic, onions if you like, and a flavouring of wild marjoram (oregano) or, for a change, tarragon.

Simmer the sauce until it is well reduced, amalgamate it with the cooked courgettes, then mix both with the beaten eggs, cheese and parsley, and cook as above.

This *tian*, with the red-gold of the tomato, and the green of the courgettes, is just as handsome as the first one.

TIAN WITH SPINACH AND POTATOES

Wash 500 g (1 lb) of fresh spinach, cook it very briefly in just the water clinging to the leaves. Season with a little salt. Drain and squeeze dry. Chop it roughly, adding a little garlic if you like, and half a dozen anchovy fillets torn into short lengths. Stir this mixture into the beaten eggs and cheese, then add the cubed potatoes, and cook the *tian* as before. If you can lay hands on a few pine nuts, they make a delicious and characteristic addition to this *tian*. An alternative to the potatoes is cooked rice. Allow about 100 g (3½ oz), uncooked weight, for this size of *tian*.

---

* *See also* the different version – *Tian* or gratin of courgettes, tomatoes and eggs on page 42.

GRATIN OF RICE AND COURGETTES

This is a rather different dish, more delicate and milder than any of the *tian* tribe.

For 4 people allow 500 g (1 lb) of courgettes, 100 g (3½ oz) of butter, 2 tablespoons of flour, ½ litre (18 fl oz) of milk, 3 tablespoons of Parmesan or Gruyère, 4 tablespoons of fine quality rice, seasonings of salt, pepper and nutmeg. A little extra butter for finishing the dish.

Prepare, grate, and cook the courgettes as described in the first *tian* recipe, but using half the butter instead of olive oil. (This is a wonderful way of cooking courgettes to serve as a vegetable on its own – but you need a large pan.)

With the remaining butter, the flour and warmed milk make a béchamel sauce. Season it well, not forgetting a little nutmeg. When it is well cooked and smooth, stir in the courgettes.

Cook the rice in boiling salted water, keeping it on the firm side.

Have ready a lightly buttered gratin dish, approximately 20 cm × 5 cm (8 in × 2 in), combine the courgette-béchamel mixture with the rice, put it all into the dish and smooth it down, lightly. On top sprinkle the Parmesan, and a little butter in tiny knobs.

Put the dish near the top of a moderate oven, 170°C/325°F/gas mark 3 and let it cook for 15–20 minutes, or 30 if the whole mixture has been heated up from cold. The top should be lightly golden and bubbly.

The first time I ever had this gratin of courgettes was at lunch in a village inn at Rians near Aix-en-Provence. It was twenty years ago and I can still remember our meal. First came a typical Provençal hors d'oeuvre – pâté, tomato salad, olives, a few slices of salami – then the courgette dish, quite on its own, followed by a daube of beef served sizzling hot in a casserole brought to the table and left on it so that we could help ourselves. Then, as an alternative to the fruit, or ice cream, one would expect at the end of such a meal we were offered little bowls of a most delicious jam, home-made from green melons. There was, by the way, no vegetable of any kind with the beef stew. We had good bread with which to mop up the juices, and that was enough.

Søndags B-T, Denmark, June 1976

Le Rouge et le Noir

Black looks give all dishes in which aubergines cooked in their skins – as with rare exceptions they should be – an alluring and dramatic appearance. To a certain extent the same applies to black olives in beef and wine stews; also to caviare and black truffles; to cèpes and flat field mushrooms stewed in olive oil in a pot lined with vine leaves; and to squid cooked in its own ink. This dish, served with the ritual slabs of marigold yellow polenta of northern Italy, has a high theatrical appeal to the eye; to the palate it is rich, strange, and worth at least a venture when one comes across it in Venice and on the Adriatic coast.

A generation or two ago I think that English people would have felt just as adventurous in approaching the ratatouille, that handsome mixture of onions, aubergines, peppers and tomatoes imported from Provence. Such is the power of a memorable name and dramatic looks that, at any rate according to Mr Egon Ronay reporting in his restaurant guide, ratatouille has become the national dish of Chelsea. If that is the case, best leave our Chelsea restaurant cooks to evolve their national dish in their own way, without worrying too much if their way is seldom recognisable as the way of Provence.

When the time comes for a change, as alluring a name on the menu and a dish which demands less ritualistic preparation and production is the bohémienne. I don't say that this is one of the world's great regional dishes; it is a relation, lighter in weight, less compact and less demanding, of the ratatouille. It is a red and green dish rather than a black and bronze one; a dish of inland and upper Provence rather than of the Mediterranean littoral. It has another name, barbouillade, as descriptive as ratatouille, which after all is only French for a stew, mish-mash, hotch-potch.

The ingredients for bohémienne, susceptible of a good deal of variation, are approximately as follows:

4 tablespoons of olive oil, 250 g (8 oz) onions, 2 small red or green sweet peppers, a clove of garlic, 500 g (1 lb) courgettes, 250 g (½ lb) skinned tomatoes, salt, a little fresh basil or parsley.

The method of cooking is much as for ratatouille: the vegetables, put into the pot with the olive oil, in the order given, are stewed gently for about 45 minutes.

The owner of the restaurant at Gap in upper Provence where I first encountered this dish informed me that the omission of aubergines is the point which differentiates bohémienne from ratatouille. René Jouveau in his recently published *La Cuisine Provençale de Tradition Populaire*, a book produced with heavy-handed luxury but into which the author has put much pains-taking research concerning every local dish mentioned in Mistral's poems and a good many others besides, gives a recipe for bohémi-enne in which aubergines are the *raison d'être* of the dish and does not mention ratatouille at all (I believe that ratatouille is technically a Niçois dish; and to the *félibriges*, the writers and poets of Mistral's Provençal revival period, Nice was not Provence); possibly bohémienne is simply the inland version of a typical southern vegetable stew.

Unexpected recipes from authors regarded as classic are always interesting. About Escoffier's work a relevant point to remember is that he was a Provençal who was born and spent his early boyhood in the village of Villeneuve-Loubet in the Alpes-Maritimes. From his post-*Guide Culinaire* cookery books and articles one has the impression that he did not ever entirely lose the taste for the village cooking of his very humble childhood and that occasionally, bored with exquisite subtlety and the standards of perfection he had himself created, he had wistful hankerings for the primitive food of his childhood. Today's interest in all regional cooking and in particular in the dishes of his own native Provence would surely have been welcome to him.

I do not know whether Escoffier's sweet pepper and onion mixture, a cross between a chutney and a sauce to be eaten with cold meat, was derived from a Provençal recipe – it is a little reminiscent of the Italian peperonata – whether he evolved it from some other source, or invented it entirely. It is an uncommonly interesting and unusual sauce. Escoffier calls it simply *piments pour viandes froides* and the recipe is to be found in his *Ma Cuisine*, published by Flammarion in 1934, the year before the author's death at the age of eighty-nine.

This Escoffier sauce, one which evidently never found its way into the bottles of the Peckham factory he founded in 1898, is one which became a favourite of mine during the years I lived in Egypt. The ingredients were all to hand, cheap and common, and the sauce was a great enlivener for the local meat. My own slightly simplified and reduced version of the recipe is no longer quite that of Escoffier.*

You need 2 large fat fleshy sweet and very ripe red peppers (about 500 g/1 lb), 250 g (8 oz) mild Spanish onions, 500 g (1 lb) ripe tomatoes, 1 clove of garlic, 125 g (4 oz) raisins, half a teaspoon each of salt, powdered ginger (or grated dried root ginger) and mixed spices such as allspice, mace and nutmeg, 250 g (8 oz) white sugar, 4 tablespoons of olive oil and 150 ml (¼ pint) of fine wine vinegar.

Melt the finely chopped onions in the olive oil, add the chopped peppers (well washed, all core and seeds removed), salt and spices, and after 10 minutes, the peeled and chopped tomatoes and the raisins, garlic and sugar, lastly the vinegar. Cook extremely slowly, covered, for at least 1¼ hours.

A tall marmite-type pot rather than a wide preserving pan should be used for this confection. The sauce does not, and I think is not supposed to, turn into a jam-like substance. It is another bronze dish, *mordoré* to use the marvellous French word.

Bottled in screw-top jars the mixture keeps well for two or three weeks, although I have never made enough at one time to report as to whether it has a more enduring shelf life. It is good with cold lamb and beef.

For an ancient black-a-vised dish, I think that a recipe from Robert May's *Accomplisht Cook* (1660) is worth consideration:

Tart Stuff that Carries its Colour Black

Take three pounds of prunes and eight fair pippins par'd and cor'd. stew them together with some claret wine, some whole cinnamon, slic't ginger, a sprig of rosemary, sugar, and a clove or two, being well stewed and cold, strain them with rose-water, and sugar.

This mixture was used as a filling for open pies, and possibly appeared on Stuart tables in company with others of different colours, for May, a writer with a great eye for drama and decorative touches (sprigs of gilded rosemary ornamenting creams, leaves of a kind of clotted cream made into a frilly cabbage shape), gives

* The Escoffier recipe was published in *Spices, Salt and Aromatics in the English Kitchen.*

recipes also for yellow, white, green and red tart stuff, all made from fruit, the red ones consisting of quinces, pippins, cherries, raspberries, barberries, red currants, red gooseberries or damsons. In effect, most of May's fruit mixtures were jams, although many were made from dried or preserved fruit – apricots, quinces, nectarines, peaches and plums.

In Turin recently I saw and bought something which I think would have pleased Robert May: black sugared fruit. They were walnuts. Gathered green, they turn black and soft when preserved. Sugar-dusted and clove-scented nuggets of onyx, these candied walnuts are a speciality unique to one and one only of the confectioners' shops for which Turin is famous.

The Spectator, 4 October 1963

Erbaggi Mantovani: Vegetables of Mantua

Bartolomeo Stefani's *L'arte di ben cucinare* first appeared in Mantua in 1662. Stefani, who was Bolognese by birth, had trained with his uncle, a master cook working in Venice. At the time his book was written and published Stefani was chief cook to the ducal house of Gonzaga in Mantua. The family's glory and prosperity had long since departed, but that they were still able on occasion to entertain on a splendid scale can be seen from descriptions of some of the state banquets included by Stefani in the *Nuova Aggiunta* or *New Additions* to the third edition of his work which appeared in 1671. One such occasion was the visit in November 1655 of Queen Christina of Sweden when, Stefani says, he personally served all the ceremonial and ornamental cold dishes and presented the numerous and grandiose *trionfi* of sugar work and also of pleated linen. On the whole, however, the Gonzaga in Stefani's day seem to have eaten quite frugally, and few of his recipes are for rich or complex dishes. Compared indeed to the styles of cooking described in contemporary French and English works such as Robert May's *Accomplisht Cook* of 1660 and La Varenne's *Le Cuisinier François* of 1651, Stefani's is almost modern, distinguished particularly by many interesting vegetable dishes and a number of unusual sauces and relishes in which fruit plays an important part.

The Italian love of both vegetables and fruit and their skill in growing them is of course apparent in all their cookery manuals from the days of Apicius to the publication in 1570 of Scappi's magisterial *Opera*, and in all those stewards' handbooks which were such a notable feature of Italian publishing from the second half of the sixteenth century right up to the end of the seventeenth. But in Stefani's work a new, and intensely personal, approach is evident. He picks and chooses his ingredients and his words with equal care, puts them together thoughtfully, weighs and specifies his quantities, explains his methods clearly. He loves his work and is proud of his profession. Altogether he is making a great effort to fulfil the promise carried in his title of 'instructing the less expert' in the art of good cooking. 'This little book,' he says in his address to the readers, 'does not come from an academy but from a kitchen.' It certainly reads as though he had been writing close to the cooking pots and the fire, the spice boxes and the knives, the scales and the strainers. That ever-present sound of all kitchens of his day, of weighty pestle pounding in huge mortar is still in his ears as he composes his book. In seventeenth-century Italy that quality is uncommon. Since 1570 Scappi's great work had stood alone in dealing directly with practical cookery, and in having been written by a practising cook. Physicians, chemists, scientists, agricultural and horticultural experts, and above all the stewards and professional carvers had all had their say on household and domestic matters, some of them at considerable length. But among them all none since Domenico Romoli, author of *La Singolare Dottrina*, a work first published in 1560 and reprinted in 1570, appear to have personally come to grips with the realities of the kitchen proper as distinct from the work of the Credenza or Pantry, in which the salads and cold dishes, the desserts and fruit were prepared.

Of the following brief selection of vegetable recipes from Stefani's *L'Arte di ben cucinare*, the *minestra d'erba brusca* is from the *Additions* to the 1671 edition, all the others having already appeared in the original 1662 edition.

MINESTRA DI FINOCCHIO
(a dish of fennel)

Take well cleaned fennel and wash it in cold water, and having first cooked it in a vegetable broth and cut it into mouthfuls, you are to put it in a glazed vessel with a little capon broth, and when hot put in a few gooseberries (*uva spina*), a glass of cream, two ounces (60 g) of pine nuts steeped in rosewater, crushed in the mortar, and thicken the sauce with four egg yolks beaten with lemon juice, and under the fennel in the dish put slices of bread fried in butter; thus you may make a most delicate minestra, serving it hot, powdered with cinnamon.

MINESTRA D'ERBA BRUSCA E DI BORAGGIO E CIME DI FINOCCHIO E CIME DI BIETA
(minestra of sorrel, borage, fennel shoots and beet shoots)

Take these four varieties of herbs well cleaned and washed in plenty of water; you mince them all very small, in quantities which you must judge by your own eye, knowing how much minestra you need to make, and when they are minced you put them in a two-handled soup pot (*pignatta*), adding capon broth, or else beef broth, enough to cover the herbs by half, not to rise above them; put the *pignatta* over a charcoal fire and as soon as it boils the broth reaches perfection.

To season the minestra you take fresh eggs, grated cheese in proportion, and cook as already instructed; if you like to add asparagus tips in the season, you may put them in, but first having cooked them in water, then plunged them in fresh cold water, so that they lose that particular odour which they give the water. There are many cooks who first cook the fresh herbs in the same way, thereby throwing away the best part, for they throw away the first juices given out by the herbs, leaving them with less aroma and less goodness.

ZUCCHI TENERE, O ZUCCOLI DA FRIGGERE
(young tender marrows, or small marrows for frying)

Take the marrows, free of skin and cut in slices, steeped and softened with salt, and well drained, arrange the slices one on top of the other, put a weight on them so that the moisture is pressed out, and carefully flour them. Put these slices in a frying pan with clarified butter, when they are cooked take them from the pan and prepare the following sauce.

Take a little basil, a leaf or two of sage (*erba amara*), a few fennel seeds, all well pounded in the mortar, and for every pound of *zucchi*, take four ounces (125 g) of soft cheese, pound it well in the mortar with the other ingredients, then allay it with the juice of verjuice grapes, the juice to be first diluted with water; add nothing else, but if the juice has not been diluted you may add two ounces (60 g) of sugar with four yolks of fresh eggs well beaten, put all in a *cazzetta* (a water bath) on the fire with three ounces (90 g) of butter, stirring with a wooden spoon, and when you perceive that it has cooked into a thickened broth, then cover the dish of marrows with this sauce and serve it cold with powdered cinnamon.

If the marrows are fried in oil, make the sauce in this fashion. Instead of soft cheese take crumb of bread steeped in verjuice, with the same aromatic herbs, and instead of eggs use almond milk, and cook the sauce in the same way. But when the marrows are larger, you may cut them in the fashion of lardoons. They may also be stuffed, as I have told you. Patty cases may be made from them, and in fine they make such a diversity of dishes that they could constitute an entire course.

VIVANDA D'AVENTANI
(a dish of eggplants)

Providing a rare variant on the Italian name of the eggplant – so rare indeed that it appears not to have been known to R. Arveiller when he wrote his nineteen-page article on *Les noms français de l'aubergine*, necessarily covering numerous Italian and Catalan variations, published in the *Revue de Linguistique romane*, Vol. 33, 1969[1] – this recipe of Stefani's is both original and easily

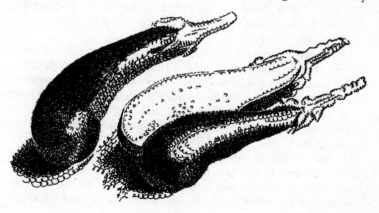

adaptable. It also tells us that this fruit was at that time, in northern Italy at any rate, cultivated in monastery gardens and was still unfamiliar enough for the readers to need a description. The name used by Stefani which derived, I think, not from the now obsolete *avelenoso* meaning something injurious, harmful, poisonous, but from *aventare*, to wind, to fill and puff with wind, or from its participle meaning windy, puffed, full of wind.[2] To judge from what Stefani says, he was approaching this fruit with caution, but not with the deep suspicion it had so often engendered in the past.

'The *aventani* are certain fruits grown in gardens and in which monks such as Capucins, Osservanti and the like are specialists. When in perfection they turn a purple colour and are smooth as ivory; they are about the size of an apple, oval in shape. Take these, remove their skins with very exact care, and having split them, take away their seeds, then divide them in small pieces, plunge them in cold water, which you must change two or three times, in order to remove their natural bitterness: take them from the water, dry them, put them in a *pignatta* or other vessel of a suitable size, with oil, salt and pepper, and set them on a charcoal fire, stirring frequently. When they are cooked, take sweet almonds, three ounces (90 g) for every pound (500 g) of eggplant, toast them in the oven, taking care not to scorch them, and pulverise them in a mortar, add a little nutmeg, and a little sugar according to your judgement, all to be tempered with the juice of bitter oranges, put this into the vessel containing the eggplants, which are to be turned into a dish and served hot.

If you wish to cook this dish with butter, do it as above, but instead of the almond sauce dress it with *piacentino* (Parmesan), with cinnamon over.'

I have many times cooked aubergines on the lines described by Stefani, but bypassing the cold water baths he recommends – I find that aubergines nowadays don't need any pre-cooking treatment to remove bitterness – and the removal of seeds (I have come across this same daunting direction in a Spanish MS recipe of about the same date as Stefani's), a refinement I have not even contemplated.

For the sauce, the three ounces (90 g) of almonds to a pound (500 g) of aubergines is rather too high an allowance, I find, particularly as Stefani appears to have been using the twelve ounces (350 g) pound, and one and a half ounces (45 g) to the juice of a couple of Seville oranges seems about right. A word of warning here. The bitter orange juice and the scrap of sugar in combination with the almonds makes a sauce so vastly superior to the same made with sweet orange juice, without the sugar but with the addition of lemon juice, that I am tempted to say don't bother to try the dish until you can lay hands on Seville oranges, but perhaps after all it is worthwhile persevering until you find some satisfactory way round the problem. A sprinkling of ground red sumac, that favourite Persian seasoning, might provide a simple lemon, sweet orange and almond mixture with just the required quality of aromatic acidity; or sweet-sour pomegranate juice could be the answer. It is a pity to have to keep so good a dish as Stefani's *Vivanda d'aventani* for just those few weeks of the year when Seville oranges are obtainable in England.

I think, by the way, that the dish is better cold than hot. And I do find that a very small amount of garlic, chopped with parsley, and added during the cooking, is an improvement, almost a necessity.

VIVANDA DI SILARI
(a dish of celery)

Take the celery well cleaned of its leaves and green stalks so that what remains is half a palm's length of the heart of the celery close to the foot; throw it into cold water and wash it; have ready a pot of vegetable broth on the fire, when it is at the height of boiling throw in the celery, let it boil until half cooked; then take it from the broth, put it in a dry vessel, squeezing lemon juice over it and adding crushed pepper; in the meantime prepare a frying pan with butter. And because celery, like many other things is calculated by the piece not by measure or weight, it is obvious that there are small and large ones, so that in some places the average ones may be larger than the large of elsewhere; and in other places so small that the largest are smaller than even the medium ones of elsewhere, so it is necessary to use judgement and to take a quantity proportioned to the ingredients here given:

For every two pounds (1 kg) of celery, therefore, prepared as above: put into a frying pan over a slow fire a *piccata* (a chopped foundation as in the modern *battuto*) of *ventresca di porco* (salt pork belly), or *panzetta* (the same cut but differently cured) as you please, and this you cook lightly, and when it is almost cooked you add the celery; and separately you beat the yolks of six fresh eggs with lemon juice, two ounces (60 g) of fine sugar, six ounces (180 g) of Genoa capers in vinegar, removing their stalks, three ounces (90 g) of crushed pine nuts, and all this you throw into the pan set over a very low fire; when you see that this composition is setting, like curded milk (*cagliata*), have in readiness a dish spread with slices of bread which you have sprinkled and rubbed with garlic cloves, then fried in butter; and on these put the celery heads with their sauce, garnishing the dish with grated Parmesan cheese and powdered cinnamon.

This is a graceful and delicate dish; serve it hot.

Note

This is perhaps an appropriate place for a note on the Italian cookery book use of the term *cagliata* and its correct meaning.

Usually taken by English translators to mean curdled in the sense of separated, as when a custard or an egg-thickened sauce or soup gets over-cooked, the direction has been a puzzle to many people. No wonder. It was not the intention, I am sure, in the minds of the people who initially recorded the recipes concerned that their sauces should be curdled. It was simply that a more precise term for describing a smooth, creamy, egg-thickened sauce or custard did not exist in Italian or Spanish culinary language – in French it was *prise* – and the nearest one to use was *cagliata* or *quagliata* in its secondary sense of congealed, set, clotted, or if you like, curded (but not curdled) as in our own lemon curd, which after all is not and never has been curdled, at any rate not intentionally. A related English usage of the term, which I came across only recently, occurs in a seventeenth-century MS receipt embodying the direction to 'whip the whites till ye come to curd'.

A good example of a recipe demonstrating that *quagliata* did not in fact mean curdled in the sense usually understood occurs in Scappi's *minestra di zucchi* with almond milk (1643 edition, p. 511). In this recipe the sliced gourd or marrow, boiled in chicken or veal broth, is reheated in almond milk based on the broth in which the marrow has boiled, plus verjuice. There are no eggs and no milk proper in the mixture, but it is to be sweetened with sugar, the cooking is to continue until it becomes thick, *venge quagliata*, and the minestra is to end up of *maggior sostanza*, of great substance. In other words you are aiming for a reduced and dense mass of syrupy marrow. It doesn't sound very enticing, but curdled in our sense of the term it is not and could not be.

Quagliata by the way derived from the Arabic *quajar*, meaning both to curdle and to congeal. I could cite many more Italian recipes, mainly from sixteenth- and seventeenth-century books, in which the term is used in a sense which can only be understood to mean thickened or congealed, as in a custard or a béarnaise sauce. Stefani's book alone contains a great number of such recipes. Now and again he even used the term *congelata*, instead of *cagliata*. Evidently the 1660s in Mantua, as elsewhere in Italy, was a great time for egg-thickened sauces, often served over bread as Stefani directs for his *vivanda di silari*. Something of the kind was of course the origin of the *zuppa inglese*, that favourite dessert of modern Italy, the *zuppa* having indicated, originally, the sup or sop of bread, not the custard sauce.

References

1. A copy of this article was most kindly sent to me by a reader, Mr C. A. Stray of Swansea, after he had read my essay on aubergines ('Mad, Bad, Despised and Dangerous', in *PPC* No. 9), to whom my very grateful thanks.

2. John Florio's *Worlde of Wordes*, 1611 and 1688 editions, and the *Grande Dizionario della Lingua Italiana*, 1972. It may be worth noting that Florio also gives what could conceivably put another interpretation on the derivation of Stefani's *aventani*. This is *aventiccio*, a foreigner, a stranger, one that hath no settled place of abode, but is going and coming, etc.

Petits Propos Culinaires, No. 12, 1989

Home Cooking

It's a dull schoolboy who doesn't collect things. Birds' eggs and butterflies are discouraged nowadays, matchboxes aren't what they were, cigarette cards and model trains are for adults who go to auction prepared to spend the year's rates three times over on a Dinky toy. The odd child prodigy does of course gather in Krugerrands, Stradivarius violins, London theatres, and lost Tom Keatings. But to collect potatoes like George V collected postage stamps it took a Scots schoolboy, now Captain Donald MacLean of Dornock Farm near Crieff in Perthshire. Not just a few varieties of potato picked up like pebbles to take home and gloat over, you understand, but potatoes to cultivate, potatoes of widely differing characteristics, colours, shapes, flavours, textures, cooking properties. Potatoes red, blue, purple, black, even ordinary potato-coloured potatoes. A splendid and rare mania. Did the youthful MacLean by any chance catch it from a boyhood reading of that extraordinary book by Redcliffe N. Salaman published in 1949 and, a trifle forbiddingly, entitled *The History and Social Influence of the Potato?*

Whatever the origin of Captain MacLean's obsession, Jane Grigson, in *The Observer Guide to British Cookery*, her latest and to date bravest book, tells us that he now has 350 varieties of potato under cultivation. Yes. Not that it's the world's largest collection, as Mrs Grigson thought when she wrote her potato piece; that's maintained by the World Potato Collection in Lima, Peru, native habitat of the potato. Still, for a start 350 will do. How many varieties of potato can a London greengrocer name by name? Two? Three? How many can any of us buy in our local shops? How often do we eat them as a dish in their own right? What's happened to the vegetable cooks in our upmarketish London restaurants, that, apart from frites or pommes Pont Neuf, engagingly offered on the menu of the old Derry & Toms roof garden restaurant as Ninth Bridge potatoes, the only potato dish they seem to know is a damp and usually inappropriate little portion of gratin which arrives on a tea-plate along with a dab of carrot purée and a couple of broccoli spears? Couldn't those cooks ever be persuaded that customers would welcome the chance of trying, let's say, real griddle-baked Irish potato cakes or the potato pancakes called boxsty? Mrs Grigson produces a plausible explanation for the name as well as a careful recipe. Why not have a go?

In France, a country to which potatoes came late, much later than to us, several localities boast of their potato pancakes. Not after all a very resounding culinary achievement, but still a worthwhile one. I remember a restaurant at Vonnas, north-east of Lyon, where back in the Fifties the patronne's potato pancakes were so famous that her establishment was awarded two Michelin stars. If you stayed there you climbed down steep stairs from your bedroom and proceeded through the kitchen to the restaurant. Adjoining it, the bar would be busy with local workmen drinking their evening aperitifs. I'm afraid it isn't like that now. The present proprietor, Georges Blanc, grandson, I believe, of the Mère Blanc of those days, currently has three stars and a helicopter pad, though I'm sure that doesn't stop him offering the family's famous potato speciality. Michel and Albert Roux, Nico Ladenis, Anton Mosimann, where are you? And Captain MacLean will you help?

As Jane Grigson reminds us, to make good potato cakes we need floury potatoes, and in our islands, even in the other one, they're rarities now. All the same, at the Kundan restaurant in Horseferry Road, Westminster, admirably cooked and wonderfully spiced potato cakes are always to be had, and I don't believe the kitchen there has any potatoes we can't all buy. Admittedly, to order Kundan's potato cakes you ask for vegetable kebabs, but the point is that they *can* be ordered, that they will arrive freshly made, sizzling in an iron pan, and you may eat them on their own. You aren't expected to have them *with* something.

I didn't intend to give the impression that Jane Grigson's *British Cookery* is exclusively concerned with potatoes – indeed I rather wish she'd given more space to the subject, potatoes being, after all, of nearly as much national interest as grain and bread – because what this new book is really about is not so much British cooking as its essential materials and the heroic efforts currently being made by British market-gardeners, fruit growers, poultry and livestock-breeders – one success there is the rearing of veal calves in decent, humane conditions – British dairy farmers and British cheesemakers. With the very properly acknowledged assistance of Major Patrick Rance of cheese-shop fame, and with the co-operation of a handful of conscientious restaurateurs and retailers, Jane Grigson has sought out dedicated small-scale producers who are constructively fighting the familiar ogres of factory farming, unworkable EEC regulations, the bureaucrats of the Milk Marketing Board and all those who push the just acceptable at the expense of the best. An appendix lists relevant addresses.

When it comes to honourable British specialities Jane Grigson knocks spots off our feeble Taste of Britain campaigns with their make-believe food and phoney regional recipes. Here, for a start, is that legendary rarity, the Lincolnshire chine of salt pork stuffed with a basinful of fresh green herbs of all sorts. Tied in a cloth, boiled, pressed, eaten cold, the Lincoln chine was described, with much relish, by the poet Verlaine when a schoolmaster in the locality in the 1870s. I suppose you could say it is England's reply to the Burgundian *jambon persillé*. An appetising photograph of this appetising speciality accompanies the recipe, and Mrs Grigson gives the address of the Lincoln butcher from whom it may be ordered, May to December.

Inevitably, in a book with origins in a chopped-up Sunday supplement series, the photographs of sheep farmers, cheese-makers, shopkeepers, seaweed gatherers tend to look folksy and contrived as though the subjects were posing for postcards. Come to that, the *Observer* could do worse than go into the food postcard business – I've often thought of doing it myself – donating a proportion of the profits to the support of some worthy cause. How about a campaign to outlaw the use of dye in the cure of smoked haddock and kippers? Or promotion of the Rare Breeds Survival Trust, a body helping for one thing, to bring back real ham pigs such as the Tamworths and Gloucester Old Spots reared by Anne Petch of Heal Farm, King's Nympton, Devon? From these pigs Mrs Petch cures hams described by Mrs Grigson as glorious, no less.

Tatler, March 1985

In the 1980s Jane Grigson, and other writers and broadcasters like Jeremy Round and Derek Cooper did their utmost to raise awareness of and promote the best of British produce. The Consumers' Association published its *Good Food Directory*, edited by Drew Smith and David Mabey, in 1986. In 1993 appeared the first edition of Henrietta Green's influential *Food Lover's Guide to Britain*, and by then Randolph Hodgson and his colleagues at Neal's Yard Dairy had further developed the market for prime British cheeses. At the end of the 1990s farmers' markets were being established across Britain, and specialist and organic producers of meat, fish, fruit and vegetables are doing booming business by mail order as well as through supermarkets and independent shops.

JN

The Great English Aphrodisiac

It was a subject awaiting an author. The potato, its history as a member of the botanical family *Solanaceae*, its adoption by man as a cultivated plant, and the record of its spread throughout the world, found a very remarkable author. He was a young doctor, whose active career in medicine had been cut short by illness while still in his twenties. By the time he was thirty-two, living a life of ease in a beautiful Hertfordshire village, happily married, free from financial worries, Redcliffe Salaman found himself completely restored to health and able once more to lead a physically active life. His winters were sufficiently taken up with fox-hunting but, lacking enthusiasm for golf, tennis and cricket, he found his summers empty of interesting occupation. After a false start in the field of Mendelian research and the study of the heredity of butterflies, hairless mice, guinea pigs and the like, this singular young man turned to his gardener for advice as to a suitable subject for research. Something ordinary, such as a common kitchen garden vegetable, Dr Salaman stipulated.

The gardener, whose name was Evan Jones, was that archetype, the omniscient one known ever since Adam vacated Eden. Jones had no hesitation in advising Dr Salaman that if he wanted to spend his spare time in the study of vegetables, then he had better choose the potato. Because, said Jones, 'I know more about the potato than any man living.' It was then 1906. Forty-three years later, in 1949, Redcliffe Salaman's extraordinary study, *The History and Social Influence of the Potato*, was published by the Cambridge University Press. 'A work of profound and accurate scholarship', commented the scientific journal *Nature*. 'A great, in many respects a noble work' was the *Spectator*'s verdict. Reprinted in 1970, and again last November, with a new introduction and corrections by J. G. Hawkes, the book remains a major work of reference on its subject.

With the exception of recipes, no aspect of the potato story was neglected by Salaman. He traces its origins in the Andes, and its deep significance in the lives of the Incas, to its arrival and reception in Europe in the second part of the sixteenth century, its fatal planting and all too rapid spread in Ireland, its entirely mythical connection with Virginia, the long unresolved confusion of identity between the tubers of the sweet potato, *Ipomoea batatas*, and those of the totally unrelated common potato, *Solanum tuberosum*, further complicated by the late arrival in Europe of a red herring in the shape of *Helianthus tuberosus*, known to us as the Jerusalem artichoke, to the French as *topinambour*, and to the Germans as *Erdbirn* or earth pear. In France arose an even odder confusion created apparently by the French horticulturalist

Olivier de Serres who, in 1600, published his *Théâtre d'Agriculture* in which he offered a description of the potato plant comparing its tubers to truffles, saying that it was often called by the same name, *cartouffles*. As to the taste, said de Serres, 'The cook so dresses all of them that one can recognise but little difference between them.'

Olivier de Serres was not alone in likening potatoes to truffles. To the Italians at the same period, common potato tubers were *tartuffoli* or *taratouffli*, and under the latter name two were sent by a correspondent to the famous Belgian-born botanist Charles de L'Ecluse in Vienna, where in 1588 he was employed working on the Emperor Maximilian's gardens. A few years later, in 1595, L'Ecluse, or Clusius as he called himself in Latin, accepted a professorship at Leyden University, and from then until his death in 1609 one of his many preoccupations was the encouragement of potato cultivation – of the common potato, that is – throughout Europe.

At the same time – although Salaman does not specifically point this out – to most Italian contemporaries of Olivier de Serres and Charles de L'Ecluse, potatoes undoubtedly meant *patatas* or sweet potatoes, not the common potato. In Spain, particularly around Seville and Malaga, *patatas* had been established early in the sixteenth century. It was probably from Spain, therefore, that they reached Italy. In both countries they were appreciated for their sweetness and the resemblance of their flesh to that of sweet chestnuts, which at the time were commonly served with the dessert fruits. Roasted in the ashes, peeled, sugared, sliced into white wine, or into a sugar-syrup, potatoes were also candied, as in those days was almost every fruit, vegetable and flower in sight, from primroses to pumpkins, lettuce stalks to wild cherries. In 1557, a Spanish writer, G. F. Oviedo y Valdes, giving an account of Hispaniola (Haiti), compared *patatas* favourably to marzipan. A higher recommendation you could not give.

In England, too, potatoes imported from Spain were quickly accepted as a delicacy. They wouldn't, of course, grow in the English climate, and the price was high. Salaman cites an instance of two pounds of potatoes 'for the Queen's table' costing, in 1599, 2s 6d per pound. Regardless of price, or perhaps because of it, they took the fancy of the luxury-loving Tudor gentry. Recipes for candying potatoes were tried out and written down in household receipt books, and before long the tubers were appearing as an ingredient in expensive pie fillings. A receipt for one such found its way into print in a little book promisingly titled *The Good Huswife's Jewell* published as early as 1596. Thomas Dawson, who claimed authorship of the book, gave the ingredients as two quinces, two or three burre roots (pears, says Salaman. But why roots?), an ounce of dates and just one 'potaton', cooked in wine, sieved, mixed with rosewater, sugar, spices, butter, the brains of three or four cock-sparrows and eight egg yolks, all to be cooked until thick enough to be consigned to the pastry case. If the sparrows' brains and the potaton didn't give the game away, the title of the receipt was clear enough. 'To make a tarte that is a courage to a man or woman' simply meant that the brew was an aphrodisiac, although just why sparrows' brains were so associated I have never discovered. How the Spanish potato came to join the list of prized English aphrodisiacs is explained by Salaman in a diverting chapter, one which he himself had clearly had a good deal of fun researching.

In the works of late Elizabethan and early Jacobean dramatists, including Shakespeare, Salaman found quite a storehouse of bawdry concerning the perfectly innocent Spanish tubers. They were of course luxuries. As such they came to have the same saucy connotation as champagne, caviar, oysters and truffles to later generations. In 1617 potatoes were included among the foods dubbed 'whetstones of venery' by George Chapman. In the same year, John Fletcher had soldiers disguised as pedlars singing licentious songs and making impudent fun of an elderly gentleman: 'Will your Lordship please to taste a fine potato? T'will advance your withered state. Fill your Honour full of noble itches.'

In only slightly less crude terms Fletcher, again, suggests the potato as revivifier of a woman's lost vigour: 'Will your Ladyship have a potato pie? T'is a good stirring dish for an old lady after a long Lent.' Not that everyone thought it necessary to abstain from this over-stimulating food during Lent. In 1634 the prolific early Stuart letter-writer, James Howell, castigated people who while abstaining from 'Flesh, Fowl and Fish' on Ash Wednesday, made up for the penance by eating luxurious 'Potatoes in a dish Done O'er with Amber, or a mess of Ringos in a Spanish dress'. Ringos were eryngoes, roots of the sea-holly, usually candied, and had long preceded the potato as a reputed aphrodisiac.

The absurdest aspect of the aphrodisiac story was that when eventually the common potato, *Solanum tuberosum*, superceded

Ipomoea batatas in English esteem, the reputation of the exotic Spanish potato was for a time transferred to our own home-grown tuber. In continental Europe the aubergine and the tomato, both members of the same *Solanaceae* family, were in their turn attributed with the possession of aphrodisiac powers.

Tatler, May 1985

Courgette dish currently popular at E.D's lunch time picnics at 24 Halsey St

garlic;

1 lb courgettes; olive oil; thick mayonnaise made with Mrs Z's olive oil, yolks of one hard boiled egg and one raw egg, lemon juice (salt not needed with this oil); pine nuts toasted in o (approx 3 tablespoons); parsley, preferably flat-leaved; salt.

Wash & trim courgettes, chop or grate them (chopped better Cook in sauté pan in olive oil with small piece of crushed garlic. After 3 or 4 minutes add salt, cover pan, leave over lo heat approx 5 minutes. Turn into white salad bowl. Stir in mayonnaise and chopped parsley. Put little heap of toasted pine nuts in centre. Eat tiepido.

E.D. March 1979

This courgette dish is one I remember eating on several occasions, and very good it was too. Elizabeth often gave typed or occasionally handwritten recipes, signed and dated, to her friends, to celebrate a birthday or as a memento of a meal. Sometimes there were different versions of a dish as she evolved and tested recipes further. In her note to Lesley O'Malley following the Fish Loaf (page 160) she makes it clear that the ingredients for the dish could be varied in many ways.

The olive oil referred to above was produced by Mrs Zyw in Tuscany, and in the days of the kitchen shop, sold there, and subsequently by the wine merchants, Haynes, Hanson and Clark.

500 g (1 lb) courgettes should be used for this dish, and the instructions for making mayonnaise are on page 122.   JN

AUBERGINES WITH GARLIC, OLIVE OIL AND TOMATOES

2 or 3 average-size aubergines, preferably long rather than round – say about 1.5 kg (3 lb) weight in all – leaves discarded but stalks left intact, 500 g (1 lb) tomatoes, about 4 cloves of garlic, salt, 2 scant teaspoons of mixed ground spice – cinnamon, cloves, nutmeg, allspice, approximately 8–10 tablespoons of olive oil, fresh basil or mint, sugar.

Slash the unpeeled aubergines lengthways and all round, without separating them at the stalk end, sprinkle them with salt. Skin the tomatoes and chop them with the peeled and crushed garlic cloves.

Put the aubergines into a casserole or baking dish with a lid, in which they will just fit lengthways. Put tablespoons of the chopped tomatoes between each aubergine division until all is used up. Sprinkle in the mixed spice, a few cut or torn leaves of basil or mint, a little more salt, a teaspoon or two of sugar. Pour in olive oil to come at least level with the tops of the aubergines. Cover the pot. Cook in a low oven (170°C/325°F/gas mark 3) for approximately an hour. The aubergines should be soft but not mushy, and the sauce still runny. Taste the sauce for seasoning, and if necessary add more salt and/or spice. Serve cold, with a little fresh basil or mint sprinkled over. Enough for 4 as a first course.

N.B. This is basically the Turkish *Imam Bayeldi* but without the onions characteristic of that celebrated dish.

Unpublished, July 1989

FAGIOLI ALLA FAGIOLARA TOSCANA
(beans in the Tuscan bean jar)

The traditional earthenware *fagiolara* or bean pot of Tuscany [seen on page 35] is shaped like a wine flask, its narrow neck and wide belly ensuring that the beans cook evenly, slowly, and with the minimum evaporation of liquid.

First you need good beans. The very small round Madagascar beans sold as haricots in most English shops are not much use for Tuscan dishes. Ask in Italian delicatessens and groceries for white cannellini or pink borlotti beans.

Soak 250 g (½ lb) of either of these types of beans overnight.

Drain them, put them in the jar with a half onion, a piece of celery, a clove or two of garlic, two or three leaves of fresh sage (the herb traditional to Tuscan beans) or, if you prefer, a sprig of wild thyme and a couple of bay leaves. Pour in about 1.2 litres (2 pints) of water, and add a couple of tablespoons of olive oil. Cook very slowly in the covered jar, starting off over a very low heat and setting the jar over a mat when the water has reached simmering point. In just on 2 hours the beans should be tender. About 20 minutes before cooking time is up, add a tablespoon of salt.

Drain the beans and decant them into a dish. Extract the onion and herbs. Season immediately with more salt if necessary, and freshly milled pepper. Add some very fine slivers of raw mild onion, a generous mixture of fine fruity olive oil and a few drops of wine vinegar. The beans should be served in soup plates and eaten hot, just as they are, or on a slice of bread dried in the oven and rubbed with garlic set in each plate or bowl. They can also be served cold with plenty of fine quality tunny fish in oil, divided into chunks, piled up in the centre of the beans and sprinkled with parsley.

These beans are usually served as an antipasto or first course. They are at their best when freshly cooked, and eaten almost before they have cooled.

Unpublished, 1966

CELERY AND MUSHROOMS

A fresh and quickly cooked little vegetable dish.

You need 1 large head of celery, washed, trimmed and cut in slantwise slices about 5 cm (2 in) long, 125 g (4 oz) of mushrooms, briefly rinsed, dried and sliced, stalks and all; a scrap of crushed garlic; olive oil, walnut oil or sesame oil for frying; salt, freshly milled pepper, parsley or cress.

Warm just enough oil to spread over the base of a 25-cm (10-inch) frying or sauté pan. Put in the prepared celery. Add salt. Sauté for 5 minutes. Add the crushed garlic and the mushrooms. Cook for another 3 or 4 minutes. Grind in a little black pepper. Strew with chopped parsley or cress and serve hot. Enough for three, and good with almost anything as well as on its own.

Unpublished, 1970s

SWEET-SOUR CABBAGE

For this you need a large wide sauté pan, or an old-fashioned deep fryer, more or less in the shape of a Chinese wok. The recipe however is an Italian one.

Ingredients are: a good hard little white cabbage weighing about 1 kg (2 lb), or half a larger one, olive oil, salt, wine vinegar, sugar, parsley.

Cut out and discard the hard stalk part from the cabbage. Slice the rest into thin ribbons. Heat 2 or 3 tablespoons of olive oil in the pan. Throw in the cabbage before the oil gets too hot. Sauté it quickly, turning it over and over with a wooden spatula. Add salt, say 2 teaspoons, but you have to taste. Cover the pan. Leave it for 5 minutes. Uncover it, stir, and turn again, adding 2 level tablespoons of sugar and 2 of wine vinegar. Cover and leave another 5 minutes. Taste for the seasoning. Turn into a wide shallow serving dish or salad bowl. Strew with chopped parsley.

This is good as a vegetable dish on its own. Or serve it as a salad with ham or cold roast pork.

SWEET-SOUR CABBAGE WITH SPICED PRUNES

Cook the cabbage as in the recipe above. During the final minutes of cooking add 8 or 10 spiced prunes prepared as in the recipe on page 257. A beautiful dish. But take great care that the cabbage is still a little bit crisp and that the prunes retain their identity.

A little grated lemon peel mixed in with the chopped parsley before it is strewn over the cabbage adds an agreeable tang.

Unpublished, January 1979

CREAM OF PARSNIPS WITH GREEN GINGER AND EGGS

Boil 500 g (1 lb) scrubbed parsnips in their skins, as for the Pastenak and Cress Cream on page 31. Drain, purée them in the blender. Season the purée with a little grated green ginger root, salt and freshly milled pepper. Thin with a little of the reserved cooking water and a spoonful or two of olive oil. Spoon into 3 individual egg dishes. On top of each put a halved hard-boiled egg, cut side downwards. Strew with breadcrumbs and a little more olive oil. Cook in a medium-hot oven for about 10 minutes until the purée is hot and the breadcrumbs golden brown.

Unpublished, c.1980

ITALIAN POTATO PIE

As I see it, any dish made from left-overs ought to be cheap, easy to prepare, and should not involve the opening of a lot of tins and bottles and jars just so that you can use two sardines or three cherries, or a tablespoon of tunny fish. In their turn, these things become left-overs. You are obliged to use them up whether you want to or not, and the whole operation has become a false economy.

On the other hand, I do think that a dish of left-overs can perfectly well be a good dish in its own right, as indeed is cottage pie, or the famous French *boeuf miroton*, rather than a little concoction of too many diverse ingredients put together without purpose or point.

This Italian potato recipe, typical of the inventive ability which Italian household cooks know so well how to exercise when they are obliged to make a small quantity of ingredients go a long way, is a dish which can be adapted for left-overs without ever seeming to be a makeshift. It looks handsome; and it makes a substantial and original lunch or supper dish for 4 people with quite respectable appetites.

Ingredients for the crust are 1 kg (2 lb) potatoes, 90 g (3 oz) butter, 4 tablespoons of milk, salt, freshly milled pepper, nutmeg, 3 tablespoons of breadcrumbs.

For the filling: 125 g (4 oz) – weight without skin, bone, etc. – of cooked ham, veal, lamb, pork, or chicken, plus 2 hard-boiled eggs, approximately 90 g (3 oz) of cheese which can be Bel Paese, Emmenthal, Gruyère, Parmesan or Demi-Sel cream cheese, parsley or basil.

Cook the potatoes in their skins, peel and purée them while still warm, add 60 g (2 oz) of the butter, the warmed milk, plenty of seasoning – and don't forget the nutmeg.

Spread a 20-cm (8-in) pie plate or removable base tart tin with 15 g (½ oz) of butter and half the breadcrumbs. Line the tin with one half of the potato purée – just spread it out and press it lightly down with your knuckles.

Put in the meat or chicken cut into little cubes or strips, and the chopped eggs. Then the cheese, either grated or cut into tiny cubes. Strew with a little parsley or basil.

Spread the rest of the potato purée on the top, and see that the edges are well pressed together. Brush the top with the remainder of the butter, melted. Then strew with the rest of the breadcrumbs.

Put the prepared pie on the centre shelf of a fairly hot oven, 190°C/375°F/gas mark 5 and bake until the top is pale golden-brown. It will take between 35 and 45 minutes.

Serve it on its own, sizzling hot, and have a green vegetable or salad afterwards.

Unpublished, 1960s

LEMON AND CELERY SAUCE

This is a lovely sauce and very simple, although a bit extravagant, because unless you happen to be using the lemon peel for something else it is wasted. (*See* note over.)

For 3 people you need 1 large lemon, 3 fat sticks of celery, 1½ tablespoons of sugar, 4 tablespoons of light olive oil, salt. Please note that by tablespoons I mean the present British standard measuring spoon which holds 15 ml or approximately ½ oz. It is important to bear this in mind.

Clean, trim and chop the celery. Cut away all peel and every scrap of pith from the lemon. Cut the flesh into dice, discarding pips and central core. Put the lemon and sugar into a bowl standing in a saucepan over simmering water, or in the top half of a double saucepan, and let it cook until the sugar has melted. Add the chopped celery, olive oil and a little salt. Cook for 5 more minutes.

Good hot or cold, with chicken or turkey (in treble quantities) and also with fish. Not good for fine or delicate wine.

Note

One way of using the lemon peel would be to grate it into Demerara sugar to be kept in reserve for the lemon and brown sugar cake on p. 261. Or use a couple of strips to flavour an apple purée. In that case, wash the lemon before paring it.

Unpublished, 1970s

FRESH TOMATO SAUCE

1 kg (2 lb) ripe tomatoes, 30 g (1 oz) butter, salt, sugar, dried basil, and, optionally, a tablespoon of port.

Chop the tomatoes, put them in a wide shallow saucepan or 25-cm (10-in) frying pan in which the butter is melting. Add a teaspoon each of salt and sugar and dried basil. Cook over a moderate heat until most of the moisture from the tomatoes has evaporated. Sieve, and return the resulting purée to the cleaned pan. Reheat, and just before serving add the port, which is not essential but does have a softening and mellowing effect on the sauce.

Made in this simple fashion, without the thickening of flour so often and so mistakenly recommended by professional cooks and cookery teachers, tomato sauce is delicious, fresh, appetising in colour and of the correct consistence. It is the perfect sauce with fried food such as potato croquettes and fish cakes; good with grilled fish such as mackerel and grey mullet; and combined in various ways with eggs, cream and cheese makes some of the most delicious and attractive dishes ever invented.

Unpublished, 1960s

THREE-MINUTE TOMATO SAUCE

Chop 250 g (½ lb) of fine ripe skinned tomatoes. Put them with a teaspoonful each of butter and olive oil into a heavy frying pan or small saucepan. Cook them for 3 minutes, no more. Season them with salt, sugar and a scrap of dried basil or a teaspoon of freshly chopped parsley.

This is the sauce, or fondue of tomatoes, which makes the best filling for a tomato omelette. It is also the best sauce to go over toasted or baked cheese croûtons.

Cook it in double quantities and for a little longer and have it with scrambled eggs, fried bread, and baked gammon rashers or sausages.

Nova, July 1965

SWEET-SOUR TOMATO AND ORANGE PICKLE

This is a pickle which can be made at any time and with almost any tomatoes, although very firm and slightly unripe ones are the best. Half and half green and red tomatoes produce good results.

1 kg (2 lb) of firm tomatoes, 2 small oranges, 750 g (1½ lb) of sugar, 300 ml (½ pint) of tarragon vinegar.

In a preserving pan (preferably an aluminium one, don't use an untinned copper jam pan for pickles or chutneys) boil the sugar and vinegar to a thin syrup. Pour boiling water over the tomatoes. Skin and chop them.

Slice the oranges, the peel included, first into thin rounds, then cut each round in four, discarding all pips and the ends of the oranges. Blanch the pieces in boiling water for a couple of minutes and drain them. The preliminary blanching is to soften the rinds.

Put the chopped tomatoes into the hot syrup, bring to the boil, continue the boiling, not too fast, for about 30 minutes, skimming from time to time. Add the orange pieces. Cook for another 15–20 minutes or until the mixture sets when a little is dropped on to a plate.

Pack into small jars. This is good with cold pork, gammon and ham and also with cold salt beef.

Note

When the pickle is to be made in quantity, the easiest way of preparing the tomatoes is to pack them in a big earthenware pot and let them soften in a low oven for half an hour or a little longer. Then push the whole batch through a coarse sieve or Mouli-légumes.

Unpublished, 1970s

The Besprinkling of a Rosemary Branch

To judge by the frequent references to lamb with rosemary, veal with rosemary, chicken with rosemary, which I note in recent editions of the *Good Food Guide* as dishes which invariably draw enthusiastic comment, rosemary must be a high favourite in current English cookery. I can't say I share the taste to any great extent. I have never cared for the way the Italians use it to flavour veal roasts, very often to excess. In Provence it often smothers the natural taste of lamb, and in the same region the little white goats' milk cheeses coated with rosemary spikes tend to taste of nothing else. (The alternative version, coated with *poivre d'ane* or wild savory is more to my taste, but is becoming rare.)

Then in France there is the current mania for olives packed in jars of oil crammed to the corks with *herbes de Provence* – predominantly dried rosemary and thyme – and costing twice as much as olives which actually have their own taste. It's quite difficult to overpower the flavour of those little black olives, but rosemary does the trick. Sure, rosemary is for remembrance. I'd just rather it weren't for the remembrance of those little spiky leaves stuck in my throat.

It isn't that I have anything against rosemary as a plant. In the garden it smells delicious and looks enchanting. In my cooking it has little place, although I did learn a useful trick years ago in Capri when I caught sight of an old woman dipping a branch of rosemary in oil and gently brushing it over a fish she was roasting over a charcoal fire. An excellent notion. And recently I have collected a few other forgotten uses for the rosemary which was such an important plant in the herb gardens of our ancestors.

Toothpicks, for example, and skewers for grilling small items such as chicken livers, were cut from rosemary twigs, and in the seventeenth century much use seems to have been made of rosemary as a decorative element in dessert dishes. Robert May, whose famous book, *The Accomplisht Cook*, was first published in 1660, the year of the restoration of Charles II, mentions a rosemary sprig planted upright in a snow cream, a frothy confection of sweetened cream and egg whites set on bread. I think this manner of using rosemary must have been standard practice in the seventeenth century. At any rate the 1611 edition of Cotgrave's French–English Dictionary gives an entry for '*neige en rosemarin*, the besprinkling of a Rosemarie branch with salt or froathe creame'.*

A curious and unexplained custom involving the decorative use of rosemary is one recorded in the archives of the master bakers of Paris. Every baker who had served his apprenticeship, spent a minimum of two years as a journeyman baker, and having finally passed his test as a master – he was required to make several kinds of loaves, the most difficult being the *pain coiffé*, the equivalent of our cottage loaf – was summoned to attend a convocation of the entire corporation presided over by the Grand Panetier, the Grand Pantler of France. At the ceremony, the new master baker, bearing in his hand a new earthenware pot containing a rosemary plant 'with all its root', hung with sugared peas, oranges and other fruits suitable to the season, was to stand before the Grand Pantler and say 'Master, I have done my term.' The Grand Pantler asks the Judges if this is true, and the answer being in the affirmative, he asks them if the pot is in the correct form and fit to be received. If the answer is again in the affirmative the Pantler takes the pot and presents the new master with his certificate.

The significance of the rosemary in this context is not clear, but according to Alfred Franklin, who describes the ceremony in *Comment On Devenait Patron*, Paris, 1889, the custom continued until about 1650, when the pot of rosemary was replaced with a gold louis, a more prosaic but surely easier way of paying homage to the Grand Pantler than decorating what must necessarily have been a rather substantial rosemary plant with oranges and the like, but in the hands of a skilful decorator, how charming they must have been, those rosemary bushes

* There is a recipe for Snow Cream on page 256.

ceremonially decked out with precious and brightly coloured fruits and sweetmeats.

Sir Kenelm Digby, a dashing young man at the court of Charles I, later a staunch friend to the widowed Queen Henrietta Maria, and passionately devoted husband of the legendary Venetia Stanley, was a many-sided man interested in science, alchemy, astrology and philosophy. He was also soldier, adventurer, traveller, writer, book collector, something of a medical quack, and an inspired recorder of recipes and cooking experiments. The brewing of mead, metheglin and hydromel was another of his favourite preoccupations. Into his vats went herbs and flowers by the sackful, rosemary flowers of course among them.

Rosemary itself, however, is conspicuous by its absence in all his cookery receipts with the one exception of a syllabub, when he suggests bruising a sprig in the cream 'to quicken the taste'.

It is an interesting point that Digby suggested his sprig of rosemary a little bruised to liven up the taste of the cream and wine, whereas Robert May's appears to have been only for decoration. Rosemary and wine seem in fact to have been considered to have affinities, and John Evelyn, in his *Acetaria, A Discourse of Sallets*, 1699, says that while the leaf is not used in 'A Sallet furniture' the flowers 'a little bitter, are always welcome in Vinegar; but above all, a fresh Sprig or two in a Glass of Wine'. We might not see eye to eye with that today, but then John Evelyn's wine was very different from ours, and he was not a man to treat his food and drink without due care and consideration, or to follow a custom because it was a fashionable thing to do. So we must accept that rosemary really did do something for the wine of Evelyn's day.

In the seventeenth century those pretty and 'a little bitter' rosemary flowers were also used, as were violets, carnations, roses, lilies of the valley, lavender, and a dozen other scented garden flowers, to make a kind of sugar candy.

Abridged from *Herbal Review*, Autumn 1980

Herbs, Fresh and Dried

To suppose that all fresh herbs are, *ipso facto*, better than all dried herbs is a sign of misplaced zeal. There are some herbs or part of herb plants which can only be used in dried or some other preserved form. Among obvious examples are angelica, which has a potent scent but no flavour until candied, and wild fennel stalks which must be tinder-dry for storage and for igniting under grilled fish or for scenting pork or pot-roasted chicken. On the other hand, any attempt to dry the leaves of fennel is a waste of time. They are so fragile that they turn to dust. The same can be said for parsley, chives and chervil, although for a few days after they are dried and packed these herbs do give out a faint scent. In Denmark, where chervil soup is a favourite and a very good dish, I have bought frozen chervil which turned out to be a hopeless mush, totally lacking in aroma and flavour.

Rosemary and bay leaves are both plants whose leaves contain a certain amount of essential oil which means that in their fresh state they can easily overpower a sauce or a joint of meat. Dried, they are milder and more subtle. A sprinkling of mint in its dried form is as essential to a great number of Levantine or Middle Eastern vegetable dishes as is fresh mint for English mint sauce. The wild thyme of Provence could be said to be born dried and gnarled on its native hills, so that the sun-dried twigs we buy for scenting our beef and wine stews and for making up our ritual bouquets are as nature made them.

English lemon thyme is another matter. It is at its best fresh, green and tender. Fresh basil and fresh tarragon are among the incomparable luxuries of summer. No dried versions can replace them. In their season they are treats to be savoured in the same way as the rare wild mushrooms of autumn or the first tangerines of Christmas.

Until recently the use of herbs in French cooking was very discreet. In the best French cooking it still is. A tendency to overdo the flavouring has, however, rather sadly to my mind, spread throughout France. Provision shops are crammed with bottles and packets of every herb and spice known; bottles of olive oil and jars of olives are stuffed to the corks with 'herbes de Provence', in other words spikes of rosemary and other overpowering herbs such as sage and *sarriette* or savory. In restaurants, roasts of lamb and veal are smothered in the same mixtures, steaks and ducks are submerged beneath layers of *poivre vert*, the soft green peppercorns which are so delectable when used with discrimination; even the exquisite tarragon is often administered in overdoses. Marjoram is another herb often used in brutalising quantity. It is indeed not easy to learn restraint where these sweet-smelling and potent aromatics are concerned.

The best rule to remember is that it is only when dealing with poor raw materials – battery chickens, characterless vegetables, frozen fish, eggs laid by caged, unhappy hens – that a heavy hand with herbs, spices, salt and pepper is likely to improve matters. So think twice before throwing in the extra spoonful of *arômes de Provence*, the redundant sprinkling of rosemary and chopped garlic, the uncalled for mustard in the mayonnaise, and the over-liberal administration of wild thyme to a beef stew. All these flavourings and aromatics are blessed gifts. We should certainly not neglect them. Nor should we abuse them.

Unpublished, 1970s

Green Pepper Berries

In the thirteenth century a Franciscan friar known as Bartholomew the Englishman wrote a famous encyclopedia called *Concerning the Nature of Things*. In this work he propounded the theory that pepper grew on trees on the south side of a hill in the Caucasus. This wooded hill was infested with serpents. To drive them out, so that they could harvest the pepper, the peasants set fire to the trees. In the resulting conflagration, some of the fruit of the pepper became charred and blackened, while that which escaped the fire remained in its natural white state.

Nowadays we know better. Pepper, we have discovered, doesn't come from the Caucasus. It comes from the spice merchants who grow both black and white kinds, sometimes in small berries and sometimes in powder form, in small glass jars or cardboard packets. This doesn't account for green peppercorns, which weren't known to Bartholomew the Englishman – or to anyone else in Europe – but surely he wouldn't have been too hard put to find an explanation of the nature of this kind of pepper and the reason it grows in cans.

Lacking Bartholomew's ingenious imagination, I will try to set down some bare and relatively sober facts.

All these peppercorns, then, are the fruit of the same climbing plant, *Piper nigrum*, cultivated in the East and West Indies, the Malay peninsula, Ceylon, Brazil and the island of Madagascar. Initially, like most fruit, it is green. As it ripens it turns red, when it is harvested and dried. As the berries dry they shrivel and turn from red to bronze-black. These are black peppercorns, aromatic and of comparatively mild strength. To obtain a stronger pepper, some of the berries are peeled. When dry, these berries are smooth and pale fawn or – well – pepper colour. They have more strength and less aroma than the black corns. Both variations of dried peppercorns, however, retain their properties as long as they remain whole, in so remarkable a way that ever since Roman times pepper has been one of the most valuable and universally used of all spices.

And those green pepper berries? In their soft, unripe state they have for long been used in the local cooking of the pepper-growing regions, going straight from the pepper vine into the pot. But it was not until the nineteen sixties that a French planter on the island of Madagascar started experimenting with methods of preserving the little green berries for export, thus creating fresh export markets for Madagascar pepper, and at the same time offering a virtually new spice to the kitchens of the world.

One of the first to see the possibilities of the new product was Raymond Oliver, owner of one of France's most famous restaurants, the Grand Véfour in Paris, and by 1970 several of his colleagues had followed his lead. Duckling or steak au poivre vert became immensely popular.

Preserved in a light brine, in their own natural juices, or in piperine, the extract of the pepper itself, the little green pepper berries are wonderfully aromatic without being fiery. Their applications are many, one of the best being as a fish seasoning. Or, combined with cinnamon and a scrap of garlic, they make an original and interesting spiced butter to serve with steak or chicken, or again, fish. They can be applied rather like garlic slivers to a boned loin of pork before it is rolled and tied ready for cooking, for a very successful roast.

Once the tin of green peppercorns has been opened the contents should be transferred to a glass jar with well-fitting stopper, and refrigerated. In this way they will keep for a week or so, or they can be stored in the freezer.

GREEN PEPPER AND CINNAMON BUTTER

Crush 2 teaspoons of green pepper berries with a small sliver of garlic and a half-teaspoon of ground cinnamon. Into the mixture work 45–60 g (1½–2 oz) of butter. When thoroughly amalgamated add a scant teaspoon of salt – less if you have used salted butter. Store in a small covered jar in the refrigerator, or make in larger quantities and store in the freezer, keeping a small jar in the refrigerator for current consumption.

Coriander, ground cumin and/or ginger can be combined with the cinnamon in this recipe, or used instead, and proportions of the spices can be increased or diminished according to taste.

CHICKEN BAKED WITH GREEN PEPPER AND CINNAMON BUTTER

For a 1.25–1.5 kg (2½–3 lb) roasting chicken (dressed and drawn weight) have ready 45 g (1½ oz) of the spiced butter described above.

Lift the skin of the chicken, rub salt and then the butter well over the flesh, making a few gashes with a small sharp knife in

the drumsticks and thick part of the legs so that the spices will penetrate. Put a little more of the butter inside the chicken. If possible leave for an hour or two before cooking.

Put the chicken, with a few bay leaves, into a shallow baking dish into which it will just fit. Cook, uncovered, on the centre shelf of a moderate oven (180°C/350°F/gas mark 4), allowing 20 minutes on each side and 20 minutes breast upwards. Baste with the juices each time the chicken is turned. At the end of the cooking time the skin should be beautifully golden and crisp.

Serve with lemon quarters and watercress, and the buttery juices poured into a little sauce boat.

A simple green salad with a very light dressing is the best accompaniment.

This recipe also works well with pheasant. For a young bird of about 850 g (1¾ lb) dressed and drawn weight, the timing and temperature are as for the chicken. But the pheasant should be wrapped in well-buttered paper or foil.

PORK CHOPS WITH WHITE WINE AND GREEN PEPPERCORNS

Pork is always the better for a mild degree of spicing. The following is a most successful and easy recipe.

Buy two loin chops about 2 cm (1 in) thick and if possible with the rind left on. (Nowadays English pork chops bought without the rind have been divested also of most of their fat, which results in dried out, shrunken meat.)

Rub the chops with plenty of salt and a cut clove of garlic. Sprinkle them with flour. Put them in a heavy enamelled cast-iron skillet or other pan which can be transferred to the oven and which has a lid. Add no fat or liquid. Let the chops heat gently at first, then increase the heat so that they brown a little on each side. Add 2 or 3 bay leaves and a few dried fennel stalks. Pour in a glass (125 ml/4 fl oz) of dry white wine or vermouth. Let it bubble fast for a few seconds. Cover the pan. Transfer it to the centre of a moderate oven (170°C/325°F/gas mark 3), and cook for 20–30 minutes until the chops are tender.

Remove them to a serving dish, keep them hot while the pan is returned to the top of the stove so that the juices can bubble and reduce a little. Stir in a teaspoon of strong yellow Dijon mustard. When this is smoothly blended add a heaped teaspoon (more if you like a strongly spiced sauce) of green pepper berries. Crush them slightly as you stir them into the sauce, which should be poured sizzling over the chops. Serve swiftly.

A dish of sweet eating apples, cored, peeled, sliced and gently fried in butter with a sprinkling of sugar makes a delicious accompaniment. For each chop allow two apples.

LOIN OF PORK SPICED WITH GREEN PEPPER

A most original and subtly spiced dish.

Ask the butcher for a joint of loin of pork weighing about 2 kg (4 lb). The meat should be boned and the rind should be taken off, but do not have the meat rolled or tied. It is important to cook the meat with the bones and rind in the pan, so make sure that you get these put in the parcel with the meat. Other ingredients are 2 teaspoons of fresh whole green peppercorns, a clove of garlic, salt, approximately 1 teaspoon each of ground cinnamon and ginger, bay leaves, dried fennel stalks, about 450 ml (¾ pint) of good clear jellied stock, or failing stock, a tumbler of white wine or dry vermouth and plain water.

Put the meat flat on a board, rub it very thoroughly with salt, then with the cinnamon and ginger. Spread very small thin slivers of garlic at regular intervals along the length of the joint, then press in the green pepper berries, distributing them evenly. Roll the meat into a bolster shape, tie it securely with fine string.

In a baking dish put the bones, the rind, several bay leaves and branches of dried fennel. On top put the joint.

Start the cooking with the meat uncovered and placed low down in the oven (170°C/325°F/gas mark 3). After 30 minutes add the stock or wine and water mixture. Leave another 10 minutes, then cover with foil and cook for another 2¼ hours.

Remove the meat to a dish, strain the liquid through muslin into a glass bowl or jug. When cool put in the refrigerator so that the fat sets. Next day take off the fat. (Keep it; re-melted and stored in a pot, it will make lovely fried bread.) Serve the meat cold, with the jellied stock separately in a bowl or sauce boat. Enough for 6–8 people.

The bones and trimmings of the joint can be cooked again to make a second batch of stock which can be stored for the next time you cook a chicken or piece of pork with *poivre vert*.

An extra flavouring for this pork dish is a small piece of root ginger peeled, sliced and put in the baking pan with the bay leaves and fennel, and a little extra vermouth or white wine or even Madeira can be poured over the meat during the last 10 minutes of cooking.

GREEN PEPPERCORN AND CREAM SAUCE FOR FISH

This is a simple sauce, so gently spiced that it cannot overwhelm even the most delicate of fish. The only ingredients needed are very fresh double cream (for 2 allow 150 ml/5 fl oz), 30 g (1 oz) of unsalted butter, 1 teaspoon of green peppercorns, 2 teaspoons of chopped parsley, salt.

First crush the green peppercorns in a bowl or mortar. In a small frying or sauté pan melt the butter, over low heat. Stir the crushed green peppercorns into the warmed butter.

Quickly add the cream, increase the heat, stir very thoroughly, tipping the pan so that the butter and cream amalgamate to form a sauce which, although not thickened, is coherent. Pour into a warmed sauce boat and stir in a pinch of salt and the parsley.

The sauce should be made only at the last minute, when the fish is ready to serve. It is delicious with freshwater or sea trout, baked in the oven (in buttered foil), and with white fish such as halibut and turbot, either poached or baked.

Introduction from Williams-Sonoma booklet 1974;
recipes from booklet published by
Elizabeth David 1972

Is there a Nutmeg in the House?

Joseph Nollekens, the great eighteenth-century English sculptor, was almost as celebrated for his wife's, and his own, parsimonious habits as for his splendid portrait busts of the eminent men and women of his day. After his death in 1823, an ex-apprentice, one John Thomas Smith, wrote a gossipy memoir of his late master, in no way stinting the warts. Smith's acute sense of comedy and his relish in his own jokes go far toward softening the edge of even his more malicious anecdotes. One of the most richly absurd of these reveals Mrs Nollekens scrounging free spices from the grocer while her husband filches them from the dinner table at that august establishment the Royal Academy of Arts:

The Grocer, of Margaret Street, has been frequently heard to declare that whenever Mrs Nollekens purchased tea and sugar at his father's shop, she always requested, just at the moment she was quitting the counter, to have either a clove or a bit of cinnamon to take some unpleasant taste out of her mouth; but she never was seen to apply it to the part so affected, so that, with Nollekens's nutmegs, which he pocketed from the table at the Academy dinners, they contrived to accumulate a little stock of spices, without any expense whatever.

Nollekens and his Times, 1828

I find it rather amiable of this mostly unamiable pair that they should have bothered with a half dozen cloves here, a few bits of cinnamon bark and a couple of nutmegs there. I wish that Smith had told us more. Did they secrete their little hoards in special spice boxes, did the Royal Academicians take their own pocket nutmeg graters out to dinner or were graters as well as nutmegs – no doubt for flavouring the punch at the end of dinner – on the house?

It was a civilised fad, that eighteenth-century love of portable nutmeg graters for the dining-room, and the drawing-room hot drinks, and for travelling. I see no reason why we shouldn't revive it. It is far from silly to carry a little nutmeg box and grater around in one's pocket. In London restaurants such a piece of equipment comes in handy. Here, even in Italian restaurants, I find it necessary to ask for nutmeg to grate on to my favourite plain pasta with butter and Parmesan, and for leaf spinach as well. To my mind, nutmeg is essential to these dishes, as indeed it is to béchamel sauce, cheese soufflés, and nearly all other cheese mixtures. Yet how many times, I wonder, have I been told by an apologetic waiter that there is no nutmeg in the house?

In Italy, a kitchen without a nutmeg would be a contradiction in terms, the *noce moscato* or musky nut being as necessary to Italian cooking as Parmesan cheese and oregano and for that matter salt. It isn't that the Italians have a heavy hand with spices. On the contrary they are rather sparing with them, using them in subtle combinations for flavouring delicate cream cheese and spinach stuffings for cannelloni and ravioli, sometimes producing the unexpected pleasure such as the nutmeg, white pepper and clove mixture with a distinct whiff of juniper berry which I remember as the spicing for a grilled chicken eaten out of doors at a Tuscan country restaurant now alas vanished, and tiny shreds of lemon peel with chicken livers in the sauce for home-made pasta in the same enchanting place.

In English cooking nutmeg is used less imaginatively than in Italy. It goes into pudding and cakes and sweet creams, it is grated over milk junkets, cream curds, and the Christmas brandy butter. Our savoury dishes such as potted meats, sausages, and pie fillings are seasoned with mace rather than with nutmeg. The tradition is probably based on some sort of logic. Mace is a part of the same fruit as the nutmeg and has a similar aroma but coarser, less sweet and more peppery.

To be precise as to the distinctions and differences between nutmeg and mace, the nutmeg tree, *Myristica fragrans* bears a plum-like yellow fruit which splits open when ripe to reveal white flesh and in the centre a bright scarlet lacy wrapping enfolding a single hard brown seed. The seed is the nutmeg, the lacy covering or aril, the mace.

The *Myristica* is a native of the Moluccas, the Indonesian islands known to the old traders as the Spice Islands, and although the nutmeg appeared in England at least as far back as Chaucer's day – he mentions it in connection with ale – it became generally known in Europe only much later, after the discovery of the Spice Islands by the Portuguese in 1512. Nowadays our sources of supply are mainly the West Indies and the Philippines.

Williams-Sonoma booklet, July 1975

ITALIAN SPICE MIXTURE

I noted down this formula about twenty years ago when reading through Luigi Carnacina's *Il Gourmet Internazionale*. Recently I have been mixing and grinding various blends of spices in a small electric coffee mill, and the Italian one seems to me exceptionally successful.

The original quantities were: 125 g (4 oz) of white peppercorns, 35 g (just over 1 oz) of grated nutmeg, 30 g (1 oz) of juniper berries, 10 g (⅓ oz) of cloves.

For my own use I have reduced the quantities as follows: 3 teaspoons of white peppercorns, approximately ½ a small nutmeg, 1 teaspoon of juniper berries, ¼ teaspoon of whole cloves.

Put all the spices in the coffee mill and grind them until they are in a powder. The nutmeg takes the longest, and there are moments when the coffee grinder makes a rather angry whine – which it tended to do even when used for its legitimate purpose. However, so far neither the mechanism nor the lid of the grinder (a very old and much-used Moulinex) has been affected.

The quantity makes enough to fill a little glass jar of approximately 45 g (1½ oz) capacity, and is sufficient to last about 6 months – one does not want to use the same spice so often that it becomes monotonous, nor is it advisable to make up too much of the mixture at one time. Although this particular blend is made up of spices which all retain their aromas very well, it still seems best to make it freshly from time to time.

Sprinkled on pork chops for grilling, on pork to be roasted, on lamb, on chicken for grilling, this spice gives a most delicious and subtle flavour. The small amount of trouble required for blending it is really worthwhile.

Unpublished, early 1970s

A SPICED HERB MIXTURE TO SPREAD ON BAKED GAMMON

This mixture is derived from the old recipes for the stuffing to go into a whole chine or back of bacon boiled in the Lincolnshire manner. This was a dish for harvest suppers.

I sometimes use the spice and herb mixture instead of ordinary breadcrumbs, or in place of a sugar glaze, to spread on the fat side of a piece of baked corner or middle gammon when the skin has been peeled off. A few minutes in the oven will set the mixture, and the joint will not dry out or become overcooked.

For a piece of gammon or bacon of approximately 1–1.2 kg (2½ lb) weight, a teacup of stuffing should be made up of the following ingredients: Fresh parsley, fresh or dried marjoram, fresh or dried mint, lemon thyme, chives when in season, the grated peel of one lemon and of half an orange, ¼ teaspoon of crushed coriander seeds, a scant ½ teaspoon of coarsely crushed black pepper, 2½–3 tablespoons of dry breadcrumbs, a little melted butter.

The proportions of the fresh and dried herbs can be improvised according to fancy and depending on which are most plentiful. The fresh parsley is important, the mint gives a peculiarly English flavour to the mixture, the lemon peel and the spicy coriander make up for such seventeenth-century flavourings as the violet and marigold leaves which in country districts were still used in the stuffings for boiled bacon until well on in the nineteenth century.

This mixture is delicious as a stuffing for fresh baked pork.

A variant of the recipe on p. 181 of *Spices, Salt and Aromatics in the English Kitchen*

GARAM MASALA

I have based my Garam Masala on a recipe given by Jon and Rumer Godden in *Shiva's Pigeons* (Chatto, 1973). For English households I have reduced the quantities and also slightly altered the proportions – fewer cloves and cardamoms – as follows:

4 teaspoons coriander seeds, 2 teaspoons cumin seeds, seeds from 12–15 cardamom pods, ½ teaspoon whole cloves, 2 teaspoons white peppercorns, 5 cm (2 in) cinnamon bark, ¼ nutmeg.

Roast the coriander and cumin seeds on separate ovenproof plates in a moderately hot oven, 190°C/375°F/gas mark 5, for about 10 minutes. Put them with all the other spices into an electric coffee mill and grind them to a powder. Store in an airtight jar.

Unpublished, September 1973

Relishes of the Renaissance

'A savoury addition to a meal; thing eaten with plainer food to add flavour; a savoury or piquant taste; the distinctive taste of anything.' The OED provides other definitions of the term 'relish', none of them particularly satisfactory. To those of us old enough to remember that pre-war favourite Patum Peperium, the Gentleman's Relish, there couldn't be any doubt. A relish meant a highly savoury paste compounded of anchovy, pepper, plus other ingredients, unspecified and with a rather forbidding greyish aspect but packed in an attractive china pot. Come to think of it some years ago I bought a mini-size pot of that once-loved spread, produced by the Essex firm of Elsenham. 'Original 1828 recipe',

M. BARTOLOMEO
SCAPPI

the label said. There was no reason to doubt it, and that dear old Gentleman's Relish does in fact still exist. But what has become of all those good and interesting sweet-sour relishes, neither chutneys nor sauces but something between the two, both in taste and consistency? Many people used to make them at home, from summer and autumn fruits: damsons, plums, sloes, bullaces, bilberries, blackberries, mulberries, wild rose hips, crab apples, japonica berries, quinces. Have they entirely succumbed to the all-conquering tomato product of the Heinz company?

Never popular in France, relishes were once much appreciated in Italy, and are still loved in Austria and Bavaria. John Florio, in the Italian–English Dictionary which he called *A Worlde of Wordes*, compiled for the benefit of Anne of Denmark, queen of James I, and published in 1611, translated *sapore* as 'any savour, smack, taste or relish, also any sauce to give meat a good taste' and *saporoso* as 'savoury, well tasted, full of savour'. The main distinction between a *sapore* and a *salsa*, at any rate in Bartolomeo Scappi's great cookery book of 1570 – initially it was called simply *Opera*, later elaborated to *L'Arte del Cucinare* – seems to have been 'keeping' quality. A *sapore* could be stored, a *salsa* was for relatively rapid consumption. With the odd exception, a *sapore*, relish, or condiment, was very sweet and was sometimes spread over spit-roasted meat, poultry or game birds, sometimes set on the table in saucer-shaped bowls so that people could help themselves. Here are some examples from Scappi's rich repertoire.

GALANTINA
To serve as a relish or to cover spit-roasted meat and poultry

Take one pound (500 g) of currants, pound them in a mortar with six hard boiled egg yolks, three ounces (90 g) of musk-scented biscuits (*mosiacciuoli*), three of bread toasted in the embers, steep them in rose vinegar, then temper all with six ounces (180 ml) of malmsey & four (125 ml) of clear verjuice, & pass through the sieve or strainer adding one pound (500 g) of sugar, three ounces (90 g) of sweet-sour citron juice, half an ounce (15 g) of pounded cinnamon, one ounce (30 g) of pepper, & cloves & nutmeg pounded, and when it is sieved give it a warm in the saucepan, & thereafter leave it to cool, & when it is cold serve it as a relish, with sugar & cinnamon over. But if you need it to cover poultry or game birds roasted on the spit, keep it clearer with a little lean meat broth.

Notes

Verjuice, the Italian *agresto*, was one of the essential condiments of Medieval and Renaissance cookery. It was not, as often believed, simply the juice of unripe grapes, but was made from a particular acid grape cultivated especially for the purpose, and known by the same name. The vine bearing the *agresto* grape was one on which the ripe fruit and the flowers were often seen simultaneously.

Verjuice could be preserved in small vats with wine lees, covered with a cloth. When the ferment rose, the scum sank to the bottom and the juice cleared. In this manner, it was claimed, verjuice would keep a whole year, and was used as a thirst-quenching beverage as well as in cookery. Mixed with honey, it was considered beneficial in the treatment of sore throats, mouth ulcers, and scabrous eye infections.

SWEET ALMONDS
A yellow-coloured relish to serve hot or cold

In the mortar pound one pound (500 g) of finest skinned almonds with six ounces (180 g) of crumb of bread steeped in clear verjuice, & three ounces (90 g) of *pignoccati* (small sweetmeats shaped like pine cones), & six hard egg yolks, & when all are pounded, temper with citron juice, clear verjuice, & a little trebbiano wine, or muscat, & strain through the sieve, & put in a saucepan with a pound (500 g) of sugar, adding together pepper, cloves, cinnamon and nutmeg pounded, in all one ounce & a half (45 g), but more cinnamon than the other spicery, & cook it as the relish above – that is, with ordinary red wine and vinegar, and musk-scented biscuits – & serve hot or cold as you please, with sugar & cinnamon over.

AGLIATA
Made with fresh walnuts and almonds

Take six ounces (180 g) of fresh, shelled walnuts, & four (125 g) of fresh almonds, & six cloves of garlic parboiled, or one & a half of raw, & pound in the mortar with four ounces of crumb of bread steeped in meat or fish broth, not too salty, & when they are pounded, put thereto a quarter of an ounce (7 g) of pounded ginger. This relish if well pounded, does not need to be sieved, but is simply tempered with one of the above broths, & if the walnuts are dry, leave them to steep in cold water until they are soft enough to skin. With this relish you may pound a little turnip, or cauliflower well cooked in meat broth, if it is a meat day.

FRESH CHERRIES WITH VERJUICE AND SPICES

Take four pounds (2 kg) of fresh Roman cherries, not too ripe, & cook them in a pot with a *foglietta* (i.e. half a Roman wine pint, about 8 oz) of clear verjuice & two ounces (60 g) of fine spice biscuits & four (125 g) of soft breadcrumbs, a little salt, one pound (500 g) of sugar, one ounce (30 g) of pepper, a quarter (7 g) of cloves, & nutmeg, & boil everything together with a *foglietta* (8 ounces/250 ml) of clear verjuice, & four ounces (125 ml) of rose vinegar, & when it is cooked press it through the sieve & this relish should have a little body, & when it is sieved, leave it to get cold, & serve it.

BLACK GRAPES
A relish for storing

Take black grapes which are firm, & they should be those called *gropello*, that is from Cesena, with the red stalks, press the grapes & put them to boil in a saucepan over a slow fire for an hour, & then take the juice which the grapes have yielded & pour it through a sieve, & for every pound (500 ml) of juice, take eight ounces (250 g) of fine sugar, & reboil it in a saucepan, skimming it, & finally add a little salt, & whole cinnamon, & let it boil over a slow fire until it starts to set, & when it is cooked, store it in glass vessels, or in glazed jars.

SWEET MUSTARD
The taste of the quince

Take one pound (500 ml) of grape juice & another of quinces cooked in wine & sugar, four ounces (125 g) of rennet apples cooked in wine, & sugar, three ounces (90 g) of candied citron peel, two ounces (60 g) of candied peel of *limoncelli* – Naples lemons, small fruit with thin skins and plenty of juice – & half an ounce (15 g) of candied nutmeg, & pound all the candied things with the quince, & with the rennet apples in the mortar, & when all is pounded, press through the sieve together with the grape juice, & with the said ingredients three ounces (90 g) of cleaned mustard, more or less, according to whether you want it strong, & when it is sieved put thereto a little salt, & finely pounded sugar, half an ounce (15 g) of pounded cinnamon, & a quarter (7 g) of cloves pounded, & if you have no grape juice, you may make it without, taking more quince, & rennet apples, cooked as aforesaid.

Notes
The above recipe would produce a thick sweet mostarda which must surely be the ancestor of one I bought in Venice many years ago. It was late autumn, early November as I remember, and this quince *mostarda* was to be found in just one shop near the Rialto market. I was told by the shopkeeper that only a small amount was made each year because it did not keep beyond Christmas. That Venetian *mostarda amabile* was certainly a great improvement on today's debased commercial version of Cremona *mostarda di frutta*, and as is clear from Scappi's recipe, the making of his own *mostarda* was very much a matter of what was in season. The candied nutmeg is about the only ingredient now entirely unfamiliar to us. In Scappi's day, and even for three centuries afterwards, nutmegs were harvested green and brought from Malaysia in sugar syrup, packed in small barrels. They could then be candied or crystallised or they could be left as they were and cut in small pieces to add spice to many dishes.

Taste, July 1991

Italian Fruit Mustards

The sweet mustards of Italy are survivals, I think, from the days of the Roman Empire. The great French culinary scholar, Bertrand Guégan, cites a Roman recipe for the preparation of mustard given by Palladius: 'reduce to powder a setier and a half [a setier was the equivalent of 4 litres] of mustard seed; put to it five pounds of honey, one pound of oil from Spain and one setier of strong vinegar; when all is well beat together you may use it'.[1] These Roman mixtures of honey, mustard and vinegar were sometimes mixed with pine kernels and almonds, and were also used as a kind of syrup in which roots such as turnips were conserved. We are already getting close to the fruit mustards of the Middle Ages, at that time known as *compostes*, and evidently familiar to Italian, French, Spanish and English cooks.

The famous *Ménagier de Paris*,[2] a treatise composed *c.*1393 by a middle-aged bourgeois for the benefit of his young bride, gives lengthy and perfectly clear directions for making this preserve, a mixture of green walnuts gathered around St John's Day (i.e. midsummer), steeped in water for ten days, and subsequently spiced with cloves and ginger and preserved in honey until All Saints (1 November), when you were to add peeled, quartered and boiled turnips; then carrots treated in the same way; next, pears, unpeeled, but cut in quarters; then, in due season, slices of pumpkin, unripe peaches (these obviously came into season long before November), and roundabout St Andrew's Day, 30 November, you were to add some fennel root and parsley root (that last item must have been the ancestor of the variety we now call Hamburg parsley).

Once all the fruit and vegetables were ready in the honey preserve, mustard seeds and anis, fennel and coriander seeds were all pounded together in a mortar and mixed with vinegar. Horseradish root was also pounded up and moistened with vinegar. Cloves, cinnamon, pepper, green ginger, cardamom seeds, saffron and sandalwood (for colouring) were also required to be pounded. The spices were to be added to the mustard mixture, but the saffron and sandalwood were kept separate.

The next stage in the confection of this wondrous preserve was the heating and skimming of a large quantity of thick honey to which, when cool, you added your mustard and spice powder mixed with half and half red wine and vinegar. Now the saffron was to go in, then a handful of coarse salt, and the sandalwood heated in wine. Finally, having mixed all these preparations with your preserve of fruit and vegetables, you were to take two pounds of the small seedless raisins of Digne, newly dried,[3] pound them, moisten them with vinegar, strain this mixture through a fine sieve and put it to all the other things. As a final fling, the *Ménagier* adds: and if you put four or five pints of grape must or of *vin cuit*[4] the relish will be all the better.

An English version of composte appears in the celebrated *Forme of Cury*, the book compiled toward the end of the fourteenth century by the master cooks of Richard II. The English recipe is less complex and far less precise than the French one, and the confection is made all in one operation instead of being spread over a period of several months. Walnuts are omitted, and instead of the several different operations involving the addition of honey, wine, mustard and vinegar, the ingredient specified is 'lumbard mustard'. People unfamiliar with Italian fruit mustards have taken 'lumbard mustard' to mean straight mustard seeds, without questioning what significant difference there might be between the mustard grown in northern Italy and our own native product.

In Italian, *mostarda*, of course, implied the presence in the compost of boiled and concentrated grape must or *mosto*; this, together with the honey, wine and vinegar constituted the thick sweet-sour syrup in which the medley of roots and fruits were preserved, while mustard in our terms, called *senape* in Italian, combined with the horseradish, pepper and ginger to contribute the hot element.

As far as the term Lumbard is concerned, the mustard mixture is by no means the only dish of the period to which it was applied. There were, for example, several different versions of Lumbard pies, recipes which persisted in our cookery books until well into the eighteenth century. They were huge, covered pies filled with mixtures of bone marrow, meat or fish – according to whether they were for a meat or fasting day – dried fruit, dates, pine nuts, spices and sugar. Sometimes the top crust was ornamented with a cluster of sugared and spiced pears.

In the contemporary French cookery books these pies were alternatively referred to as *tourtes pisaines*. Did they then originate in Tuscany, rather than in Lombardy? Possibly. But we have to remember that in the days when the Lumbard pies were introduced into England – it was probably a century or more before Richard's cooks recorded them – Lombardy was that part of the Holy Roman Empire which encompassed almost the whole of Italy north of Rome and the Vatican States, and excluding only the Republic of Venice. So Pisa, Florence, Lucca, Parma and Bergamo were as much a part of Lombardy as Milan is today. There is good reason to suppose that the dishes designated as Lumbard – there were also Lumbard sweetmeats, solid pastes made of fruit and honey and spices – were in fact brought to us by Lumbards, perhaps even by those merchants and moneylenders who settled in the city of London in the twelfth century and gave Lombard Street its name.

How was that Lombard compost eaten in the days of the Plantagenets? Although it is mentioned at one feast, given by a Lord de la Grey[5] early in the fifteenth century it appears bracketed with Brode Canelle (cinnamon broth) as a kind of sweet-sour hot relish, the broth itself no doubt being a sweetened one.

In England the tradition of the ancient European relishes died out, their place being taken by Indian chutneys and pickles of which English cooks made strange imitations. In France the roots and herbs, the honey and vinegar and spices were dropped and compost became *raisiné*, a sweetmeat of autumn fruits preserved in boiled-down grape must. By the end of the seventeenth century the term *composte* had come to have its present meaning of fruit cooked for current consumption. In Italy, however, the fruit mustards continued to flourish. The great French essayist, Michel de Montaigne, journeying about Italy in 1580 and 1581 remarked two or three times on the excellence of the relishes and condiments. In October 1581 for example he was in the region of San Secondo[6] and 'they put upon the table for me an assortment of condiments in the form of excellent relishes of various kinds. One of these was made with quinces.' A few days later at Borgo San Donnino, in the Cremona region, 'they put on the table a mustard-like relish made with apples and oranges cut in pieces, like half-cooked quince marmalade.'[7]

References

1. *Les Dix Livres de Cuisine d'Apicius*. Traduite du Latin pour la première fois et commentés par Bertrand Guégan. Paris, René Bonnel, 1938.

2. First printed by the Société des Bibliophiles françois, 1847. The MS was edited by Baron Jérôme Pichon, the Society's President.

3. If the preserves were being made at the end of November, it would have meant that they were very recently dried. Digne is a town in the Basses Alpes. The local raisins appear to have had a considerable reputation in the fourteenth century. It sounds as though they were rather like sultanas.

4. Newly-made wine boiled down and reduced.

5. Probably Lord Grey de Ruthyn who had been Naperer at Henry IV's coronation feast in 1399.

6. Now in the province of Parma.
7. *The Complete Works of Montaigne*. Translated by Donald
M. Frame. London, Hamish Hamilton, n.d.

MOSTARDA D'UVA
(grape must preserve)

The following Piedmontese recipe – from Anna Gosetti della
Salda's *Le Ricette Regionale Italiane* (1967) – appears to answer
almost exactly to Montaigne's description of the relish he enjoyed
at San Donnino.

Ripe but firm figs, 1 kg (2 lb), quinces 1 kg (2 lb), Martin pears 1 kg
(2 lb), grape must 10 litres (2¼ gallons), walnuts and hazelnuts, a
few.

The grape must requires very lengthy cooking, and the preserve
is one for which you really need a wood or coal fired cooking
stove. Ten litres of new must are reduced to one litre of *mostarda*.

Wash and pare the quinces and pears and cut them in pieces.
Put the must to cook with the prepared fruit, add the figs, cut up
but not peeled, the peeled walnut kernels and the hazelnuts,
toasted in the oven and then rolled back and forth on a metal
sieve so that the scorched skins rub off.

Leave the mixture to cook very slowly for several hours, until
the preserve or *composta* has reduced to a thick *mostarda*; the
fruit should be partially disintegrated. This preserve is served as
an accompaniment to hot or cold *bollito*, the mixed boiled meats
of Piedmont.

Note
Martin pears are a late autumn variety, small, russet-coloured
and with firm flesh. They are little cultivated nowadays.

MOSTARDA DI CREMONA

This is the version given by Ada Boni in her famous *Talismano
della Felicità*, 13th edition 1947 (first published 1934). The must
is omitted from this one.

You need a certain quantity of fruit such as pears, apples, cherries,
unripe figs, orange peel, etc.; and each variety should be cooked

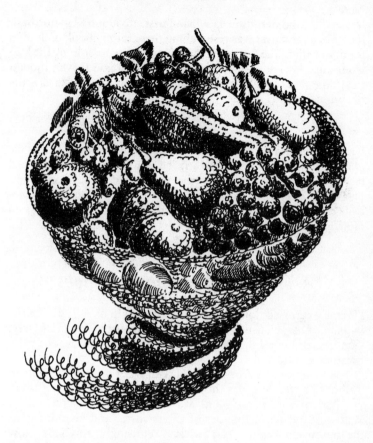

separately in a little water and sugar syrup. Cooking should be done carefully so that the fruit remains slightly hard, and not reduce to pulp.

Once all the fruit is cooked, amalgamate all the different syrups, add more sugar and reduce until you have a somewhat dense syrup to which you add mustard moistened in a little water. You put all the fruit together in a pot and cover it with the prepared syrup. Leave it several days before broaching it.

Note

It was this kind of mostarda which I first encountered in northern Italy in 1952 when I was researching there for my book on Italian food. In Milan, the Cremona mustard fruits were sold by the kilo from huge barrels. They were beautiful and good, even though the grape must had long since vanished from the mustard fruits of commerce.

Unpublished article, late 1980s

Elizabeth was always interested in Italian fruit mustards and had a file of notes about them. I think this article was written soon after she had made the revisions to *Italian Food* in the late 1980s, but it was never published. Most of her articles underwent several drafts, sometimes quite radically different, and it may be that this was an earlier version of *Relishes of the Renaissance*.   JN

A True Gentlewoman's Delight

Having expressed doubts as to the authorship of *A True Gentle-woman's Delight*, usually attributed to Elizabeth Grey or de Grey, Countess of Kent, I should perhaps explain my reasons. The story is rather an odd one.

The Countess we are concerned with was born Lady Elizabeth Talbot in 1581. She was the second daughter of Gilbert Talbot, 7th Earl of Shrewsbury, and Mary Cavendish, daughter of Sir William Cavendish, founder of Chatsworth, and his third wife, the renowned Bess of Hardwick. Confusingly, this lady, now widowed for the third time, and mother of six Cavendish off-spring, shortly married our Countess's grandfather as his fourth wife and became Countess of Shrewsbury. Not however before she had assured the marriage not only of her daughter Mary to the Earl's son Gilbert, but also of her eldest son Henry to the Earl's youngest daughter Lady Grace, the two couples being married at a great double wedding ceremony at Sheffield in February 1568. Later, after Bess had married her Earl, she contrived the marriage of another daughter, Elizabeth, to the young Scottish Earl of Lennox. (The daughter of that marriage was the celebrated beauty of James I's court, Lady Arabella Stuart.) Bess, creator of

Hardwick Hall and several other great Midlands houses, was born in 1518, lived through almost the entire Tudor age and became one of its most powerful women. Immensely rich, 'proud furious and selfish' as her biographer wrote, she died in 1608 aged ninety.

In 1601, two years before Queen Elizabeth's death, Bess's grand-daughter, Lady Elizabeth Talbot, married Henry, Lord Grey de Ruthin, son and heir of the 6th Earl of Kent. Both the young Grey de Ruthins were eventually appointed to positions at the Court of James I, Lady Grey as lady-in-waiting to the Queen, Anne of Denmark. This place she held from c.1610 until the Queen's death in 1619, when she is recorded as having followed her late mistress's coffin in the funeral procession.[1]

As one of her father's co-heiresses,[2] the Countess of Kent – her husband succeeded to the title in 1623 – must have been a very rich woman, and the Kents evidently kept up some state, maintaining a large household of waiting women and gentlemen (the youthful Samuel Butler was a page in the Countess's household, so Aubrey recorded). As legal adviser and steward at Wrest Park in Bedfordshire, the family seat, the Earl employed John Selden, the distinguished lawyer and historian. Concerning this gentleman and the Countess, Aubrey has a typical piece of scandal to recount. The Countess, he says, 'being an ingeniose woman and loving men, would let him lie with her and her husband knew it. After the Earle's death he married her.'

The Earl of Kent died in 1639, and whether or not she then married Selden, the Countess evidently continued to live in the grand style, for it was about 1642, at the time of the outbreak of the Civil War, that she employed Robert May, author of the famous *Accomplisht Cook* of 1660, and May was certainly not the man to tolerate a household where the provisions were less than lavish or the hospitality in any way second rate. May was accustomed to grand and noble households and a numerous staff of under-cooks and servants, and it was in a note at the beginning of his book listing some of his richest employers and signed W.W. that he was recorded as having worked for the Countess of Kent 'at the beginning of these wars'.

Curiously, given her evident love of good living and Aubrey's gossip concerning her promiscuous ways, it was for her generosity to the poor and her medical cures and receipts that the Countess seems to have been best known. It is an aspect of her character

which at first sight accords uneasily with her formidably commanding appearance – her portrait by van Somer, painted when
she was about forty, is now in the Tate – and reports of her
unpopularity at Court. 'The Lady of Roxburgh is gone from
Court' wrote one John Chamberlain to Sir Dudley Carleton in
October 1617 'and the Lady Grey de Ruthyn, though with much
opposition, succeeds in her place.'[3] She certainly looks a very
imperious lady, our Countess, and it comes as no surprise that
she was unloved by her colleagues. All the same, tartar though
she may have been, van Somer's portrait shows that she was lively
and intelligent – as Aubrey says, ingeniose – with it. She must also
have performed her duties efficiently and have been liked by the
royal family, for she seems to have returned to Court to serve
Queen Henrietta Maria, perhaps at the time in 1626 when Charles
I packed off his wife's troublesome French retinue of four hundred
courtiers and hangers-on, brought with her at the time of their
marriage in the previous year. It would have been during this
period that the young Sir Kenelm Digby knew the Countess,
noting how she cooked her nourishing broth for consumptions
'in a close flagon *in bulliente Balneo*, as my Lady Kent, and my
Mother used'[4] and that a certain W.H., one of Henrietta's scribes,
or perhaps an apothecary, recorded the recipe for a powder
presented by the Countess to the Queen. This was a concoction
of white amber, crab's eyes, red coral, harts-horn, saffron and
pearl dissolved in lemon juice, the whole lot made into a paste
and dried.[5] This powder was a specific 'against all malignant and
Pestilent Diseases' including 'French Pox, Small Pox, Measels,
Plague, Pestilence'. It was known as My Lady Kent's Powder, or
Gascons Powder.

In December 1651 the Countess died at her London house at
Whitefriars. Aged seventy, and childless – her husband's title had
passed to a cousin, Anthony Grey – she bequeathed most of her
personal property, including the Whitefriars house, to Selden. It
was only then, according to Aubrey, that Selden made public his
marriage to the Countess. Aubrey further recounts that Selden had
been carrying on with the women of the Countess's household,
including 'my lady's Shee Blackamore' and a certain Mistress
Williamson, 'a lusty bouncing woman, who robbed him on his
death-bed'. With his customary relish for scandalous tittle-tattle,
Aubrey adds that his saddler, who had also served the Kents, had
said that 'Mr Selden had got more by his Prick than he had done

by his practise'. An envious allusion, no doubt, to the considerable fortune left him by the Countess. Selden, however, lived only three more years to enjoy his wealth and his bouncing Mistress Williamson. Afflicted with dropsy, he died at the Whitefriars house in November 1654.

In 1653, a year before Selden's death and two years after that of the Countess, the book of medical receipts which bears her name was published. It was entitled *A Choice Manual, or Rare Secrets in Physick and Chirurgery Collected and practised by the Right Honourable the Countess of Kent, late deceased*. My edition, the 19th, carries the further subtitle *Whereto are added several Experiments of the Vertue of Gascons powder, and Lapis contra Yarvam by a Professor of Physick. As also most excellent ways of Preserving, Conserving, Candying etc.* The Nineteenth Edition, London, Printed for Henry Mortlock at the Phoenix in St Paul's Church-yard, 1687. In all editions except the first, at any rate according to Oxford, there was a portrait of the Countess of Kent. This portrait is often missing, as it is in my copy, but I have seen three different versions of it. All three could, possibly, be extremely crude drawings taken from the van Somer portrait, since in one of them the Countess appears to be wearing the same cap with the aigrette on the back of her head. The portrait was in the collection of Charles I, and sold during the Commonwealth.

The 1687 edition is a tiny 24mo volume, in two quite separate parts. The medical receipts run to 238 pages, of which 43 contain the additional Experiments announced on the title page. There is also a Table of Contents of the Additions running to five unnumbered pages. Then comes the cookery part, separately paginated, and titled *A True Gentlewomans Delight. Wherein is contain'd all manner of Cookery Together with Preserving, Conserving, Drying, and Candying. Very necessary for all Ladies and Gentlewomen.* Published by W. G. Gent[6] London. Printed for Henry Mortlock, at the Phoenix in St Paul's Church-yard, 1687. There is a dedicatory Epistle addressed 'To the Virtuous and Most Hopeful Gentlewoman, Mrs Anne Pile, Eldest Daughter of the Honourable Sir Francis Pile Baronet, Deceased', signed W.J., and another addressed 'Friendly Reader' and signed W.L. The Table of Contents follows, again unnumbered, then the receipts, running to 140 pages.

At no place in the book, then, is there the slightest printed claim that the cookery receipts were those used by the Countess of Kent or that they came from any MS. found among her papers. It seems fairly likely that the MS. receipt book was the property of W.J., the gent of the title pages, or of some friend of his, and that the Countess of Kent's book of medical secrets had also fallen into his hands. When he decided to publish it, whether with or without Selden's consent we do not know – the two MSS. were put together in order to increase the size of the volume or to make it more complete and thus attract more sales.

The sole connecting link between the two books is provided by the dedicatory Epistle to the *Choice Manual*, addressed to the 'vertuous and most Noble Lady, Laetitia Popham, wife of the Honourable and truly Valiant Col. Alexander Popham'[7] and like the one addressed to Mistress Anne Pile in *The True Gentlewoman*, signed W.J. The same W.J. – the initials were on the title page of the earlier editions of the *Choice Manual* – also signed the Epistle introducing the additional *Experiments* of the later editions of the book. From this we learn that the said W.J. had been given some of these receipts for 'select cordial spirits' by a certain Dr Samuel King who had them from Sir Walter Rawleigh, with whom he had 'lived long time in the Tower, and in his Expeditions'. This Samuel King, continues W.J., was 'my loving friend, and School-fellow both in Canterbury and Westminster Schools'. It sounds very much as if W.J. were himself a physician, the 'Experiments of Gascons powder, or the Countesse's', having been tried 'upon several persons by my self and divers others by my directions'. Could W.J. perhaps have been a doctor or apothecary in the Kent household, assisting her in her ministrations to the sick, and therefore having access to her book of medical receipts and rare secrets?

When it comes to the famous receipts and secrets, many of them turn out to be for delightful herbal mixtures and syrups, compounded of flowers and spices, oils and beeswax, almonds, milk, honey, ale, cordial waters, French white wines, muscadine, malmsey. There are broths of chicken and raisins, distillations of water-cresses, water-mint and spearmints. Honeysuckle, celandine, comfrey, cowslips and wild white roses all make their appearance among the commoner herbs such as marjoram and wild thyme, parsley root, marigold flowers and violet leaves. The receipts are written literately and with much style. Reading them one appreciates once again how closely the arts of medicine and cookery were related in the Countess of Kent's day, although it has to be admitted that the less enticing brews of the period are not absent from the Kent manual. 'Take three round Balls of Horse-dung, boil them in a pint of white wine'; 'Take a Hound's turd'; and for a Pin or Web in the Eye 'take two or three lice out of one's head, and put them alive into the eye that is grieved, and so close it up and most assuredly the lice will suck out the Web in the eye and will cure it and come forth without any hurt'. Such were conditions and the state of medicine in Stuart England.

Reflecting on the Countess of Kent's haughty appearance and scandalous sexual conduct (Aubrey was not alone in reporting it) I think they are less incompatible with her ministrations to the sick and her charitable hospitality to the poor[8] than it would at first seem. The Countess was rich, she was childless, all châtelaines of great houses were expected to be conversant with medicine, the arts of distilling cordials and healing waters and the cooking of restorative broths.

Charity was a natural duty, and if the Countess practised it on the scale reported by de la Pryme then she was exercising the organising capacity and administrative ability of a high-powered woman such as the one depicted in the van Somer portrait. The Countess had certainly inherited some of her famous grand-mother's commanding characteristics. As for brazenly cuckolding her husband and subsequently living with John Selden in 'open whoredom' as de la Pryme wrote in his Diary, at the period neither circumstance was any great rarity. The Jacobeans were not prudish about sex. As Oliver Lawson Dick wrote in the foreword to his edition of *Aubrey's Brief Lives*:[9] 'In the seven-teenth century sex had not yet been singled out as the sin par excellence, it was merely one among many failings, and Aubrey no more thought of concealing it than he dreamed of avoiding the mention of gluttony or drunkenness.' Or, it might be added, the presence of 'lice in one's head'.

What then of the little book of cookery receipts which for so long had gone under the Countess of Kent's name? Whatever its provenance, *A True Gentlewoman's Delight* is a collection of much charm, someone's personal receipt book not written for publication any more than was the *Choice Manual*.[10] Like many such family receipt books it is somewhat higgledy-piggledy and inconsistent. Some of the receipts date back to Tudor days, a few are survivals from medieval cookery, others are for the typical dishes of the first Stuart period – delicious creams and junkets, spiced yeast cakes, pottages enriched with raisins and dates, an artichoke pie, 'a potato pie for supper', a tart with green pease and a tart of hips. Many other receipts reflect that preoccupation with preserving, candying, crystallising and comfit-making common during the first half of the seventeenth century and stressed in the sub-title of the book.

Together with the medical receipts of the first part those were evidently the ones which the publishers counted on to sell the book. And sell it they did. By 1654, a year after its first appearance, it had already gone into four editions, and by 1659 into twelve. At some time between the appearance of the fourth and eleventh editions (also 1659) the Additions to the medical receipts supplied by W.J. were inserted. The latest edition of which I have heard is the twenty-first, published in 1708. From 1658 to 1708 makes a remarkably long life for so small a book, and is perhaps a testimonial to the selling power of the Countess of Kent's name.

It is unlikely that we shall ever know the identity of the *True Gentlewoman*. One thing I think I can say with certainty. *If* the Countess of Kent wrote the medical receipts then she did not write the cookery receipts. The style of the two books is quite different, a point I have only recently perceived. Nor is it the cookery receipt book of a rich noblewoman who entertained sixty or eighty poor people every other day and sent out food to those who could not come (de la Pryme again). I would say that the collection came from a much more modest household, and this is very much part of its appeal. I have owned the little book for about fifteen years, have studied the cookery receipts – and used some – always with joy and fascination, but only lately have I thought to read the medical ones with anything other than passing curiosity.

References
1. John B. Nichols, FSA, *The Progresses, processions . . . of King James the First . . . collected from original mss, etc*, London 1828.
2. The Countess's elder sister, Lady Mary Talbot, married William Herbert, 3rd Earl of Pembroke, in 1604.
3. Nichols, op. cit.
4. *The Closet of the Eminently Learned Sir Kenelme Digbie, Kt. Opened*, 1669, p. 141 of the 1910 edition.
5. The Receipt of the Lady Kent's powder presented by her ladyship to the Queen. *A Queen's Delight*, 1658 edition. First

published 1655. This version differs slightly from the one in the Kent manual.

6. The G. is evidently a misprint. In earlier editions it was W.J.

7. Born 1605, one of the three brothers Popham who fought for the Parliament in the Civil War.

8. *The Diary of Abraham de la Pryme*, ed. Charles Jackson, Surtees Society 1869–70, Vol 54. In the year 1686 de la Pryme reported that his aunt, who knew the Countess, said 'that she spent twenty thousand pound a year on physick, receipts and experiments, and in charity towards the poor'.

9. Secker and Warburg, 1949, and Penguin Books, 1962. It is from this edition that all passages quoted in this article have been drawn.

10. Whoever described the Countess of Kent as an 'authoress' in the D.N.B. cannot have examined the book.

RECEIPTS

Here are two brief recipes, interesting, although not typical ones (since most of these are too long for quotation here), from the Kent medical collection, followed by two from *The True Gentle-woman*.

To take away Hoarseness

'Take a Turnip, cut a hole in the top of it and fill it up with brown sugar-candy, and so roast it in the embers and eat it with Butter.'

A Strengthening Meat

'Take Potato roots, roast them or bake them, then pill [peel] them, and slice them into a dish, put to it lumps of raw Marrow [i.e. bone-marrow] and a few Currants, a little whole Mace, and sweeten it with sugar to your taste, and so eat it instead of buttered Parsnips.'

To boil a Capon or Chicken in White broth with Almonds

'Boil your Capon as in the other, then take Almonds, and blanch them and beat them very small, putting in sometimes some of your broth to keep them from oiling; when they are beaten small enough, put as much of the uppermost broth to them as will serve to cover the Capon, then strain it, and wring out the substance clear, then season it as before [i.e. with grated Nutmeg, Sugar, and Salt], and serve it with marrow on it.'

How to make a Florentine

'Take the Kidney of a Loin of Veal, or the wing of a Capon, or the leg of a Rabbet, mince any of these small, with the Kidney of a Loin of Mutton; if it be not fat enough, then season it with Cloves, Mace, Nutmegs and Sugar, Cream, Currans, Eggs and Rosewater, mingle these four together and put them into a dish between two sheets of paste, then close it, and cut the paste round by the brim of the dish, then cut it round about like Virginal Keys, then turn up one, and let the other lie, then pink it, bake it, scrape on sugar, and serve it.'

This last recipe is particularly interesting for the manner in which the pastry is cut (I have made it. It does indeed resemble virginal keys) and because Robert May has a picture (p. 265 of the 1685 edition) of just such a pie – although not the recipe. The edition of May's book, *The Accomplisht Cook*, in which two hundred additional and very interesting Figures, as he calls them, first appeared, was published in 1664, a long while after that of *The True Gentlewoman*, so it looks as though May borrowed the idea from her book – I have not seen it described in any other work – forgetting to insert the recipe, or finding the obviously left-over wing of capon or leg of rabbit beneath his style of cooking. His two Florentine recipes are predictably more complex and on a grander scale.

One more slender connecting link between May and the *True Gentlewoman* are the recipes for black tart stuff and yellow tart stuff which appear in both books but not in others of the period which I have seen. These pie fillings are, respectively, mixtures of raisins and prunes cooked and sieved to a purée, and a rich egg custard sweetened with sugar and sack. May has three variations on the black one [*see* the recipe on page 59], one of them very similar to the *True Gentlewoman*'s. Their yellow tart stuffs differ in that the lady's calls for 24 eggs and a quart of milk, May's for 12 eggs and a quart of cream. May also has red, white, and green tart stuffs, made from quinces, cherries, red currants, red gooseberries, damsons, pippins, barberries, raspberries for the red ones; for the green, spinach, peas, sorrel, green apricots, peaches, green nectarines, green gooseberries, green plums, the juice of green wheat; for the white, just whites of eggs and cream sweetened with sack and sugar, and perfumed with rose-water, musk and ambergris.

Did May borrow the black and yellow mixtures from the *True Gentlewoman* and then concoct his green, red and white mixtures? Useless speculation. But not entirely irrelevant, for it has to be said that although May's book will always be immensely interesting, the man himself was a great boaster and a bit of a fraud, who slammed French cooks and cooking and nearly all the books written by his predecessors and contemporaries, at the same time coolly admitting that he had helped himself from the best French, Italian and Spanish works, although he was careful not to say on what a wholesale scale he had lifted, appropriating for example the entire chapter on egg cookery from La Varenne's *Le Pastissier François*. As for English books, the only one for which he had a good word was the *Queen's Closet* published in 1655 by Nathaniel Brook, by coincidence his own original publisher.

It is a curious point that while the modest little Kent book ran into twenty-one editions and lasted for over half a century, May's far grander and more important one, with its beautiful illustrations, ran into no more than five editions and had a life of only twenty-five years. And, unjustly, May was ignored by the compilers of the D.N.B.

Petits Propos Culinaires, 1979

Quiche Lorraine

It was in the classrooms of upper-crust English cookery schools of twenty years ago that the ex-debs of the time learned to make great thick open pies crammed with asparagus tips, prawns, mushrooms, crab-meat, olives, chunks of ham, all embedded in custard as often as not solidified with cheese. In directors' dining-rooms and later in expensive delicatessens and in the new-style London wine bars they dubbed those creations 'quiches'. It was libel really, but the British have never been too particular in such matters. As far as imported foreign specialities are concerned it's the name they fancy, the substance isn't of much account. It's not difficult to see why the girls picked on those hefty pies as their *pièces de résistance*, and called them quiches. The name is catchy and they hadn't been taught what the real thing was.

The Constance Spry quiche lorraine recipe published in the Cordon Bleu cookery school bible in 1956 has cheese and onions in it: a young girl I knew attending classes given by a respected Kensington teacher circa 1960 was taught to make quiches with a filling of evaporated milk and processed Cheddar; so when the time came the young women who graduated into the genteeler areas of catering found that they could get away with putting anything they chose into a pastry shell and calling it a quiche.

In 1966, via Penguin paperback, Julia Child's *Mastering the Art of French Cooking* began to reach a massive British audience. From that formidably detailed manual, cookery students now learned that a quiche was 'an open-faced tart', that it was 'practically foolproof', that 'you can invent your own, anything combined with eggs, poured into a pastry shell'. Mrs Child and her collaborators had provided a sound enough recipe – classic they called it – for quiche lorraine, its filling just eggs, cream, bacon. No cheese, they emphasised. Few British readers can have paid attention to that instruction. They didn't want to, any more than they had wanted to when in my own *French Provincial Cooking* (1960) and *French Country Cooking* (1952) I had published recipes for the regional quiche lorraine which didn't call for cheese. What the catering girls went for was the licence provided by Mrs Child to print the word quiche in connection with any and every open-faced tart – if that's the only alternative description one sees why it was discarded – filled with any one of fifty-seven different combinations of fish, fowl, vegetable, cured pork and cheese.

Those confections were immensely convenient. The ingredients for the fillings were as variable and interchangeable as anyone could wish. As Mrs Child had promised, quiches were all but foolproof. They could be made in the cook's own time, on her own premises, they were easy to transport, safe to warm up, saleable in wedges, and extraordinarily profitable. Those little bits and pieces encased in good stout pastry walls are a lot cheaper to buy than the double cream and eggs which are the main ingredients of the traditional quiche of Lorraine. No wonder that that one was quickly rejected as a profit-making proposition for wine bars and delicatessens. Besides, like so many seemingly easy dishes, the simple version of quiche lorraine is quite tricky to get right. It needs accurate timing. It isn't too successful when reheated. Anyway, British cooks tend to mistrust simple recipes calling only for a minimum number of ingredients. They suspect there's something missing. So they supply the lack.

In 1932, Marcel Boulestin, whose cookery books were by then well known to connoisseurs of good food, came up with a quiche lorraine recipe. It appeared in a little volume called *Savouries and hors-d'oeuvre* (reprinted in 1956), and figured among the hot hors d'oeuvre. Boulestin's recipe called for flaky pastry and a filling composed of a tumbler of cream, a quarter pound of grated Gruyère, and just one beaten egg. A few pieces of bacon chopped fine were optional. Not a compulsive recipe. The cheese, like the flaky pastry, was quite alien to the rustic nature of the original,

This postcard made Elizabeth laugh, and she kept it for many years

but it probably appealed to English cooks. The anachronisms had undoubtedly come via Paris chefs.

As far back as 1870 Jules Gouffé, head panjandrum of the kitchens at the very grand Paris Jockey Club, had published an appropriately sumptuous and imposing *Livre de pâtisserie* in which he had re-interpreted the quiche lorraine according to the lights of the grande cuisine of the period. Gouffé spelled the word 'kiche' and made its base of puff pastry instead of the piece of leavened dough which formed the mainstay of the original. For fillings for his 'kiches' Gouffé gave several variations. One called for parmesan cheese, one was sweetened with sugar and scented with orange flower water, one was perfectly straightforward, consisting of butter, eggs and cream in generous quantities and without redundant frills. Gouffé – who had served his apprenticeship with Carême and whose brother Alphonse was in charge of Queen Victoria's pastry kitchens – had all the same taken the first step in the Parisianisation of the primitive galette or quiche as it used to be made in the villages of Lorraine before the Franco-Prussian war of 1870. But Jules Gouffé can hardly be held responsible for the fate which overtook the quiche a hundred years after his book was published at the hands, not of his own culinary heirs, but at those of Albion's cooking daughters.

It's too late now to restore the ravaged image of the quiche as we know it in British take-aways and wine bars, 'made up of egg, cheese, milk and ham and seasoned with herbs, part-cooked and ready to eat after 20 to 30 minutes in an oven'. No comment, but here, for the record, is a description of how the quiche lorraine was made in its days of innocence.

The recipe was recorded by the French académicien André Theuriet and contributed by him to a wonderful treasury of recipes and food lore put together by his friend Edmond Richardin – both men were natives of Lorraine – and published in 1904 under the title *L'Art du bien manger*. 'The quiche or galette lorraine was the delight of my childhood,' Theuriet wrote, remembering back some forty or more years. 'You take a piece of bread dough, you roll it out as thin as a two sous piece and you spread it out very carefully in a shallow fluted toleware tart tin, previously dusted with flour. On this round surface you arrange, chequerboard fashion, fresh diced butter. This preliminary effected, in a salad bowl beat an appropriate number of eggs, adding a bowl of thick ripe cream of the previous day's skimming. When this filling is thoroughly blended and just sufficiently salted, pour it over the prepared dough. Now carry your galette to the blazing oven of the neighbourhood bakery. Leave it five minutes, no longer. It will emerge puffed up, golden, blistered, alluring, filling the house with its savoury aroma. Eat it scalding hot, with it drink one of the light pineau wines from Lorraine and you will appreciate what good cheer means.'

Indeed, yes. But I suggest we keep that from the pizza houses or next thing we know it'll be pizza lorraine and back we'll be with that old dream topping of Carnation and Kraft.

To be fair to the gentrifiers of the quiche, even when Jules Gouffé came on the scene the basic bread dough version already had a gone-up-in-the-world local rival. Jules Renauld, historian of drinking and eating customs in Lorraine and author of *Les Hostelains et Taverniers de Nancy*, published in 1875, described the quiche lorraine as being a very thin round of ordinary tart pastry spread with an equally spare dressing of cream and eggs no thicker than a sheet of paper laid over the pastry. The quiche had been known in Lorraine, he claimed, for at least 300 years. As evidence he cited a payment for quiches supplied by Charles Duke of Lorraine's household steward for his master's table on 1 March 1586. So quiches were then accepted as Lenten fare.

It may be worth making the point that it's not easy to appreciate what well-made quiches are like today unless you go to Lorraine and eat them on the spot. The pastry is always very thin; it's always baked in shallow tart tins; the filling is always composed of eggs and cream; it never contains Gruyère or Parmesan cheese; and usually there's a small amount of streaky bacon – another local product – in small pieces.

In the villages of the Vosges you may discover older versions without the bacon but with plain, fresh, skimmed-milk curd cheese mixed with the cream and eggs. I suppose someone might even consider reviving the ancient bread dough version. I'm told they still make one in some parts of Alsace. It's rectangular, and as the bread dough bakes in a very hot oven its dressing of fresh curds and cream integrates with its base and appears as inviting as the bronzed and blistered quiche of André Theuriet's childhood. In Alsace it's called *Flammen Kuchen* or tarte à la flamme, it's eaten bubbling hot, and with it, of course, you drink a cool aromatic local white wine.

Tatler, September 1985

Hand-made Mayonnaise

Those who make their mayonnaise in the electric blender will perhaps think it very quaint that anyone should still use the old method of stirring by hand. In some ways I would agree. The electric blender has, after all, revolutionised our cooking lives during the past three decades, and it is only sensible to take every possible advantage of its labour-saving benefits. I would certainly, for example, use the blender when making a mayonnaise in large quantity. Given time, however, I still take pleasure in settling down to make this extraordinary sauce by the old method which to many people now seems laborious. The following notes, therefore, are concerned mainly with hand-made mayonnaise. They may prove useful to those who already know the theory but still find the practice tricky – and there are, I think, many young people today who prefer hand-made to mechanical methods; there are even people who don't possess or can't be bothered with electric blenders and mixers.

1. The fresher your egg or eggs, the easier and quicker it will be to achieve a mayonnaise of the right consistency. Just what this should be is fully described in note 5 below.

2. If you use an olive oil of good quality with a delicate and true taste of the fruit, mayonnaise needs no seasoning other than lemon juice or a very little wine vinegar. With rare exceptions, as for example when destined for a celeriac salad, mustard is ruination to mayonnaise. Pepper is redundant, and surprisingly so is salt, although that is no doubt a matter of taste. Strong condiments are needed only for mayonnaise made with totally tasteless oil. Even then they should be used very sparingly indeed. In a mayonnaise all seasonings and flavourings are much intensified. Overdone, they produce a sauce approaching perilously near the bottled stuff.

3. Before starting on a mayonnaise, make certain that eggs and oil are both at room temperature. There is no surer way of curdling the sauce than by using ice-cold ingredients, or an ice-cold with a warm one. So if you store your eggs in the refrigerator, remember to take out however many you need in good time. If you have forgotten this precaution, put your egg or eggs in a bowl of warm water for a few minutes before you start work on the sauce. As

for the oil, it would be absurd to refrigerate it, and my advice is don't. Instead, keep it at a moderate and constant temperature.

4. The fewer eggs you can manage with, the better the mayonnaise. Beginners may need the reassurance of using two yolks for a small amount of sauce, but with experience most people discover that one large yolk will serve to thicken up to 300 ml (½ pint) of oil and often more. Much depends on the quality of both ingredients. And, again, a fresh egg with a good plump yolk works twice as fast as a stale flat one and goes much further.

5. The solid, jelly-like consistency of a true mayonnaise does, of course, take a little longer to achieve by hand than in the blender. Some people never do achieve it, because – lacking faith perhaps – they give up before the stage of maximum absorption and expansion has been reached, thus producing a pouring sauce rather than the emulsified ointment-like substance that a mayonnaise should be. This was very graphically defined in a recipe I came across recently in Cassell's *Book of the Household*, published in 1889, as being 'quite as thick as a pat of butter on a hot day in August. Indeed it would stand up in a tablespoon, so that you could put three or four tablespoons in one spoon at a time, and hold it up in the air and it would not run over.'

The thickening and expanding process starts only when the egg has absorbed a certain quantity of oil, and at this stage the beginner has to have faith and patience. Quite suddenly you find that the sauce has changed from a thick cream into a smooth, shining ointment. From there you persevere until the ointment is so thick and stiff that it is quite difficult to stir in more oil.

6. Experienced mayonnaise-makers tend to plop oil straight from the bottle, not worrying too much about that drop-by-drop business – except for the first minute or two – but probably the most satisfactory and the simplest method is to use a measuring jug. Any jug with a good pouring spout will do – if it is a bad one you waste a lot of oil – and some kitchen shops probably still stock glass oil pourers imported from Spain. These are very effective, and although they slow up the process rather, do give a feeling of safety to the beginner.

7. Separating the eggs is such a basic kitchen operation that it is surprising to find that people are actually frightened of it. Indeed special gadgets have been invented to help the nervous and the inexperienced. In this respect, the best gadget I know is a good fresh egg. Give it a sharp, decisive tap – in the centre – on the rim

of the bowl waiting to receive the white. Passing the egg from one half shell to the other, let the white fall into the bowl, giving it a bit of assistance with the shell. The shell can also be used to scoop out any scrap of yolk which has found its way into the white, but with a really fresh egg this doesn't happen, and it hardly takes more than five seconds to separate the egg. For mayonnaise, by the way, it doesn't matter if a little of the white gets into the bowl with the yolk. It can happen, of course, that a stale egg, on being cracked, falls plop into the bowl and cannot thereafter be separated, so you have to start again with another egg. Or give up the whole enterprise and resort to the blender which obligingly makes mayonnaise from the whole egg. It won't make a very good one though, not with a stale, flat egg.

8. The bowl you use for making mayonnaise should be a fairly solid one, one which does not slide about the table as you stir, and if it is wide in proportion to its depth, so much the better. It will be easier to stir the mixture as it thickens. Professional chefs tend to use a balloon whisk for mayonnaise, so they also need a rather large, deep bowl. Old-fashioned home cooks often used to beat the oil into the egg with a fork. Personally I use a tough little boxwood spoon with a rather long handle. It's a question of finding out what suits you best.

9. I find that adding the oil to the egg drop by drop is necessary only in the very early stages, until yolk and oil are securely amalgamated. After that you can plop it in in quite large spoonfuls. The important thing is to stir very firmly after each addition and to wait until the oil is properly integrated before adding more. The stirring or beating must take in *all* the sauce, from the bottom of the bowl and round the sides as well as the top surface. As the sauce thickens and its volume increases, the oil can be added, if you like, in a steady thin stream. On the whole, though, I find it easier to continue with the system of alternately adding and stirring, a system which creates its own rhythm. Every now and again stir in a little lemon juice. Quite quickly, if all has gone well, the mayonnaise becomes so stiff that it is quite difficult to stir. If you think you have enough, stop now. Taste the mayonnaise, add more lemon juice or a few drops of vinegar if necessary. (Careful about the vinegar though. Nothing is easier than to wreck the entire batch of mayonnaise by the careless addition of vinegar. So measure it out into a teaspoon.) If, however, you still need more, you will find that you can go on incorporating oil for quite a long

time after the final stage appears to have been reached, and certainly for long after your arm has started to ache. 300 ml (½ pint) of oil per egg yolk seems to me about the right proportion, but you could use much more. The stories you hear about people making a washbasin-size bowl of mayonnaise based on a single egg yolk are not just myths. Given the rarity, though, and the huge cost of good olive oil, it would be a bit reckless to use more than you need just for the sake of a dare, or because you find the process so mesmerising you can't stop the pouring and stirring.

A very important point remains to be made: one of the major troubles about mayonnaise is that when it's good there is seldom quite enough. So don't stop before you are sure there really *is* enough. But be cautious once you have passed the half-pint-to-one-egg level.

10. If you have a mishap and the sauce does separate, the remedy is to start again with a fresh egg yolk in a clean bowl. Add the curdled sauce a little at a time to the new egg. It will soon thicken and solidify.

11. Once your mayonnaise is soundly and securely integrated, it takes really careless treatment to spoil it.

12. If you need to keep the mayonnaise overnight, possibly the most effective way is to cover the whole surface with, first, a thin film of oil, then with a piece of plastic wrap. Store it in a cool place – say about 15°C/60°F – but not in the refrigerator. (Mayonnaise doesn't like extremes of temperature either way.) The idea of the sealing film of oil is to exclude the air and prevent the formation of a skin which often causes the downfall of the sauce. When the time comes to serve it, simply stir in the oil in the routine way and all should be well. I find this method a very useful one. Another way is to stir a tablespoon of boiling water into the mayonnaise when it is ready. This stabilises it, but does thin it very slightly. To some people this is an advantage, and it does make the sauce go further. So much depends upon what it is to accompany.

13. That last sentence brings me to the olive oil itself. I have deliberately left it to the end of these notes. Olive oil addicts and connoisseurs will have their own views and preferences and experience to draw on. They will also, no doubt, have their own sources of supply. Good and authentic olive oil is now so rare and so expensive that advice to use a heavily fruity, green, first-pressing Tuscan or Italian Riviera oil, or a slightly more refined and subtle golden oil from Provence for a mayonnaise to go with

this or that or the other given dish is about as meaningful as telling people that a Chambolle-Musigny 1967 might be better with the pheasant and chestnuts than a Romanée-Conti 1964.

So from my own experience, and for the benefit of the few who are interested enough to search out, and both able and willing to pay for, supplies of good olive oils, I'd say it is by no means essential to use a particularly fruity olive oil for mayonnaise, although I do have to say again that it does depend upon what food the sauce is to go with. For coarse white fish, for example, a fruity oil is an advantage. For salmon trout or a delicate poached chicken I use a milder Provence oil. For salmon, which has its own richness, I'd also use a mild oil, or perhaps equal quantities of a fruity oil and a refined, light and fairly tasteless one of a reliable and uniform quality. To the inexperienced I should add a warning about olive oils blended with other oils, usually corn or sunflower seed oil. Not so long ago, in a friend's house, I made a mayonnaise with this type of oil. I came to the conclusion that the blend must have been in the proportion of a quart of sunflower to an ounce of olive oil. A waste of the olive oil, in fact. It must be remembered that in a mayonnaise the taste of the oil is much intensified. Consequently the flavour of the mayonnaise I made with the blended oil was solely of sunflower seed. No amount of extra seasoning in the form of mustard, lemon juice, salt, pepper, could make it edible.

14. Finally, a method of making mayonnaise using one raw and one hard-boiled egg yolk. This combination makes the basis of the modern sauce rémoulade, in other words a thick mayonnaise to which chopped herbs, capers, and sometimes anchovies are added. But there's no reason why the basic sauce shouldn't be regarded just as a mayonnaise which is amazingly good tempered, and one which in my experience it is almost impossible to curdle. It's a bit creamier than an ordinary mayonnaise, but particularly useful when you have to make the sauce in advance and keep it overnight.

All you need to do is extract the yolk from a not-too-hard-boiled egg, mash it to a paste in a bowl, stir in the raw yolk, and when the two are thoroughly blended start adding the oil. Proceed as usual, adding lemon juice or a few drops of vinegar from time to time as the sauce thickens. You need stop only when you think you have enough sauce, or when your arm aches too much to continue, whichever is the soonest. Cover, as before, with a thin film of oil and then with plastic wrap. Leave in a cool place, but not in the refrigerator.

If you are intending to treat the sauce as a rémoulade rather than as straight mayonnaise, add the rémoulade part about an hour before serving. In their simplest form the flavourings consist of a teaspoon each of rinsed, carefully drained, and chopped capers, chopped fresh tarragon, and chopped fresh parsley. Optionally, a few chives cut small, a de-salted and chopped anchovy fillet or two, a very little yellow Dijon mustard (an authentic French one, not an imitation). Should you happen to have rocket, that neglected salad and sauce herb, growing in your herb patch, use a chopped leaf or two instead of mustard. The sauce is good with cold chicken and with the breast of lamb dish called *à la sainte Ménéhould*, in other words braised and cooled breast of lamb, boned, cut into strips, breadcrumbed, and grilled on an iron grid over direct heat. An admirably economical dish.

Masterclass, 1982

Poached Eggs

Over the years I think that I have received more pleas for advice on the technique of poaching eggs than on any other aspect of cookery, with the possible exception of how to get the brûlée part on crème brûlée. But that's another story.

In his book, *A Complete System of Cookery*, published in 1759, William Verral put the matter in, one might say, an eggshell.

'Be sure the eggs are fresh; for, from the experience I have had, I am sure it is not in the power of the best cook in the Kingdom to poach stale ones handsome, notwithstanding they may come all whole out of the shell.'

There you have it. To produce neat, plump, well shaped and comely poached eggs it is essential to start off with fresh eggs. Not *too* fresh though. A really new-laid egg is not a good subject for poaching. The white separates too easily from the yolk. Three-day-old eggs are the ideal, although how, unless one keeps hens, one is ever to know the exact age of an egg is not a problem I can solve. But, like many people who live in big towns, I find that it pays to go to some trouble to discover a shop where the supply of eggs is limited, and the turnover rapid, so that one can always be reasonably sure that the eggs are fresh. And when friends arrive from the country with their own fresh eggs I find that the best way to ensure a few days' supply of nicely poached eggs is to cook them immediately and keep them in a bowl of acidulated water in the refrigerator. This is a most successful system. With the help of Parmesan cheese, breadcrumbs, butter and fresh parsley or tarragon, possibly a little cream, or freshly made tomato sauce, or chopped spinach, delicate and appetising little poached egg dishes can be produced for lunch in a few minutes.

Here is the method. Apart from the fresh eggs – for poaching choose small ones whenever possible – a certain knack is needed. It is one which is easily acquired, but until the simple technique has been mastered it is advisable not to attempt to poach more than two or three eggs in one go.

Utensils required are an ordinary saucepan of 1½–2 litre/3–4 pint capacity and with a cover, a long-handled perforated metal spoon, a bowl and a couple of small cups or saucers. I find that a timer is also indispensable.

Three-quarters fill the saucepan with water, bring this to simmering point, add a tablespoon of wine vinegar. Break the eggs into the cups or saucers, slide them into the gently simmering water. Count thirty. Turn off the heat. Quickly, with the edge of your metal spoon, roll each egg over once or twice. This sounds dangerous but – always provided that the eggs are in the right condition – I assure you that it works. If any of the white of the eggs has separated and floated to the surface, skim it off.

Now cover the saucepan and leave the eggs for three minutes.

Have ready a bowl of cold water to which you have added a few drops of wine or tarragon vinegar.

With your perforated spoon lift out the poached eggs and drop them gently into the cold water. This immediately arrests the cooking, so that when you come to reheat the eggs they will still remain tender and soft. Any trimming of the whites which may be necessary can be done at a later stage.

Cover the bowl and store the eggs on the bottom shelf of the refrigerator. If not used within two or three days, renew the slightly vinegared water and return the bowl to the refrigerator.

A week is the maximum time I have stored poached eggs in this manner.

Notes

1. I find that it is not very practical to make more than one batch of poached eggs without boiling fresh water and vinegar. The water becomes cloudy, and requires much skimming, and often the second or third batch of eggs looks messy. So the sooner one can acquire the knack of poaching several eggs at a time in a large pan, the quicker it will be to poach say half a dozen eggs, so often called for in those recipes which start off by telling you in such a wonderfully carefree way to 'have ready ten nicely poached eggs'.

2. No matter how fresh eggs may be, some are just better than others – plumper, with whites which coagulate more perfectly, so sometimes it is not necessary to turn the eggs over in the water. One sees that the whites have of themselves formed a beautiful, shapely covering for the yolks.

3. Some cooks use a shallow sauté pan rather than a saucepan for the poaching of eggs. I find that it matters little which is used. Possibly a sauté pan is best for a quantity of eggs, a saucepan for just two or three. Just as for scrambled eggs, omelettes, fried eggs and boiled eggs, the choice of pan is a matter of personal preference. Any law laid down would be arbitrary.

Masterclass, 1982

TORTILLA – SPANISH OMELETTE

A Spanish tortilla is a thick, unfolded omelette, consisting only of eggs, potatoes and seasonings. It is cooked in olive oil, should be compact and have almost the appearance of a cake, can be eaten hot or cold, and makes a splendid picnic dish, especially for a car journey. A big tortilla will keep moist for three days.

The following recipe, in note form, is exactly as I wrote it down while watching Juanita, the village girl who once cooked for Anthony Denney in his house in the province of Alicante. The notes seem to me to convey the essential points about making a tortilla more vividly than would a conventional recipe, and I have used them often without in any way altering the method, except to cook the potatoes rather more gently than Juanita did – she was never a patient girl.

About 500 g (1 lb) of potatoes for 4 eggs.

Potatoes all cut up small. Soaked in plenty of water (like for gratin Dauphinois).

Cooked in olive oil (she lets it smoke) in shallow earthenware dish directly on butagaz. Tiny piece of garlic. Stirred fairly often, and pressed with flat, iron spatula-spoon. Salt. In the end the potatoes are almost in a cohered mass. If any pieces too big she cuts them as they cook with her iron implement.

She beats the eggs in a bowl, tips in the potatoes (slightly cooled; they have been transferred to a bowl) and mixes them well.

The tortilla is cooked in an iron omelette pan with smoking oil. It puffs up. She holds a deep plate in her left hand and turns the tortilla into it. Then back into the pan. And process repeated (sometimes twice, it depends if she is satisfied with its appearance).

Notes

As a tortilla is a very filling dish, I find that half Juanita's quantities, i.e. approximately 250 g (½ lb) of potatoes and 2 eggs make enough for two or three people. It is of course easier to handle in this smaller form, for which I use an iron pan of 20-cm (8-in) diameter, measured at the *top*. For a 4-egg tortilla use a 22-cm or 24-cm (8½-in or 9½-in) pan.

For the initial cooking of the potatoes I still use a Spanish earthenware dish over direct heat, as did Juanita (it is a delicious way of cooking potatoes, and need not necessarily be reserved for the tortilla) although an ordinary frying pan serves perfectly well.

About that spatula-spoon: this is a characteristic Spanish kitchen implement, a round flat pusher, as it were, with a long handle, used mainly when the paella is cooking, and just right for moving the rice and other ingredients around in the pan. I use a thin wooden spatula or palette knife instead.

Really fresh eggs are necessary for a tortilla. Stale ones don't puff up, and so produce a flat omelette.

Recipe recorded at La Alfarella, 1964

CHEESE PUDDING

This is a very old English dish and a very useful one. Something like a soufflé, but quicker to prepare and better tempered, it *can* be kept waiting. And precise timing is not important. I think it was probably devised in the days when coal-burning kitchen ranges were so temperamental, and when hot dishes were required to withstand the long journey from country house kitchens to dining-rooms. It's just as good and useful nowadays when, although most of us take our food straight from the oven to the table, everybody needs dishes which demand little preparation, and without anything very difficult in the way of ingredients.

You need 180 g (6 oz) of any decent English cheese – Cheddar, Cheshire, Double Gloucester, Leicester, Wensleydale, Lancashire (don't use processed cheese. It simply doesn't taste of cheese), 2 tablespoons of dried breadcrumbs, just over 300 ml (½ pint) of cold milk, 2 large or 3 average whole eggs, 1 teaspoon of made mustard – French or English, plenty of freshly milled pepper, salt, cayenne if you have it. The dish to use is either an ordinary English pie dish of 900-ml (1½-pint) capacity or a soufflé dish of the same capacity. If I'm making the pudding in double quantities, I prefer to use two, side by side in the oven, rather than one large one. They don't have to be buttered.

Put the breadcrumbs into the dish, pour the milk over them. Stir in the grated or chopped cheese and the seasonings. Not too much salt but the amount depends on the saltiness of the cheese used, so taste as you go.

Separate the eggs, beat the yolks very thoroughly, stir them into the cheese mixture. Whisk the whites to a stiff froth. Stir a spoonful or two into the cheese mixture, then tip in the rest, lifting and folding with a metal spatula or a spoon, as lightly and quickly as possible.

Put straight into the centre of the preheated oven, 180°C/350°F/ gas mark 4 and cook for 25–30 minutes. The top of the pudding should be well risen, golden and spongey. Leave it for 5 minutes or so before serving. By that time the inside should be rather like a thick creamy custard. Enough for 3.

Notes

1. If it happens to be convenient, the main ingredients of the pudding – the breadcrumbs, cheese, milk and seasonings – can all be mixed in the dish well ahead of time. Only the eggs need to be

added just before cooking. While you are doing this heat up the oven.

2. Borrowing an idea – a rather expensive one – from the Swiss cheese fondue, a liqueur glass of Kirsch can be added to the mixture. This gives a delicious flavour, but if you use it leave out the mustard. Another alternative, if you like the taste of caraway, is kümmel, or just a teaspoonful of the seeds or cumin seeds if you have them.

3. If possible serve fingers of crisp toast, preferably from brown bread, with the pudding.

4. In the twenty or so years I've been using this recipe (I published it in an article in the *Sunday Times* in October 1955) it has failed me only once. That was when I made triple quantities, using one very large soufflé dish, and got the timing wrong. So what my guests ate on that occasion was cheese and egg soup. Hence my preference for two small dishes rather than one large one. The same applies to soufflés.

This version written in 1970s

One William Verral

At Halland, in Sussex, one of the country estates of that Thomas Pelham-Holles, Duke of Newcastle, who was for thirty years Secretary of State and who finally came unstuck over the loss of Minorca and his contemptible part in the Admiral Byng affair, one William Verral was the young assistant to St-Clouet, the Duke's French cook. Halland is some ten miles from Lewes, where Will Verral was born and where in due course he succeeded his father as master of the White Hart Inn (the place was also Pelham property) and, in 1759, published a book called *A Complete System of Cookery*. It is one of the most diverting and outspoken in the history of English cookery writing.

Like all cooks who undertake the catering for special occasions in other people's houses, Verral invariably found the kitchen equipment placed at his disposal totally inadequate – and didn't hesitate to say so in print. In the house of one of the 'best families hereabouts' he finds, typically, a larder crammed with 'a vast plenty of good provisions', enough for a dinner of ten or twelve people; so having made the routine tactful approach to the resident cook – she is called Nanny – he asks to be shown the apparatus, as he calls the kitchen battery; all Nanny can produce are 'one poor solitary stewpan' and a frying-pan 'black as my hat and a handle long enough to obstruct half the passage of the kitchen'. Verral wastes no time. He sends to the inn for his own equipment and gets to work on his initial preparations. Presently he asks Nanny for a sieve and when she gives it to him infuriates her by complaining that it is gravelly. Nanny blames the housemaid. 'Rot our Sue, she's always taking my sieve to sand her nasty dirty stairs.' She gives the sieve a thump on the table, rinses it in a cauldron in which pork and cabbage are boiling and hands it back. It is now coated with pork fat. Verral rejects it – Nanny flounces off to the scullery fuming about fussy men cooks – 'There was no more sand in the sieve than would lay upon a sixpence' – and Verral has to wheedle her back into good humour by showing her how to cut up chicken for a fricassee.

Later in the evening, the dinner having proved a success, the company stays on for supper, and the host asks for another fricassee. Ever tactful, Verral supervises the making of it by Nanny, waits until the gentlemen, by that time fairly mellow one supposes, declare it even better than the one they had for dinner, and sends Nanny to the dining-room to take credit and the tip. Not unexpectedly, the master of the house presently decides to install more suitable equipment, Nanny is on the way to becoming a more civilised cook, and Verral goes on to tease more of the Sussex citizenry about the meanness and squalor of their cooking arrangements. In one house he finds the kitchen fireplace reduced to the size of a salt-box – just to save coals – and the master of the house ignorant of the meaning even of the word stove. Verral strides off, the gentleman pursuing. Verral shall have *carte blanche* to order whatever he wants.

A good agent for the local Sussex ironsmiths, our Verral; he appears to have been for ever calling them in to install new stoves and kitchen equipment; and at Anne of Cleves House in the Southover district of Lewes, given to the Sussex Archaeological Society in 1925 by a latter-day member of the Verral family, can be seen a wondrous collection of local kitchen machinery – cradle-spits, fan-spits, clockwork spits, bottle-jacks, heat-driven and weight-driven spits, chimney-cranes to hoist the iron pots and kettles which were too heavy to lift by hand, and an iron salamander for browning the top surfaces of dishes such as crème brûlée, a perfect little brute to wield single-handed. One sees what those female cooks and servant girls were up against – with that kind of equipment to cope with, sheer physical strength would have been the very first requisite of a cook.

Among the less unamiable characteristics of the Duke of New-castle, Verral's original employer and patron, were, according to Walpole, extravagance and love of ostentatious entertainment. His reputation had evidently reflected upon his cook, for in his book Verral is at some pains to vindicate French cooking in general and his former master, Clouet, in particular from charges of wastefulness. The gossips of the period were fond of spreading tales about the arrogance and extravagance of the French cooks employed by English noblemen. The reduction of a whole ham into one small phial of essence or of twenty-two partridges into a sauce for a brace was, according to tattle, common practice; cooks would think nothing of demanding that dining-room doors be widened and ceilings heightened to allow for the passage of *pièces montées*; such stories, Verral says firmly, 'were always beyond the belief of any sensible person. Much has been said of his [M. Clouet's] extravagance . . . but I beg pardon for saying it, he was not that at all . . . that he was an honest man I verily believe . . . he was of a temper so affable and agreeable, as to make everybody happy about him.'

Now this charmer had already, when Verral wrote his book, left the service of Newcastle and, returning to France, entered that of the Marshal Duke de Richelieu, he who in 1756 com-manded the French forces besieging the British at Port Mahon in Minorca, and whose cook, it is said, brought back to Paris the secret of mayonnaise sauce. Was Clouet that cook? And was Newcastle, a man in a constant fret over trivialities, exasperated that his famous cook should have defaulted to his victorious enemy?

That Clouet was at any rate an intelligent, enlightened and most meticulous cook one can see from the notes and recipes which Verral records as being those of his teacher. From him Verral learned to cook vegetables such as asparagus and French beans only to 'a crispness and yellow' and to serve them 'as [the French] do many other vegetables, for a hot sallet'. He learned to make 'a better soup with two pounds of meat, and such garden things as I liked, than is made of eight pound for the tables of most of our gentry and all for want of better knowing the uses of roots and other vegetables'; he learned not to boil the meat to rags as was the common practice and 'makes the broth both thick and grouty – and hurts the meat that thousands of families would leap mast-high at'; he noted that M. Clouet never made use of powerful herbs such as 'thyme, marjoram or savory in any of his soups or sauces, except in some few made dishes' and that in roasting a loin of veal which had been marinated overnight in milk flavoured with onion, bay leaves, shallots, salt, pepper and coriander seeds Clouet would cover the meat with buttered paper but would not have it basted with the marinade, 'never, nor with anything else'.

At a time when a tremendous quantity of materials was wasted on decoration and garnish, Verral obviously had a great feeling for the proper appearance of his dishes; of that chicken fricassee of which he was so proud he says that anyone can make a fricassee which tastes well, but it must be a good cook to make it look well; 'and for the goodness of this dish half depends upon its decent appearance'. Of a Julienne soup, 'you may fling in a handful or two of green pease, but very young, for old ones will thicken your soup, and make it have a bad look', and of a hare cake you are not 'so to smother it with garnish but every one at table may see what it is'.

The spirit of Verral was certainly not presiding over the dressing of the smoked trout I ate last time I lunched at the White Hart. Fairly festooned with sallet stuff it was, watercress and lettuce, tomatoes and cucumber, and the fish itself diminished nearly to vanishing point. But then at the White Hart today nobody has so much as heard of Clouet or of Verral; if they had they might (since the inn is French-owned) make a bit of capital out of its past associations ('*le White Hart, son ambiance historique, ses salles fleuries, son rôti de veau à la broche à la façon du bon maître Clouet, ses primeurs du Sussex, son parking*'), hang pictures of the Pelham family and their cooks in the bar, revive the Shoreham scallop industry, keep crayfish in the nearest dewpond on the Downs and cook their sheep *aux aromates du pays* and their hams in the local cider (Merrydown, what else?). I'd be all for it myself, so long as the goings-on didn't upset the waitresses; for what is an ancient English country-town coaching inn without a waitress to look you straight in the eye and tell you that 'you'll take your coffee in the lounge, now, won't you, that's right, make yourselves comfortable'?

Spectator's Choice, 1967

Edible Maccheroni

During the 1914 war Norman Douglas was staying in Rome and recounts (in *Alone*) how he goes in search of 'edible maccheroni – those that were made in the Golden Age out of pre-wartime flour'. Eventually, acting upon a hint from a friend, he finds them at Soriano, a village lying on the slope of an immense old volcano. The surroundings were sombre, the weather stifling, but 'those macaroni – they atoned for everything . . . the right kind at last, of lily-like candour and unmistakably authentic . . .'

To those who have not experienced pasta at its best, or who have never acquired a taste for it, Norman Douglas's hankering after the right kind might seem somewhat perverse. But that description – 'lily-like candour' explains a good deal. It would be hard to find better chosen words in which to convey the extraordinary charm of those pale, creamy, shining coils of pasta filling a big deep soup plate, in the centre a little oasis of dark aromatic meat sauce, crowned with a lump of butter almost whiter than the macaroni and just beginning to melt.

Whether or not your macaroni, spaghetti, noodles or any other variety of commercially produced pasta has the right attributes depends, as Norman Douglas was naturally aware, even more upon the flour used in its manufacture than upon careful cooking. The most satisfactory flour is that milled from a variety of wheat called Durum. As its name implies this is a hard wheat yielding a flour which, while unsatisfactory for bread-making, imparts those qualities to pasta products which enable them to retain their firmness when subjected to the drying process and their shape when they are cooked. Softer flours, while adequate for the kind of pasta freshly made at home and cooked the same day, are inferior for the manufactured variety because they will not dry evenly, the pasta made from them will splinter, and when cooked will disintegrate and turn to a mush. So, far from presenting that lively and lily-like candour of appearance they will be grey, sticky, and dead looking.

The water used in the manufacture of pasta dough is also said to play an important part in the quality of the finished product, and that made in the Naples district is claimed to owe its superiority to some constituent of the water in the neighbourhood. However, there are flourishing pasta industries in other parts of Italy, notably in Parma and Bologna, and it is doubtful if any but a most expert connoisseur would be able to detect the difference between, say, the spaghetti made by the Neapolitan firm of Buitoni and that of Barilla or Braibanti of Parma.

First-class imported Italian pasta products sold in packets bear the information that they are made from '*Pura semola di grano duro*' which means that the flour used, like that of the English products, is milled from the cleaned endosperm or heart of the

Durum wheat grain, of which a certain quantity is grown in southern Italy, although it is not always the amber variety. The words *semola* and *semolina* used in connection with spaghetti and macaroni imply that the grain is treated in a particular way so that only the finest and most nutritious part, the cream, in fact, of the wheat, very finely sieved, is used.

The best of those kinds of pasta in which eggs are an ingredient are made from the same flour; in Italian egg noodles, tagliatelle and similar products, five eggs to the 1 kg (2 lb) dough are the standard proportions.

Few English shops would find it worthwhile to stock all the varieties such as bows and butterflies, shells, knots and wheels, melon seeds, stars, ox-eyes and wolf-eyes, rings, ribbed tubes and smooth tubes, cannelloni, little hats, marguerites, beads, miniature mushrooms, quills and horse's teeth, green lasagne and tagliatelle, twists and twirls and whirls and all the other ingenious inventions which turn an Italian pasta shop into a place of such entrancing fantasy. And incidentally, where all these different shapes and sizes are concerned, it is difficult to give precise definitions, because the names vary both according to regional tradition and to the individual fancy of the producer, so that one particular type may have two, or three or more names. Equally two or three varieties may go by the same name in different districts.

SPAGHETTI ALLA BOLOGNESE

Possibly this is the best known of all Italian pasta dishes but recipes vary very much, and it would be a mistake to suppose that every dish bearing this name, even in reputable Italian restaurants, is cooked as it should be.

Allow 90–125 g (3–4 oz) of long spaghetti per person. For 250–280 g (8–9 oz) bring 4.5 litres (8 pints) of water, plus 2 tablespoons of salt, to a fast boil. Put in your spaghetti unbroken. Within a few seconds it will coil down into the pan. Bring the water back to the boil as fast as possible. Cook steadily for 10–12 minutes. During this time the spaghetti should grow, or swell, to twice or even three times its original volume. Stir once or twice with a wooden fork, just to make sure that no pieces are sticking to the pan. Take a little piece out and taste it. When it is tender, but still firm to the touch, with an almost imperceptible white core in the centre, it is done. Drain it in a colander. Have ready a heated dish, in which you have warmed a little olive oil or butter. In this turn your spaghetti over and over for a few seconds, rather as if you were mixing a salad. If possible, keep the dish on a table heater while this is being done.

Pile your hot sauce (recipe below) in the centre. On top put a lump of butter. Have ready your hot plates, soup plates for preference, and keep your dish on the heater while the spaghetti is served.

The sauce is made as follows.

RAGU BOLOGNESE

This is the sauce for Spaghetti Bolognese as it is made in Bologna, at the restaurant of Zia Nerina, now in the Piazza Galileo. I have not visited this restaurant since Zia Nerina moved into her new premises, but I fancy it is unlikely that any amount of success could spoil her delicious cooking.

For 4 people the ingredients are 180 g (6 oz) of good quality lean minced raw beef, 90 g (3 oz) of chicken livers, 60 g (2 oz) of uncooked ham or gammon, a carrot, an onion, a little piece of celery, 2 teaspoons of concentrated tomato purée, 1 small glass of white wine and 2 of beef stock or water, seasonings of salt, pepper and nutmeg, about 15 g (½ oz) of butter.

Heat the butter in a small saucepan, add the chopped ham or gammon and when the fat starts to run put in the finely chopped onion, carrot and celery. When they have browned a little add the minced beef, stirring it round so that it all browns evenly; next stir in the chopped chicken livers, then the tomato purée, then add the wine. Let this bubble a few seconds, add the seasonings and the stock or water. Cover the pan. Simmer very gently for 30–40 minutes. Sometimes Bolognese cooks add a cupful of cream before serving, which makes a thicker and richer sauce.

TAGLIATELLE AL MASCARPONE

Mascarpone is a pure, double cream cheese made in northern Italy and sometimes eaten with sugar and strawberries in the same way as the French Crémets and Coeur à la Crème. We have several varieties of double cream cheese here. It makes a most delicious sauce for pasta. The ordinary milk curd cheese now usually sold as cottage cheese can also be used for a pasta sauce, but the double cream variety produces a dish altogether more subtle.

Tagliatelle are narrow ribbon noodles (the green ones are particularly attractive for this dish because of the contrast of the green pasta with the cream sauce), but one or other variety of small pasta such as little shells, pennine (small quills) and so on can equally be used.

The tagliatelle will take about the same time to cook as spaghetti, 10–12 minutes. Some of the other shapes are much harder, and may take as long as 20 minutes, and although they are small, need just as large a proportion of water for the cooking.

The sauce is prepared as follows: in your serving dish melt a lump of butter and, for three or four people 125–180 g (4–6 oz) of double cream cheese. It must just gently heat, not boil. Into this mixture put your cooked and drained pasta. Turn it round and round, adding two or three tablespoonfuls of grated Parmesan. Add a dozen or so shelled and roughly chopped walnuts. Serve more grated cheese separately.

This is an exquisite dish when well prepared, but it is filling and rich, so a little goes a long way.

SALSA ALLA MARINARA

When pasta is served with a sauce based on a certain quantity of olive oil it is not always considered necessary to serve cheese as well. Some Italians, indeed, consider it absurd to mix cheese and oil; either ingredient, they say, provides, with the pasta, sufficient nourishment to make a balanced dish.

To make the marinara sauce, heat 4 or 5 tablespoons of olive oil in a frying-pan. When it is hot but not smoking, throw in several sliced cloves of garlic; after a few seconds add 750 g (1½ lb) of ripe skinned tomatoes, roughly chopped. Let them cook about 3 minutes only. Season with salt and pepper, and then add a few coarsely chopped leaves of fresh basil, or failing that, some parsley. The sauce is now ready to be served with your pasta, or for that matter with boiled rice or haricot beans. The amount of garlic used is entirely a matter of taste, and those who like only a faint flavour can remove it from the pan before putting in the tomatoes, for it will already have scented the oil.

MINESTRA ALLA VERONESE

This is an example of the way Italian cooks will embellish a chicken and noodle soup with a small quantity of extra ingredients, making it almost into a meal.

For each 600 ml (1 pint) of clear chicken broth the other ingredients are about 45 g (1½ oz) of very fine noodles or vermicelli broken up small, 4 or 5 chicken livers, 200–250 g (7–8 oz) of shelled green peas, butter, Parmesan cheese.

First boil the noodles or vermicelli in boiling salted water for 5 minutes. Drain them. (If cooked direct in the broth they would make it cloudy and starchy.) Heat the broth, add the peas, then the pasta. Cook gently until the peas are quite tender.

Meanwhile clean the chicken livers, fry them gently in butter, chop them fairly small and add them to the soup. Stir in a tablespoon or so of grated Parmesan before serving.

MACARONADE

In Italy pasta is absolutely never served as an accompaniment to a meat dish or in the guise of a vegetable. It comes as a first course, either *asciutta* or dry, that is, with a sauce or simply with butter and cheese, or *in brodo*, in a broth or consommé, which may or may not also contain vegetables, as in the recipe above. This applies both to pasta as we know it and to all the tribe of stuffed pastas such as ravioli, tortellini and anolini.

In France, both in the southern regions of Provence and the Niçois country (where cooking is very much Italian influenced) and in the eastern provinces of Alsace and Lorraine, where the habit was no doubt acquired from Germany and Poland, some forms of macaroni or noodles do sometimes figure as part of the main course. The traditional *macaronade* of the Nice district consists of small macaroni or noodles served with some of the sauce from a *daube* or *estouffade* of beef plus a little grated cheese. Originally this dish was served as a first course, with the beef to follow. Nowadays the two dishes often come together, and the noodles make an admirable accompaniment, preferable to potatoes, to the rich wine and garlic-flavoured stew. What seems to me a mistake is to serve pasta as an accompaniment to a dry dish, such as fried escalopes of veal or steak.

House & Garden, May 1958

Do not Despair over Rice

Every amateur cook, however gifted and diligent, has some weak spot, some gap in her knowledge or experience which to anyone critical of her own achievements can be annoying and humiliating. To some it may be a question of not being able to get a roast precisely right; to others, a cream sauce which only spasmodically comes off; and even to those who admit to having little talent for pastry or cakes, it is irritating to be defeated by a process which to others appears so effortless. Some regard the confection of a mayonnaise as the easiest thing in the world, some with terror and despair. There are those who have a talent for perfect rice dishes, while for others the stuff invariably turns to a mush. And it is no coincidence that when dishes go wrong, it nearly always happens when they are cooked for guests, and consequently in larger quantities than those with which one is accustomed to dealing.

Sometimes this is due to something so obvious as cooking for eight in the same utensils as those normally used for four, or to the cook having overlooked the fact that even a good-tempered dish like a meat and wine stew may disloyally change its character and appearance, losing all its professional-looking finish, if kept waiting too long in the oven. Or perhaps the joint, twice as large as usual, has been cooked twice as long, whereas what should really have been taken into consideration was not the weight but the shape and thickness of the joint.

Sometimes, of course, the trouble is more psychological than technical. Take rice, for example. Because a rice dish has gone wrong once, no doubt because the cook had no experience of cooking the particular rice she was using, she will ever after be scared stiff of making it. There *is* something rather specifically dismal about a failed rice dish. And I would never recommend anybody to cook a risotto for a dinner party which had to be managed single-handed, because it is a bad dish to keep waiting. But there are so many other ways of cooking rice and some of them appear to be specially designed for the kind of meals we all cook these days – meals consisting of dishes which simply must not be of the kind requiring split-second timing. Good quality rice is essential, though. The two kinds to look for are the long-grained

Patna type and the round-grained Piedmontese rice called Avorio or Arborio, which has a hard core in the centre of the grain so that it is almost impossible to ruin by overcooking. The flavour of this Piedmontese rice is also much more pronounced than that of the Patna type, which makes it a good one to use when the rice itself, rather than any flavouring or sauce, is the main point of the dish.

All the following recipes are ones in which the rice can be kept waiting, not indefinitely it is true, but long enough to give you a chance to have a drink before your meal, without keeping an eye on the stove.

A good point to remember about the boiling of rice is that ten times the volume of water to that of rice is an ample quantity to calculate. So measure the rice in a cup or glass, and then reckon the amount of water accordingly.

CHICKEN PILAU (1)

For 4–6 people the ingredients are 2 scant teacups (250–280 g/ 8–9 oz) of Patna long-grain rice, 3 teacups of chicken stock from which the fat should not be removed, since it helps to lubricate the rice, salt, pepper, about a teaspoon of mixed spices (cardamom seeds, a scrap of grated green ginger root, allspice, mace, pepper, cumin seeds or whatever mixture happens to suit your taste), approximately a cupful of meat from a cooked chicken cut from the bone into neat little strips.

Two-thirds fill with water a very large saucepan of about 4.5 litres (8 pints) capacity. Bring it to the boil and throw in a heaped tablespoon of salt, then the rice. Boil it steadily for exactly 7 minutes after the water has come back to the boil. Drain the rice into a small mesh sieve or colander in which the holes are not so large as to let through the grains of rice, for being only partly cooked, they are not yet swollen. Hold the colander under the cold tap and rinse until the water runs clear. Turn the rice into an earthenware pot or other fairly deep fireproof dish, of about 1.7-litre (3-pint) capacity. Stir in the spices all pounded together – the quantity can be increased if you like – and add the chicken meat and the hot stock. Bring just to simmering point on top of the stove. Have ready a clean, dry, folded linen teacloth and put this over the rice. Cover with the lid of the pot. Put in the centre of a low oven, preheated to 170°C/325°F/gas mark 3. In just 20 minutes' time the rice should be swollen and tender, all the liquid absorbed. The rice is ready to serve on a heated shallow dish with, if you like, a few slivers of almonds or some pine nuts lightly browned in the oven on the top, and some chutney and lemon separately. It will, or should, serve 6 people as a first course, 4 if it is the chief dish.

Be sure that your teacloth is one which has been properly rinsed when it was washed and does not smell of soap powder or detergent, for there is a risk of this communicating itself to the rice.

If the dish has to be kept waiting, take it from the oven once it is ready, but leave it covered with its cloth and its lid. For 10 minutes at least it will keep hot without spoiling. But do not attempt this system of cooking with poor quality, small-grain pudding rice, nor with any of the American patent rices for which the amounts of liquid to rice and the cooking times are given on the packets.

CHICKEN PILAU (2)

Supposing that your oven is occupied by another dish cooking at a temperature much higher or lower than the one at which the pilau is to cook, here is another method, using the same ingredients.

Boil your rice for 10 minutes instead of 7, rinse and drain it. Heat 30 g (1 oz) of butter, or a tablespoon of oil, in a pot or bowl or saucepan which will stand inside another one. Put in the pieces of chicken and, on top, the rice into which you have stirred the seasonings and spices. Pour in, for 2 cups of rice measured before cooking, 1 cup of hot stock, and another tablespoon of butter or oil. Cover with a folded teacloth and a lid. Steam in your improvised bain-marie for about half an hour.

This is also an excellent method for cooking moist rice to serve with a meat or chicken dish.

If you want your rice coloured and spiced with saffron, pound up about half a dozen of the little filaments, pour the warmed stock over them before you start cooking the rice, and strain them off when you add the stock to the rice.

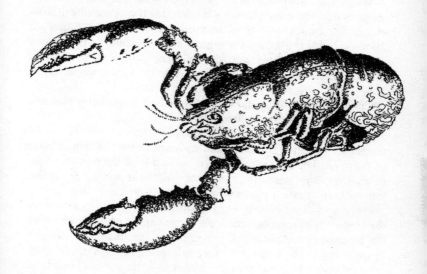

LOBSTER WITH CREAM SAUCE AND RICE

Here is a lovely dish for a dinner party, for which all the main preparations can be made in advance.

For a first-course dish for 4 people allow 1 large cooked lobster or crawfish, a hen one if possible, for the coral improves the flavour of the sauce; 60 g (2 oz) of long-grain Patna rice, and, for the sauce 90 g (3 oz) of butter, 2 level tablespoons of flour, 300 ml (½ pint) of milk, 4 tablespoons of white wine or dry vermouth, 150 ml (¼ pint) of cream, seasonings, breadcrumbs.

Melt 45 g (1½ oz) of the butter in a thick saucepan, stir in the flour off the fire; when smooth add the heated wine or vermouth and then a little of the milk, also heated. Return to the fire, gradually adding the rest of the milk, stirring all the time. Season with a little salt, freshly milled pepper, nutmeg and a scrap of cayenne. Turn the flame very low and leave the sauce cooking over a heat diffuser.

If you have a hen lobster, extract the coral and the creamy parts from the shell and pound them up with 30 g (1 oz) of the butter. Cut all the white flesh of the lobster into small neat pieces.

When the sauce has been gently cooking for about 10–15 minutes add the cream and let it cook another 5 minutes. Now stir in the butter and coral mixture. After another couple of minutes press the sauce through a sieve. Return it to a clean saucepan and, if it is being made in advance, cover the sauce with a film of melted butter, which will prevent the formation of a skin on the top.

Cook your rice in plenty of boiling salted water for 7 minutes only, rinse and strain it quite dry.

When the time comes to finish cooking the dish, allow 10–15 minutes for heating the sauce and 20 minutes for the dish to bake in the oven. The sauce should be re-heated with the pan standing in another one containing hot water. When it is hot, stir in the lobster flesh. Taste for seasoning.

Have a shallow buttered gratin dish ready. Spread the rice at the bottom. On top pour the lobster mixture, without disturbing the layer of rice. As with all gratin dishes, the dish itself should be quite full to the top. Strew fine, pale golden breadcrumbs over the mixture; add the remaining butter in little knobs. Heat in a low oven, 150°C/300°F/gas mark 2 for 15–20 minutes. At the end of this time the rice will be quite tender, and because it has been so slowly heated in the cream sauce the lobster will not have toughened and dried as it does when re-heated too abruptly; but do not be tempted to put more rice or to make a thicker sauce – you will get a stodgy dish.

To get a good glazed surface on the top of the dish, it can be put under a hot grill for a minute or so until it is blistering and bubbling. If you are going to make this dish in larger quantities, make sure you have the appropriate size of dish, or do it in two dishes rather than cram it into one which is too deep.

RICE WITH CHEESE SAUCE

This is a first course adapted from an Italian one – one in which the sauce, being a fondue of cheese and eggs, is just the kind of thing which turns malicious when you do it for guests, either refusing to thicken, or curdling when you try to hurry it up. So instead of this unreliable mixture, make a cream sauce strongly flavoured with Gruyère or Parmesan cheese. The rice is cooked *in bianco* – in other words, plainly boiled.

Ingredients for 4 good helpings are: 300 g (10 oz) round-grain

Piedmontese Avorio rice and, for the sauce, 45 g (1½ oz) butter, 1 level tablespoon of flour, 300 ml (½ pint) milk, 150 ml (5 fl oz) single cream, 90 g (3 oz) coarsely grated Gruyère cheese or 60 g (2 oz) grated Parmesan, salt, pepper and nutmeg.

The cream sauce can be made in advance in the way described for the lobster recipe above, and left until it is needed, with a film of butter over the top. It must be re-heated in a bain-marie, and the cheese added and stirred smooth when the sauce is hot. See that it is rather highly seasoned, and leave it with the water simmering very gently underneath until you are ready for it.

The rice is cooked in approximately 10 times its volume of water, with 1½ tablespoons of salt. Avorio rice takes longer to boil than Patna – about 18 minutes. Rinse under the tap and drain in a colander. Have ready a lightly buttered soufflé dish, cake tin, or fireproof bowl. Put your cooked rice into this; on the top put a folded teacloth. Put it in the oven, turned right down to its lowest temperature. There you can safely leave it for 15–20 minutes, before turning it out on a shallow and well heated dish and pouring the sauce over and round it.

Vogue, January 1959

How Versatile is Risotto?

Those who prefer their risotto anglicised will never lack for recipes. Only the other day (I am writing in 1978) the London *Times* published a recipe for a dish called 'A Versatile Risotto'. The rice specified was long-grain, there were 4½ bacon rashers and ½ lb mushrooms to ½ lb of rice. It was suggested that a sliced green pepper could be included 'for colour'; scraps of cooked chicken, a few cooked peas, some floured and fried chicken livers could be thrown in. In due course, the inevitable chicken stock cube made its appearance in the list of ingredients. So did grated Cheddar cheese.

The method of cooking was in a tightly covered saucepan, approximately that used for a pilau – it could be that the author of the recipe had discovered that long-grain rice just does not respond to the Italian risotto method – and having at last added the chopped cooked mushrooms (their cooking liquid strained off – and presumably thrown down the sink) and half the cheese to the rice the final directions strike a note of almost sublime absurdity. 'Serve just as it is – preferably with a crisp salad.' Just as it is. It's difficult to see what else you could add. A nice tomato sauce? A few Brussels sprouts?

Now I am well aware that such a dish may have its appeal to those with more appetite than discrimination, and especially to those brought up in the British tradition of jumbling together a number of incompatible ingredients and eating them all at once off the same plate. These readers would not surely be interested in knowing whether they were eating a kedgeree, a chop suey or a pilaff? Why then tell them that it is a risotto? It is, to say the least, discourteous to those readers who look to a responsible newspaper for information to so mislead them. Not long ago I tangled with the *Guardian* over a preposterous recipe for a Quiche Lorraine containing mushrooms, scraps of ham from the delicatessen (it sounded very unhygienic), stale cheese, and sundry other ingredients made into a custard and poured into ready-prepared pie shells.

Although the *Guardian* did have the grace to publish my letter of protest, the perpetrator of the recipe wrote to invite me to eat her creation which she assured me was 'really very tolerable'. No doubt, no doubt. At any rate to those tolerant of jumbled up leftovers. What the lady had failed to appreciate was that my real complaint was based on her choice of nomenclature. Tolerable the concoction may have been to her friends. A Quiche Lorraine it could not be to anybody. In the same way Miss Katie Stewart's 'versatile risotto' may well be 'tolerable'. A risotto it cannot conceivably be called. If Miss Stewart had just named her creation 'a bacon and rice dish' I don't suppose anyone would complain or think twice about it. Is it that the word risotto sounds more glamorous than just English rice? But what, I wonder, would an Italian reader make of the *Times* recipe?

I wonder too what would be an English reader's reaction – even an uninformed one – if, in a respected Italian newspaper, he were to come across a recipe for let us say English marmalade made with sweet oranges, macaroons, and ricotta cheese, chopped spinach and dried figs. I can assure you that such a mixture is no scrap more preposterous in its relation to marmalade than is the *Times* formula for a risotto to any authentic version – and heaven knows there are many to choose from of this famous and very fine Italian invention.

Unpublished, 1978

VEGETABLE AND SHRIMP RISOTTO

To achieve a true risotto, the very first requisite is the right type of rice. Italian rice is quite unlike any other. The grains are large, round and pearly, with a clearly defined hard white heart which prevents the rice turning mushy and is responsible for the characteristic flavour and for the unique consistency of a risotto – a dish which in Italy is invariably eaten as a first course and in restaurants is listed on the menu with the soups. Indeed, a risotto almost *is* a soup. Almost – but just not quite.

If you have never eaten a risotto correctly cooked in Venice or in Milan it is difficult to appreciate that there is a split-second in the cooking of the rice – just as for scrambled eggs – when the consistency is exactly right. It is neither too liquid nor too compact. It is light, every grain is separate although bound together in a homogeneous whole by the starch which has amalgamated with the cooking liquid. Suddenly, dismayingly, all is lost. Your risotto has become heavy, stodgy. It is still perfectly eatable and probably tastes very good. It is just that its elegance and distinction have vanished.

Shellfish and fresh green vegetables are the two staple flavourings of the Venetian risotto. Both are used in astonishingly small quantity in proportion to the rice. Both make dishes of great finesse.

While it is vain to hope to reproduce an Adriatic shellfish dish unless the Adriatic coast is where you live, it does seem feasible to attempt a vegetable risotto cooked along the lines of the Venetian one, even though the vegetables will be different and the end-product possibly unfamiliar to a Venetian.

For 2: 150–180 g (5–6 oz) of Piedmontese Arborio rice, 75 g (2½ oz) of butter, 2 tablespoons of grated Parmesan, 600–750 ml (1–1¼ pints) of water, 1 small onion, approx. 5 lettuce leaves, 1 leaf of a fennel bulb, 5 dried shrimps, 5 dried mushrooms, salt, nutmeg.

Use a 16-cm (2½-pint) heavy saucepan. Soak the shrimps and mushrooms in warm water for half an hour. Drain and cut very small. Shred the lettuce leaves and finely dice the fennel. Peel and chop the onion.

Melt 45 g (1½ oz) butter in the pan and cook the lettuce and fennel until soft. Lift out the vegetables, leaving behind the butter. Put in a little more butter if necessary and cook the onion for 1 minute until translucent. Add the rice, and stir it around until it glistens with butter. Pour in 450 ml (¾ pint) of boiling water and cook, uncovered, over medium heat until all the liquid is absorbed. It will take about 15 minutes.

When it begins to look dry, stir in the shrimps and mushrooms, 1 teaspoon of salt and another 150 ml (¼ pint) of boiling water. At this stage it needs watching. With a wooden fork, which doesn't break the grains, stir the rice and taste to see how tender it is. The grains must retain a slight resistance and the risotto must be liquid.

Stir in the lettuce and fennel with the Parmesan cheese, a generous grating of nutmeg and the remaining butter.

GREEN VEGETABLE RISOTTO

For 4: 300–350 g (10–12 oz) of arborio rice, 2 shallots, 3 small courgettes, 1 bunch of watercress, 100 g (3½ oz) of butter, 1.2 litres (2 pints) of water, 3 tablespoons of grated Parmesan, nutmeg, salt.

Use an 18-cm (4-pint) heavy pan.

Peel the courgettes in alternate strips, slice lengthways into four pieces, then cut into tiny dice. Cook them in 30 g (1 oz) butter in a small pan until just soft. Clean the watercress, discard all cottony and ragged parts of the stalks, cook the remainder in 15 g (½ oz) butter for 1 minute, then chop. Melt another 45 g (1½ oz) butter in the heavy pan and cook the chopped shallots for 1 minute. Stir in the rice and add 600 ml (1 pint) of boiling water. Cook as described above.

The courgettes and watercress go in at the end; to reheat the watercress before adding to the risotto, put it into the pan with the courgettes. Finish the risotto with the Parmesan, remaining butter and a grating of nutmeg.

Note

Stock is not necessary for these risottos, but there should be plenty of grated Parmesan on the table for those who like it.

Unpublished, written 1970s

Excerpt from a letter to George Elliot,

17 February 1984

Last week we made it to Hiély in Avignon. I'm happy to say it's still a lovely restaurant, the food is still good, the people charming, the service remarkable, the wine delicious and the atmosphere altogether right. None of that chilly ungenerous attitude of the place at Vézelay. At lunch the menu is 180Fr (now about £16). For that you get an hors d'oeuvre, some hot, some cold – I had pâté aux herbes, Jean had home-made nouilles with fish and a very delicious tomato coulis. Then she had a sauté of lamb and I had boned saddle of rabbit stuffed with its own liver and some bits of morille. Gratin dauphinois came with both. Then there were two enormous trays of local cheeses to choose from. Then an extraordinary array of ice creams, an amazing chocolate cake. All included. Service as well. Coffee at nearly £1 each was the only over-the-top item. But it *was* delicious coffee.

The wines were a white Lirac (Rhône) and a red Châteauneuf du Pape de l'année, en carafe, one of the most gorgeous wines I've drunk for a long time – 80Fr (say £7.00) for a 70cl carafe. So you see, I was really pleased to find it still so good, and so free of nouvelle cuisine affectation.

Here in Uzès we eat mostly vegetables, eggs (free range), local cheeses – quantities to choose from in the Saturday market, sheep's milk, goat's milk, cow's milk – salads, the occasional corn-fed chicken roasted on Patrick's electric spit, ditto the most beautiful fat red peppers from Spain (much the best way of doing them, if only I hadn't given away my own Cannon spit-roaster to Marion years ago). We buy blettes and those dog-bone shaped pumpkins, and sometimes sorrel, fresh fromage blanc, either cow's or goat's milk, and a rather remarkable confection called a tarte à la crème which is not a custard pie but a light yeast dough affair, the dimensions of a sponge cake, obviously sliced in half, filled with a very good sweet cream cheese mixture, for once not drowned in vanilla. This we buy from a woman in the market who sells good little farm cheeses and little raviolis filled with cream cheese and parsley.

Next door to the house is a boulangerie where apart from the usual baguettes and pains de ménage they make about five different kinds of biologique loaves – wholemeal bread – all of them light and *really* good. If I could buy just one at J de B's Walton St bakery I wouldn't have to make my own. The French have been very slow getting in on the wholefood business, but once they've cottoned on they've done it well. Even if what they produce isn't strictly biologique by the standards of Cranks, it's a vast deal more edible.

In the market we can buy about seven or eight kinds of olives, black and green. Even the newly-brined ones, but they're very tough. There's a good greenish extra-vierge olive oil too, but last week we went to an oil mill near Fontvieille (where Daudet's windmill is, the Anne Hathaway cottage of Provence) and bought a litre, unfiltered – they don't have a filter they said – about £3.00. Very good. They were selling soap too, made for them on a basis of their residue. We bought some. It smells good but I haven't tried it yet.

Mistress Margaret Dods

Christina Jane Johnstone, whose *Cook and Housewife's Manual*, published in 1827 under the pseudonym of Mistress Margaret Dods, was the wife of John Johnstone, a Dunfermline school-master who became editor and proprietor of the *Inverness Courier* and subsequently joint editor with his wife of the *Edinburgh Weekly Chronicle*. Mrs Johnstone took her pen name from Meg Dods, landlady of the Cleikum Inn in Auldtown of St Ronan's, a character created by Sir Walter Scott in *St Ronan's Well*. It was brave of Mrs Johnstone to use Meg's name; she is one of Sir Walter's more rugged characters, raw-boned, hideous, with the manners of a fishwife and a shrewish way of dealing with any customers she might consider unworthy of the hospitality of her Inn. 'Troop off wi' ye to another public,' she would screech, in a voice to be heard from the Kirk to the Castle of St Ronan's.

The grisly exterior, however, concealed a heart of gold and a magic touch with the saucepans; a fierce pride in her kitchen was combined with a profound respect for the art of cooking; the excellence of her table was renowned and her cellar stocked with good wine.

Mrs Johnstone, in contrast, appears to have been an amiable and accomplished woman; De Quincey refers to her as practising the profession of writing with absolutely no sacrifice of feminine dignity; her cookery book was an instant success, and ran into ten editions during her lifetime.

It is especially in the preparation of the wonderful natural foods in which Scotland abounds, salmon, grouse, venison, and in the great national dishes such as haggis, cock-a-leekie, Friar's chicken and sheep's head broth that Mrs Johnstone, 'Meg Dods', stands supreme.

On the salting, curing and smoking of meat and fish as practised in Scotland, Mrs Johnstone is particularly interesting. Notes on salted mutton and goose as well as on hams, beef, sausages and a 'Yule Mart or whole Bullock', figure in the *Cook's and House-wife's Manual*. 'Mutton, either ribs or breast', says Mrs Johnstone, 'may be salted and served boiled with roots, making at the same time potato soup, seasoned with parsley or celery.' A dish called 'Colliers roast' was a leg of mutton salted for a week, roasted and served with mashed turnip or browned potatoes; in Caithness 'geese are cured and smoked and are highly relishing. Smoked Solan geese are well known as contributing to the abundance of the Scottish breakfast.'

The *Manual* includes no detailed prescription for the salted and smoked goose (an excellent recipe for a similar dish, brined goose as prepared in certain parts of Sweden is given by Sir Harry Luke in his very original and informative *The Tenth Muse*) but Mrs Johnstone gives illuminating notes on the wood used for smoking, and the salt and spices then in common use for the curing of meats: 'green birch, oak, or the odoriferous woods, as juniper etc., are an immense improvement to all dried meats. And no sort of meat', she adds, 'is more improved by smoking with aromatic woods than mutton.'

From the following recipes the clarity of Mrs Johnstone's style can be appreciated; her directions are precise and still perfectly practical; she describes the appearance of a dish and the pitfalls to be avoided, and adds the little details so important to the successful presentation of her food, a precaution seldom observed by the experts of her time.

To boil Salmon and other Fish. There are many excellent ways of dressing this favourite fish, but perhaps none equal to plain boiling when well performed. Scale and clean the fish without unnecessary washing or handling, and without cutting it too much open. Have a roomy and well-scoured fish-kettle, and if the salmon be large and thick, when you have placed it on the strainer and in the kettle, fill up and amply cover it with cold spring water, that it may heat gradually. Throw in a handful of salt. If a jole or quarter is boiled, it may be put in with warm water. In both cases take off the scum carefully, and let the fish boil slowly, allowing twelve minutes to the pound [500 g]; but it is even more difficult to fix the time fish should boil than the length of time that meat requires. Experience, and those symptoms which the eye of a practised cook alone can discern, must fix the point, and nothing is more disgusting and unwholesome than underdone fish. It may be probed.

The minute the boiling of any fish is completed, the fish-strainer must be lifted and rested across the pan, to drain the fish. Throw a soft cloth or flannel in several folds over it. It would become soft if permitted to soak in the hot water. Dish on a hot fish-plate under a napkin.

Besides the essences to be used at discretion, which are now found on every sideboard of any pretension, shrimp, anchovy and lobster sauce are served with salmon; also plain melted butter; and where the fish is got fresh, and served in what is esteemed by some the greatest perfection – crisp, curdy and creamy – it is the practice to send in a sauce-tureen of the plain liquor in which it was boiled. Fennel and butter are still heard of for salmon, but are nearly obsolete. Garnish with a fringe of curled green parsley and slices of lemon. The carver must help a slice of the thick part with a smaller one of the thin, which is the fattest, and the best-liked by those in the secret. Sliced cucumber is often served with salmon, and indeed with all boiled fish.

To fry Venison Collops. Cut oblong slices from the haunch, or slices neatly trimmed from the neck or loin. Have a gravy drawn from the bones and trimmings, ready thickened with butter rolled in lightly-browned flour. Strain into a small stew-pan, boil, and add a squeeze of lemon or orange, and a small glass of claret. Pepper, to taste, a salt-spoonful of salt, the size of a pin's head of cayenne and a scrape of nutmeg. Fry and dish the collops hot, and pour this sauce over them. Garnish with fried crumbs. This is a very excellent way of dressing venison, particularly when it is not fat enough to roast well.

Cock-a-Leekie. Boil from 4–6 lb [2–3 kg] of good shin-beef, well broken, till the liquor is very good. Strain it, and put to it a capon, or large fowl, trussed for boiling, and, when it boils, half the quantity of blanched leeks intended to be used, well cleaned, and cut in inch-lengths [2 cm], or longer. Skim this carefully. In a half-hour add the remaining part of the leeks, and a seasoning of pepper and salt. The soup must be very thick of leeks, and the first part of them must be boiled down into the soup till it becomes a green lubricous compound. Sometimes the capon is served in the tureen with the cock-a-leekie. This is a good leek-soup without a fowl.

Some people thicken cock-a-leekie with the fine part of oatmeal. Those who dislike so much of the leeks may substitute shred greens, or spinach and parsley, for one half of them. Reject the coarse green part of the leeks.

Friar's Chicken. Make a clear stock of veal, or mutton-shanks, or trimmings of fowls. Strain this into a very nice saucepan, and put a fine white chicken, or young fowl or two, cut down for curry, into it. Season with salt, white pepper, mace and shred parsley. Thicken, when the soup is finished, with the beat yolks of two eggs, and take great care that they do not curdle. Serve with the carved chicken in the soup.

The stock may be simply made of butter, and the meat may be nicely browned in the frying-pan before it is added to the soup. Rabbits make this very well. Some like the egg curdled, and egg in great quantity, making the dish a sort of *ragout* of eggs and chicken.

It is interesting that neither Meg Dods nor any other of the notable cookery books of the period mentions the scones, girdle cakes, bannocks and pancakes which are universally considered part of Scotland's gastronomical heritage. Here are two recipes quickly made, excellent for hungry breakfasts and hearty teas.

Scotch Pancakes or Drop Scones. 250 g (8 oz) of plain flour, ½ teaspoonful of bicarbonate of soda, ½ teaspoonful of cream of tartar, 60 g (2 oz) of granulated sugar, 2 eggs, 300 ml (½ pint) of sour milk (fresh milk can be used but sour milk makes the scones lighter). Sieve the flour, bicarbonate of soda and cream of tartar. Add the sugar, then the beaten eggs and the sour milk, gradually. Stir quickly until the batter is the consistency of very thick cream. The scones should be cooked on a girdle, the advantage of which is that it is quite flat and so several can be done at once, but a heavy frying-pan can be used. Dip a screw of kitchen paper into good dripping and rub the girdle or the pan with it, so that there is the merest film of fat. Let it get warm but not too hot. Drop tablespoons of the mixture on to the girdle and cook about 2 minutes. Then lift them up with a palette knife and put them under the grill to toast the upper side. If you have no grill they can be turned over on the girdle or pan. They should be buttered at once and eaten hot. Take care not to let the girdle get too hot as the cooking progresses, as the underside will get burnt before they are sufficiently cooked inside. These quantities will make 20–24 scones.

Scotch Oatcakes. 250 g (½ lb) coarse oatmeal, 30 g (1 oz) of butter or dripping, 1 teaspoonful of salt, a pinch of bicarbonate of soda, 150 ml (¼ pint) of boiling water. Rub the butter into the oatmeal, add the salt and the bicarbonate of soda. Pour the boiling water on to the mixture and mix to a stiff paste. Roll out thinly on a floured board, cut into rounds and cook them on a greased girdle, on one side only. When they are to be eaten, toast the top side under the grill. They have a pleasant smoky flavour which goes well with bacon. Enough for a dozen oatcakes.

Harper's Bazaar, August 1951, with additional unpublished paragraphs

Kedgeree

Among the famous rice dishes of the world, from the beautiful and simple saffron risotto of Lombardy to the reckless blend of fish, chicken, vegetables and rice which makes the Spanish paella, from the spiced pilafs of the Near East to the delicious Chinese sticky fried rice, one English invention, the kedgeree, holds a very high place. For English it is, despite its name. The Indian kitchri from which it derived its name is an entirely different dish, a mixture of lentils, rice and spices; and to English cooks must go the credit of having thought of combining smoked haddock with rice and eggs to make one of the best breakfast and supper dishes.

SPICED KEDGEREE

Cut a medium-sized smoked haddock in 6 slices, put it in a deep dish, pour over sufficient boiling water to cover it completely, cover the dish and leave for 10 minutes. Then drain off the water and flake the fish, removing all skin and bone. Boil 200–250 g (7–8 oz) Patna rice in a large amount of boiling salted water for 10 minutes and strain it.

In the top half of a double boiler melt a lump of butter. Add a sliced onion, previously fried, a teacupful of raisins soaked in water, and the haddock. Into the rice stir either a little grated green ginger or a teaspoon of turmeric. Pile the rice lightly on top of the fish, add 2 tablespoons of melted butter, put a folded teacloth over, then the lid of the pan and steam until the rice is tender, about 30 minutes. Turn out on to a hot dish so that the fish, raisins and onions come out on the top, and decorate with 2 sliced hard-boiled eggs. Serve with halves of lemon and chutney.

CRAB OR PRAWN KEDGEREE

A quickly prepared version which produces a creamy rather than a dry dish. Boil 250 g (8 oz) Patna rice for about 15 minutes until just tender. Drain, spread on a shallow dish and put into a cool oven for 5 minutes to dry. Melt 2 tablespoons of butter in a thick saucepan, add the rice, season it with pepper, salt and nutmeg or pounded coriander seeds. Stir round with a fork, then add 125 g

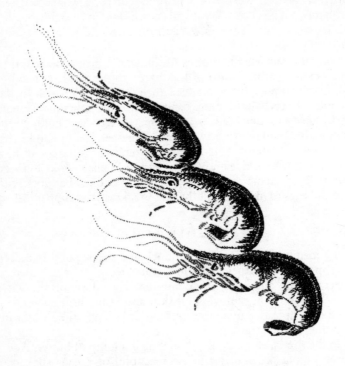

(4 oz) flaked crabmeat or shelled prawns. Shake the pan and stir again with the fork until the rice and fish are mixed. Add one well-beaten egg, or two if prawns are used, and remove from the fire as soon as they show signs of thickening. Transfer to a hot dish for serving and strew the top with chopped chives or spring onion tops.

Sunday Times, 1950s

SMOKED HADDOCK SOUFFLÉ

Make a white sauce with 30 g (1 oz) of butter, 1 heaped tablespoon of flour, 150 ml (¼ pint) of warmed milk; add half an average-sized cooked smoked haddock, boned, skinned, and flaked. Stir until well amalgamated and put through a food mill, or in the electric blender. Return to the cleaned saucepan, stir in the yolks of 2 well-beaten eggs and 60 g (2 oz) of grated Cheddar or

Gruyère. Season well with freshly milled pepper, but salt will probably not be necessary. When cooled, fold in the stiffly beaten whites of 4 eggs. Turn into a buttered 600-ml (1-pint) soufflé dish; stand the dish in a baking tin containing water. Cook in the centre of a preheated oven at 180°C/350°F/gas mark 4 for 30 minutes.

This is enough for 3 people; for 6 or 7 people, double the quantities exactly and make two soufflés simultaneously. This is not a spectacular soufflé, but it is a reliable one, creamy in the centre, and with a delicate flavour.

Vogue, March 1957

SCALLOPS WITH WHITE WINE AND BACON

Here is an excellent little scallop dish; the mixture of pork or bacon with the fish sounds odd, but it is an old-fashioned and good one.

For 2 people the ingredients are 4 large scallops, 60 g (2 oz) of streaky salt pork or unsmoked bacon, a shallot or two, butter, flour, a small glass of dry white wine, parsley.

Melt the butter in a frying pan, put in the finely chopped shallots and the pork or bacon cut into tiny cubes. Cut the cleaned scallops into larger cubes, season them with pepper but no salt, sprinkle them with flour and put them in the pan when the shallots have turned pale yellow and the pork is beginning to frizzle. Cook very gently for 2 to 3 minutes, then lift the scallops out with a slotted spoon and put them in a serving dish. Add the wine to the pan, boil to reduce a little while stirring; pour the sauce over the scallops and serve, garnished with parsley.

Sunday Times, 1950s

MOULES À LA RAVIGOTE

Put large well-cleaned mussels into a saucepan to open over a fairly fast flame. Shell them, mix them with a vinaigrette sauce to which have been added chopped hard-boiled egg, parsley, tarragon and a little pickled cucumber. Serve cold.

Elizabeth David's Menus and Recipes,
pamphlet presented by Lambert & Butler, n.d.

FISH LOAF

750 g (1½ lb) monkfish (gross weight) cooked approximately 45 minutes, covered, in oven at 150°C/300°F/gas mark 2 with approximately 450 ml (¾ pint) of fish stock made from fish carcase, head, etc, with garlic, saffron, white wine, (no onion), bay leaf, a few fennel seeds, water, very little salt. Stock to be strained through muslin.

When the fish is cooked, remove the central gelatinous bone and the skin. Pour off the cooking liquor into a saucepan, and reduce to concentrate it, but don't cook for too long.

Put the cooked fish flesh into a high-speed blender with 2 small boxes of buttered shrimps, with all their butter, plus approximately 150 ml (5 fl oz) cream, 150 ml (½ pint) fish stock, 4 whole eggs. The whole lot should come to approximately 1 litre (1¾ pints). Add extra seasonings as necessary, more salt, some cayenne, lemon juice, Pernod or another aniseed liqueur, i.e. Spanish anis – this in *half-teaspoons* not tablespoons. Madeira is another possible one, instead of the anis liqueur. Grated ginger is useful too.

Chill well in fridge and taste again for seasonings. Have ready a 1.2-litre (2-pint) non-stick loaf tin, brushed with oil. Prepare foil for a cover, also oiled on the side to go over the fish. Pierce a few holes in this prepared cover, using a skewer. (The holes are to allow steam to escape.)

Fill the tin with the fish mixture (but leaving a little space for it to rise), place in a roasting tin three-quarters filled with water, put the foil cover over the fish, if possible doming it up a little so it doesn't fit too closely.

Consign to oven (170°C/325°F/gas mark 3), lower centre, and cook for approximately 1½–1¾ hours. Test by raising the foil cover, touching top of fish loaf. If just firm, it should be done.

If it is to be eaten hot, leave for a few minutes in the roasting tin in water before turning out. If it is to be eaten cold, take it out of the roasting tin, and leave until wanted, but not in the fridge. When the loaf is to be served, put the tin in hot water for a few minutes. It should then turn out perfectly easily.

If to be eaten cold, have a simple mayonnaise with it, or a sauce verte, or the vinaigrette with a soft-boiled egg and lots of parsley from page 122 of *French Provincial Cooking*. If to be eaten hot, I make a sauce of the rest of the stock, much reduced, with the addition of cream, some anis or other such, and perhaps a few chopped buttered shrimps.

Unpublished, 20 May 1983

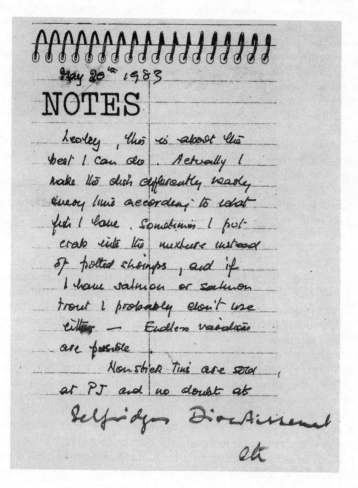

Lesley was Lesley O'Malley who lived in the basement flat of Elizabeth's house for many years.

JN

PRAWN AND MELON COCKTAIL

125 g (4 oz) peeled prawns, half a small honeydew melon, 150 ml (5 fl oz) each of yogurt and single cream, 2 teaspoonsful each of olive oil and tarragon vinegar, seasonings of ground ginger or turmeric, salt, sugar, and freshly milled pepper; chives, mint, or parsley. Ample helpings for 4.

Peel the melon and cut the flesh into small cubes. Mix the yogurt and cream together, add the oil and vinegar and seasonings – the amount of ginger or turmeric you use is a matter of taste, so it's best to start with not more than half a teaspoonful of either and then add more if you want – and about 2 teaspoonsful of sugar.

Mix the prepared melon and the prawns with this sauce, and as it needs time for the flavours to blend and to mature, leave, covered, in the refrigerator for several hours.

Finally taste again for seasoning, turn into glasses, or small bowls for serving, and add a sprinkling of chives, or chopped fresh mint, parsley, or fennel to each.

LETTUCE AND ANCHOVY SALAD

This recipe is Mrs Benny Goodman's, and the ingredients are a cos lettuce, a 50 g (approx. 2 oz) tin of anchovy fillets in oil, a clove of garlic, 3 tablespoons of olive oil, the juice of one lemon, salt, pepper, the raw yolk of one egg, and one tablespoon of grated Parmesan.

First crush the garlic clove and put it with a little salt and freshly milled pepper into a cup with the olive oil and leave to stand a while.

Pull the washed and drained lettuce into small pieces. Put them in a bowl, pour in the oil, leaving the garlic behind. Then the lemon juice. Add the anchovy fillets plus a little of their own oil. Next, the egg yolk. Turn the salad over and over until the egg has blended with the oil. Lastly add the Parmesan and mix again.

With bread and cheese, I find this salad makes almost a meal in itself for it is both refreshing and satisfying.

Recipes from *Sunday Dispatch*, 1950s

Two Cooks

Angela was Maltese and a born cook; she was scatter-brained and excitable, she never could be made to understand that my sister, for whom she worked, did not appreciate the smell of beef dripping being rendered down permeating the house from morning till night, and she seldom remembered that the English take it for granted that potatoes are served with every meal and so do not include them in the orders for the day; meal-times were frequently attended by the drama of 'Where are the potatoes, Angela?', 'Oh, Madam, I forgot'.

Angela had spent her life working for naval and military families in the island of Malta, and it was something of a mystery as to how she had retained a sincere and undimmed enthusiasm for the art of cooking. Always delighted to try out a new recipe, she usually succeeded brilliantly; occasionally there was a disastrous flop, usually due to her erratic reading of instructions, 'Perhaps you didn't beat the whites of egg enough, Angela?' 'Whites of egg? Oh Madam, I never noticed.' In those days food was absurdly cheap in Malta, drink was untaxed, and entertaining was easy and immense fun. Marketing was carried on with an oriental approach to the delights of haggling and the triumphs of carrying off a melon a penny cheaper than the original price. In the market one could buy ready boned quails for about sixpence each, chickens could be bought by the leg or the wing, you could even buy half a pigeon if you pleased; there was a prodigal supply of fruits and vegetables grown on the neighbouring island of Gozo; the local oranges were sweet and delicious, there were figs, grapes and exquisite wild strawberries.

One of Angela's triumphs was small, sweet melons, one for each person, stuffed with wild strawberries and peeled white grapes, flavoured with maraschino. As I have said, she was a born cook, otherwise how could she have known the secret of that dish of Marcel Boulestin's which has poached eggs in the middle of an airy cheese soufflé mixture – she cooked it to perfection, and never were the poached eggs too hard or the soufflé undercooked. She made milk bread and drop scones for tea which would have made a Scotch cook look foolish.

Angela gave me my first cooking lessons and to her I owe the initial understanding that to a good cook such drawbacks as tough meat and bony old hens are of little account; they existed as a challenge to Angela's pride and ingenuity. My sister's table was probably the only one in Malta where the Army ration, consisting of a hunk of beef of no recognizable origin, was not hopefully presented as the Sunday roast, for Angela made good use of the crude local wine for rich stews in the Italian manner. Elderly veal was spread with mushroom stuffing, sandwiched between slices of ham and cooked in paper; stringy birds emerged as creamy soufflés and mousses.

Angela's passion for a gossip sometimes led to trouble; the day when, recklessly disregarding my sister's repeated instructions about the cat, she went out leaving the kitchen door open and the quails for dinner exposed on the kitchen table, was a memorable one for us all. We had an honoured and greedy guest coming to dinner, and one of his favourite dishes was Angela's way of doing quails, boned and stuffed with sweet corn and wrapped in bacon. By the time that Angela returned from her chat with the next door cook the cat had got three or four of the quails. Piercing wails rent the air, the market was closed, the council that followed was one of desperation. When dinner time came and the unfortunate member of the family who had been chosen as a sacrifice ('Isn't it a bore, I'm on a diet and can't eat quails') was handed his eggs, Angela gave the whole show away by winking, nudging, and finally quaking with laughter.

My sister brought Angela home to England and for some time she was blissfully happy in a series of different houses in the neighbourhood of Salisbury Plain. She seemed to have reached the pinnacle of human happiness in that damp and clammy atmosphere; she thought the little red bungalows on the road to Andover the most beautiful houses in the world and she continued to cook like an angel. On English mutton and most un-Mediterranean vegetables her talent thrived. Alas, she had never been a methodical girl, and I think in the end it was the orderly life of an English village which got her down. You cannot haggle with a village grocer, and she began to pine for the shouting and the noise and the disorder of Valetta's market, the incessant gossip, and the fun of preparing immense quantities of food for the parties which had been an almost everyday occurrence in Malta; the deep nostalgia of every true Maltese for their little island overwhelmed her, and in the end she went back, leaving us all bereft. If she is cooking her lovely food and losing the shopping list and leaving the door open for the cat for some English family still, I hope they appreciate their good fortune.

Kyriakou was a Greek from the Dodecanese island of Simi. He was a sponge-fisher and he had escaped twice from the Italians, for whom he had a boundless contempt. When they declared war he had sailed his boat to Mersa Matruh, and when Mersa Matruh was captured he sank his boat in the harbour rather than let the Italians get it, and escaped with the British Navy, carrying with him a sack of electrical equipment he had looted from an Italian store. How he came to be a cook general in our absurdly grandiose Alexandria flat is no longer very clear, and, devoted and charming as he was, a dedicated cook I cannot claim him to have been. He was not entirely of this world, perhaps it was being so much under the sea that made him so dreamy when he was on land. He would sweep the carpet with his gaze fixed on the ceiling, as if he expected any minute to swim to the surface.

The Greeks are the most democratic people in the world and a

Greek servant is in every sense a member of the family; the money spent on housekeeping they regard as their own, and every detail of expenditure is discussed with the same passion which they apply to politics. Together, conversing in unlikely French and fantastic Greek, Kyriakou and I went shopping. It was a time when supplies of Greek olive oil, cheap Cyprus and Italian wines, and imported cheeses were still plentiful, but prices were rising and we knew that soon there would be no more.

Kyriakou's grief as the cost of a bottle of olive oil crept up from ten piastres to twenty, and finally, giving up all pretence, leapt to eighty, was tragic to watch, and he often had to be consoled with a stiff drink of *ouzou* in the market after spending my money in this reckless fashion. The rising cost of living was considerably augmented by the alarming quantity of breakages in our hideous but lavishly appointed flat. This turned out to be due to the fact that poor Kyriakou, already affected by the disease which finally gets all deep sea divers, would sometimes have a spasm of terrible pain in his right arm, most often when he was carrying a laden tray . . .

Even this, however, did not account for the number of teapots which he managed to get through in a few weeks; going into the kitchen one day at tea time I found him in the act of putting the teapot, in which there was half a pound of tea and a little cold water, straight on to the gas.

As a ladies' maid Kyriakou made stupendous efforts, and would tiptoe into my room in the morning in the most elaborate manner, only to drop the tray on the floor with a tremendous crash. Sometimes his housekeeper's pride got the better of him, and there would be a faraway look on his face as he brought in my morning coffee. With a happy smile he would empty the contents of a shopping basket on to my bed, 'Fresco, Madame, Fresco', he would coo; fresh was an understatement, for these were live fish, prawns and crabs and crayfish, slithering and gangling across my eiderdown at seven o'clock in the morning.

We were working erratic hours in Government jobs, and Kyriakou took much of the responsibility for our social activities into his own hands; our friends were his friends, so he would telephone those he liked best and inform them there was a good dinner on that night; not unnaturally the people he favoured were usually Greek-speaking or connected in some way with the Greek cause, so it happened that now and again the chromium and mirror bar, the road-house splendour of our flat took on the atmosphere of a *taverna*. Kyriakou would sit and drink with us, pouring out the drinks and fetching clean glasses with that grace of a host which is instinctive to every Greek ever born.

One day Kyriakou had news that his wife and children, left behind in Simi, had escaped to Palestine, and he intended to celebrate, he said, by giving a party for us and our friends. Nothing would stop him and we were not allowed to buy a single bottle of wine or contribute in any way to the expense. When a Greek sets out to give a party there is no cheese-paring. Where he went to do his marketing that day I never discovered, because when I asked him he giggled coyly and disclosed nothing, but I suspect that some of it at any rate was an underwater affair, for he returned home with a bucket of shell-fish the like of which had never before been seen in Alexandria; from this he concocted a pilaff which would have made a Spanish paëlla seem positively penny plain. It was a fish dinner, for as well as the pilaff there were mountains of fried fish (in Greece they like fried fish cold) with a great basin of *skordalia*, the Greek garlic sauce, and the masterpiece of the evening was an octopus stew. With passionate concentration he prepared it, and I watched him build up in a deep pot a bed of branches of thyme on which to lay a huge quantity of onions, tomatoes, garlic, bay leaves and olives, and then the octopus. Gently he poured red wine over his carefully constructed edifice, stirred in the ink from the fish, and left his covered pot to simmer the rest of the afternoon.

If I have given the impression that Kyriakou was not a very good cook I have done him an injustice; the loving devotion with which he prepared that dish was worth all the professional skill in the world. The flavour of that octopus stew, the rich wine dark sauce and the aroma of mountain herbs was something not easily forgotten.

Later in the war Kyriakou went off to join the Greek Navy, giving me as a parting present a miniature electrical Caffé Espresso machine which made wonderful coffee and which accompanied me throughout the rest of the war. We never saw him again, but to this day I cannot see a row of sponges displayed in a shop window without wondering what became of that Chaplinesque sponge-diver who was so enchantingly not of our world.

Wine and Food, Autumn 1950

Letter to Jack Andrews and John Flint

November 21st 1973

Dear Jack, dear John

What a wonderful evening – your hospitality is a joy, and I don't know how to say adequate thanks –

The first time I've had partridges this year, and what a treat. Once I had to make that dish, with lentils, for a lunch given by André Simon, for eight people. He had nobody to cook for him in his London flat – and that was the dish he requested – so I had to get it all half ready, and then transport it to his kitchen and finish it there. What a worry *that* was. I thought your artichoke purée was a marvellous idea. And the pomegranates – my beloved Suleiman couldn't have done them better. I was sad not to be able to eat as much of that dish as I would have liked, for fear of damage to fillings and crowns (had been to the dentist that morning).

I have evolved some new methods with bread and I think they might interest John – maybe you should come round one baking day, and take photographs for the record? I have a whole mass of stuff for my new book, only half-written, so not yet typed, or in any presentable form. Also, have done quite a bit of research re different mixtures of flours, useful when you can't find supplies of strong plain. Will communicate.

Very much love to you both

Liz

Christmas in France

Dinner on Christmas Eve in a French farmhouse of the pre-1914 era was a succession of homely country dishes for which almost every ingredient would have been produced on the farm itself. A characteristic menu, sustaining and solid, reads as follows:

Poule au riz à la fermière

Jambon cuit au foin

Petits pois jaunes en purée

Dindonneaux farcis aux marrons

Salade de céleris et betteraves

Poires étuvées au vin rouge

Galettes à la boulangère

Fromage de la ferme

Café. Vieux Marc

Vins: Moulin-à-Vent et . . . eau de puits

Escoffier, recording the dinner in a professional culinary magazine in the year 1912, thought it, in its 'rustic simplicity', worthy of inclusion among the festive menus of the Majestics, the Palaces, the Ritz-Carltons, the Excelsiors of Europe. How many of these menus, he asks, would be in such perfect taste? One senses a hint of envy in his words, for any chef who served such a menu in an English restaurant of the period would have been a laughing stock. The Carlton (where Escoffier was then presiding) Christmas menu for that year started with the inevitable caviare and turtle soup, and went on through the fillets of sole with crayfish sauce, the quails and stuffed lettuces, lamb cutlets, out-of-season asparagus, the foie gras and frosted tangerines, to start again with the truffled turkey, celery salad, plum pudding, hot-house peaches, *friandises*. At an elegant Paris restaurant, the Marguery, the Christmas Eve dinner at the same period consisted of one service only. Oysters, consommé with poached eggs, timbale of lobster, truffled chicken or pheasant, green salad, pâté de foie gras (in those days served after the roast rather than as an hors-d'oeuvre), an ice, plum pudding or *bûche de Noël*, fruit. The only concession to the festive season is the inclusion of the plum pudding and Yule log, otherwise it might have been a well chosen dinner for any winter's evening. For Christmas in France has never been quite the occasion for the prodigious feasts of the Germanic and Anglo-Saxon countries. A people for whom food is one of the first considerations every day of the year tend to regard the English preoccupation with eating for one week only out of the fifty-two, as rather gross.

Alfred Suzanne, whose book on *La Cuisine Anglaise* (he had been chef to the Duke of Bedford and the Earl of Wilton) is still the chief source of information to the French about English cooking, referred to the 'hecatombs of turkeys, geese, game of all sorts, the holocaust of fatted oxen, pigs and sheep . . . mountains of plum puddings, ovens full of mince-pies'. Philéas Gilbert, another well known contemporary chef, went to some trouble to prove that '*le plum pudding n'est pas anglais*', but graciously conceded that, being already so rich in national dishes, the French could afford to leave the English in possession of their national Christmas pudding.

In most French country households the *réveillon* supper, however elegant the rest of the food, includes ritual dishes of humble origin such as boudins or blood puddings in some form or other, and various kinds of bread, biscuits, and galettes to which some ancient religious significance is attached. In Provence no fewer than thirteen of these desserts are traditional, while the main course is always a fish dish, usually salt cod, accompanied by snails, potatoes and other vegetables, salads and big bowls of the

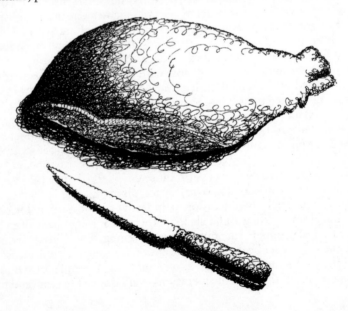

shining golden aïoli for which the finest olive oil has been reserved. For here the Christmas Eve supper is eaten before the celebration of Midnight Mass, and is therefore a *maigre* meal, shared by all the family, attended by the ceremony of sprinkling the Yule log with wine before setting it upon the fire, and the pronouncement, by the master of the house, of the prayer 'May God grant us grace to see the next year, and if there should not be more of us, let there not be fewer.'

When, as in Gascony and parts of the Languedoc, the ritual Christmas dish is one of those beef and wine *estoufats* which has been giving out its aromatic scents from the hearth where it has been simmering all day long, it will probably be eaten at one o'clock in the morning after the family comes back from Mass. The recipe for one such dish, from the Albi district, is so beautifully simple that its possibilities during the days of busy preparations for the festivities will be readily appreciated. For the rest, French turkeys, geese, hams and chickens are cooked much like our own, although the stuffings may vary, and the accompaniments are very much simpler – potatoes and a salad, a purée of dried split peas or a dish of rice, rather than the sprouts, the peas, the bread sauces, the gravies and sweet jellies of the English Christmas table.

Vogue, December 1957

Untraditional Christmas Food

If I had my way – and I shan't – my Christmas Day eating and drinking would consist of an omelette and cold ham and a nice bottle of wine at lunch time, and a smoked salmon sandwich with a glass of champagne on a tray in bed in the evening. This lovely selfish anti-gorging, un-Christmas dream of hospitality, either given or taken, must be shared by thousands of women who know it's all Lombard Street to a China orange that they'll spend both Christmas Eve and Christmas morning peeling, chopping, mixing, boiling, roasting, steaming. That they will eat and drink too much, that someone will say the turkey isn't quite as good as last year, or discover that the rum for the pudding has been forgotten, that by the time lunch has been washed up and put away it'll be tea-time, not to say drink or dinner time, and tomorrow it's the weekend and it's going to start all over again.

Well, I know that any woman who has to provide for a lot of children or a big family has no alternative. The grisly orgy of spending and cooking and anxiety has to be faced. We are so many fathoms deep in custom and tradition and sentiment over Christmas; we have got so far, with our obsessive present-buying and frenzied cooking, from the spirit of a simple Christian festival, that only the most determined of Scrooges can actually turn their faces to the wall and ignore the whole thing when the time comes. All the same, there must be quite a few small families, couples without children and people living alone, who like to celebrate Christmas in a reasonably modest and civilised way: inviting just a friend or two who might otherwise also be alone (well, maybe, like you and me, they'd *rather* be alone, but this is an eccentricity not accepted at Christmas time) – and for such small-scale Christmas meals at least the shopping and cooking marathons can be avoided, the host and hostess can be allowed to enjoy themselves, and the guests needn't have guilt about the washing-up.

For such a meal, I'd make the main dish something fairly straightforward and conventional, the colour and the festive look being supplied by something bright and beautiful as a garnish. Not inedible decorations, but something simple and unexpected such as a big bowl of crimson sweet-sour cherry sauce with a roast duck; a handsome dish of tomatoes stuffed with savoury rice with a capon; a Madeira and truffle-scented sauce with a piece of plain roast beef; sliced oranges with a pork roast or a ham.

The first course I'd make as painless as possible for the cook: if money were no object, lots of smoked salmon or Parma ham to precede the duck; before the beef, a French duck pâté with truffles and pistachio nuts, avocado pears, or simply a lovely dish of egg or prawn mayonnaise. Or, if you'd cooked a ham or piece of gammon or pickled pork to last over the Christmas holiday, then a few finely carved slices of that, with a bowl of cubed honeydew melon or some pickled peaches – there's no reason why English cooked ham shouldn't make just as good a first course as the raw Parma or Bayonne ham.

As for pudding, unless you feel you absolutely have to have at least the traditional mince pies (those who only eat the Christmas pudding because of the brandy or rum butter will find it equally delicious with mince pies), most people will be grateful if you skip straight to the Christmas dessert fruits. Usually one is too full to appreciate the charms of Malaga raisins, Smyrna figs, almonds, glacé apricots and sugar plums; or you could perhaps finish up with a big bowl of mixed fresh pineapple and sliced oranges.

BAKED FILLET OF BEEF WITH TOMATO FONDUE

Fillet is not a cut I often buy; it is expensive and always has to be ordered in advance because there is such a big demand for it and only a small piece in each animal, and then one gets so sick and tired of the fillet steaks which are often the only safe thing to order in restaurants. But Christmas weekend, when so many families are buying poultry, hams, gammons, spiced beef and legs of pork instead of the usual weekend joint, is a good moment to try for a really fine piece of fillet. It is so easy to cook and carve, and provides such an excellent contrast to cloying Christmas food.

Suppose you have a fillet weighing about 1.2 kg (2½ lb) which should provide two meals for four people, all you have to do is to brush the joint with olive oil or melted beef dripping, stand it on a grid in a baking tin, put it in the centre of a pre-heated moderately hot oven, 190°C/375°F/gas mark 5. There you leave it, without basting or turning it over or paying the slightest attention to it for 45 minutes to an hour, according to whether you want it very underdone or only moderately so. You put it on a long hot serving dish (let it stand a few seconds before carving) with watercress at each end, and, separately, serve the following tomato fondue, which can be made in advance if it's more convenient and then gently heated up.

In a small saucepan heat 45 g (1½ oz) butter: in this melt 2 finely sliced shallots or 1 very small onion: add 4 large skinned and chopped tomatoes, a seasoning of very little salt, nutmeg and dried basil. Cook gently for a quarter of an hour. Add 1 tablespoon of brandy or Armagnac and simmer slowly another 10 minutes. Finally, add a tablespoon of Madeira, a little chopped parsley, a small lump of butter and the small quantity of meat juices which have come from the meat; the fondue is ready.

But if you feel like an extravagance buy a small tin or jar of black truffles, add the juice from the tin at the same time as the brandy, then the sliced truffles. Serve in a little sauce tureen. And as an alternative choice for a guest with traditional tastes, have either some horseradish sauce as well, or plenty of parsley butter, and potatoes, either plain boiled – or, easier still because they won't get overcooked while you aren't looking – boil the potatoes in advance, keeping them somewhat under-done, cut them in quarters and bake them with butter or beef dripping in a shallow dish in the oven while the beef is cooking.

Either with or after the beef, a very simple salad of Belgian endives sliced into 1-cm (½-in) chunks, with an ordinary dressing of olive oil and wine vinegar or lemon juice to which a pinch of sugar as well as salt and pepper is added, will be very welcome. Then cheese, perhaps a beautiful piece of Lancashire instead of the conventional Stilton, and fruit.

ROAST CAPON, AND TOMATOES WITH RICE AND WALNUT STUFFING

Put a lump of butter worked with tarragon or parsley inside a 2.5 kg (5 lb) capon (about 1.8 kg/3½ lb dressed and drawn weight), rub the bird generously with butter, stand it on a grid in a baking tin and roast it slowly on its side in the centre of a very moderate oven, 170°C/325°F/gas mark 3, for 1½ hours altogether, turning it over at half time, then breast upwards for the final 10 minutes, and basting from time to time with melted butter (about 60 g/2 oz) warmed in a little pan on top of the stove. Add a couple of tablespoons of white wine to the buttery juices in the pan, let them bubble a minute or two over a fast flame and serve in a sauce boat. A plain giblet gravy as an alternative to the rich buttery one can be prepared the day before by cooking the giblets with an unpeeled onion, a sliced tomato, a small piece of celery, two or three springs of parsley, and water just to cover. This needs about 3 hours' extremely slow cooking, and is best done in the oven. Then all you have to do is to strain the gravy, season it, and heat it up and reduce it a little when the capon is ready.

For 8 to 10 large tomatoes, the ingredients for the stuffing are 90 g (3 oz) of rice, a chopped shallot, 60 g (2 oz) shelled and chopped walnuts, a dessertspoon of currants, the grated peel of half a lemon, 30 g (1 oz) of butter, pepper, salt, nutmeg and 1 egg, a little olive oil or extra melted butter. Boil the rice, keeping it slightly under-done. Drain and while still warm mix with it all the other ingredients. Slice off the tops of the tomatoes, scoop out the pulp, add it to the rice mixture, fill the tomatoes, piling the stuffing up into a mound, replace the tops, put them in an oiled baking tin or dish, pour a few drops of oil or melted butter over each and bake in the oven while the chicken is cooking: about half an hour should be sufficient.

ROAST PHEASANT WITH CHESTNUT SAUCE

A young but fully grown pheasant will weigh about 750 g (1½ lb) and takes approximately 45 minutes to roast. Put a lump of butter inside the bird, wrap it in well-buttered paper, place it on its side on a grid standing in a baking tin and cook in the centre of a preheated fairly hot oven, 190°C/375°F/gas mark 5.

Turn it over after the first 20 minutes, after another 15 minutes remove the paper and turn the bird breast upwards for the last 10 minutes.

For the chestnut sauce, which can be made a day or two in advance and slowly reheated, the ingredients are 250 g (½ lb) chestnuts, 2 sticks of celery, one rasher of bacon, 45 g (1½ oz) butter, about 6 tablespoons of port, a little cream or stock.

Score the chestnuts on one side, bake them in a moderate oven (180°C/350°F/gas mark 4) for 15 minutes, shell and skin them. Chop them roughly. Heat the butter, put in the chopped celery and bacon, add the chestnuts, the port, an equal quantity of water, and a very little salt. Cover the saucepan and cook very gently for about 30 minutes until the chestnuts are quite tender. When reheating, enrich the mixture with either a couple of tablespoons of rich meat or game stock or double cream.

This mixture is fairly solid, really more like a vegetable dish than a sauce proper, but whatever you like to call it, it goes to perfection with pheasant. A good creamy bread sauce or simply crisp breadcrumbs put in a baking tin with a little butter and left in the oven for about 15 to 20 minutes could provide an alternative, and personally I always like a few fried or baked chipolata sausages with a pheasant.

If you prefer to have your pheasant cold, a bowl of those beautiful Italian fruits in mustard syrup (*see* page 106) would be better than the chestnut sauce. And have a hot first course, an egg dish perhaps (a spoonful of the tomato fondue described on page 173, with a little cream, added to baked eggs is a good one); or some scallops, or a creamy vegetable soup.

Vogue, December 1959

SPICED BAKED CARRÉ OF LAMB

A carré of lamb is the row of best end of neck cutlets trimmed right down to the bone. You will need a rack of lamb of 8 bones weighing not more than 750 g (1½ lb) when trimmed, 1 medium-small clove of garlic, ½ teaspoon each of coriander and cumin seeds, and dried coriander or thyme, 2 teaspoons of salt, 2 tablespoons of olive oil, 2 bay leaves, and 150 ml (¼ pint) of dry white wine.

When you order or buy your joint, make sure that the bones and trimmings are included in your parcel. Weigh the joint before you start operations.

To prepare the meat for cooking, skin and halve a rather small clove of garlic. With one half, rub all the exposed surfaces of the meat and the bones. Cut the other half into very small slivers, insert one close to each bone. Pound or grind a half teaspoon each of coriander and cumin seeds, mix these spices with 2 teaspoons of salt, and a half-teaspoon of oregano or crumbled dried thyme and 2 tablespoons of olive oil. Rub this mixture, like the garlic, over the meat.

Put all the bones and trimmings of the meat into an oval, enamelled cast-iron baking or gratin dish. On top put the little joint, fat side up. This preparation can, if it suits your timetable, be done well in advance.

When the time comes to cook the lamb, set the dish over a low heat for about 5 minutes, until you hear the fat from the trimmings begin to sizzle. Quickly pour over the white wine. Let it bubble for not more than one minute before moving the dish from the top of the stove and putting it under the grill, which should already be hot. This part of the cooking is simply to brown the top surface of the meat and takes only about 4 minutes – but that depends upon the workings of your grill.

Now cover the meat with a sheet of foil and transfer it to the centre shelf of a moderately hot oven, 180°C/350°F/gas mark 4. A carré weighing 750 g (1½ lb) will take 60–70 minutes to cook so that it is beautifully pink all through.

Remove the meat to an ovenproof serving dish, cover it and keep it warm while you give the juices in the cooking pan a very quick boil; and pour them into a heated sauce boat.

Notes

1. Timing given is for a joint of say six months old lamb. Very young, new season's lamb would make a thinner joint, would need much less cooking and would not be quite suitable for this recipe. As with all recipes for oven-roasted meat, it should be borne in mind that the timing and temperatures given are those which apply to the ovens of household cookers. Professional chefs, writing for restaurateurs, give shorter times and higher temperatures because they use much larger ovens in which there is plenty of room for the heat to circulate, so the meat does not burn nor the fat fly at a high temperature. When giving recipes for the general public, chefs rarely take this factor into account. In their turn, they are incredulous when they read a household cook's instructions for oven roasting.

2. The trimmings and bones which have enriched the gravy for this dish of lamb still have meat on them and goodness to give out. The meat trimmings can be used for pilau, or the whole lot can be utilised to make a small quantity of stock which will give a good flavour to a barley, lentil or bean soup.

3. Those who like a flavour of garlic but prefer not to find pieces of the bulb, however small, in their meat, could simply rub the meat with the cut clove and put the rest of it underneath the meat with the trimmings.

Unpublished, 1970s

BONED LOIN OF LAMB BAKED IN A CRUST

This is a dish which needs a certain amount of care and attention, but the results make it well worthwhile.

Ingredients are approximately 1 kg (2¼ lb) (weight after boning – but more rather than less) of kidney end of loin of lamb, boned; the kidneys with their fat removed, sliced and put back inside the meat, which is then rolled and tied in a sausage shape. (A good butcher will do all this for you.) For cooking the meat you need butter, 1 clove of garlic, salt and herbs, and for the final operation a mixture of 2 chopped shallots, parsley, 2 tablespoons of bread-crumbs and 15 g (½ oz) of butter. For the crust, 250 g (8 oz) of plain flour, 150 g (5 oz) of butter, salt, water, milk.

Before cooking the meat, rub it with salt and chopped marjoram or thyme. Wrap it, with a large lump of butter and a whole clove of garlic, in two layers of greaseproof paper or foil, put it in a baking dish or other baking tin, and cook it in a preheated fairly hot oven (190°C/375°F/gas mark 5) for 45–50 minutes. Remove from the oven and leave about 15 minutes before unwrapping it and removing strings. (It should be warm when wrapped in the pastry, but not too much so.)

Have the parsley and shallot mixture prepared in advance, as follows: chop the shallots very finely with about 3 tablespoons of parsley, a little salt and freshly milled pepper. Melt the butter in a small pan, let it just cook a minute or two, stir in the breadcrumbs.

When the meat is unwrapped incorporate its juices – minus the garlic clove – into the mixture. Coat the fat side of the meat with this preparation.

For the crust, which is also prepared in advance, put the flour into a bowl, add a good pinch of salt, crumble in the softened butter – thoroughly but very lightly – add sufficient cold water (half a cupful at most, probably less) to make a soft dough. Knead a few moments, shape into a ball, wrap in greaseproof paper and leave in a cool place for at least 30 minutes.

Flour a board, roll out the dough fairly thin and to a rectangular

shape, sprinkling it with flour if it is sticky. Put the meat in the centre, lift up the sides and ends of the dough and join them along the top and at the sides, moistening the edges with cold water and pinching them well together. Place on a baking sheet already rubbed with a buttered paper. Prick the dough all over with a fork (this is to allow steam to escape and thus prevent the pastry from being soggy) and paint it with a pastry brush dipped in milk.

Put in the centre of a hot oven (200°C/400°F/gas mark 6) and leave for about 35 minutes. When you take the dish from the oven, let it stand 5 minutes before carving it into fairly thick slices. The pastry should be short and light and crisp, the meat inside very full of juices and still just faintly pink. It shouldn't really need any extra sauce, but redcurrant jelly can be served with it if you like, and Belgian endives stewed in butter.

Unpublished, 1970s

APPLES STUFFED WITH SPICED LAMB

This is a Persian dish. The original recipe came from Mr Arto Haroutunian, proprietor of The Armenian Restaurant in Kensington Church Street, where I had the dish for the first time. I have made my own variations in the spicing and flavouring of the lamb and of the tomato and red wine sauce in which the apples are cooked. It is an interesting and attractive dish.

For the stuffing for 8 eating apples (use well-shaped red apples such as Star King or perhaps Worcester. Avoid the insipid Golden Delicious). Other ingredients are 250 g (½ lb) of minced lamb, raw or cooked, 1 small onion, 1 clove of garlic, 30 g (1 oz) of shelled walnuts, 2 tablespoons of chopped parsley, 1 tablespoon of dried mint, 2–3 teaspoons of powdered cinnamon, 1 teaspoon of powdered cumin seed or mixed sweet spice (the kind sold as pudding spice), salt, cayenne pepper, olive oil for frying the meat and a little water or stock to moisten it.

Ingredients for the sauce are 250 g (8 oz) of fresh tomatoes and a small tin (250 g/8 oz size) of Italian peeled tomatoes, olive oil, garlic, a small tumbler of red wine, salt, sugar, water. The sauce, which emerges a deep, dark red and is quite unlike any other tomato sauce I have ever cooked or eaten, seems to me to improve and mellow on reheating, so it is a good idea to make it a day ahead.

Pour boiling water over the tomatoes, skin them, chop them roughly. Into a sauté pan or skillet pour a good measure of olive oil, heat it, put in the fresh tomatoes, let them cook until most of the moisture has evaporated. Pour in the tinned tomatoes and their juice, together with 2 or 3 cloves of garlic, peeled and crushed with a knife. Season with salt. Leave to bubble gently until the sauce is about the consistency of a thick soup. Add the wine, then the sugar. Again leave to reduce. If the sauce has been cooked in an enamelled or earthenware pan, it can safely be left in the pan until next day, otherwise transfer it to a bowl. In any case, keep it covered.

To prepare the lamb stuffing, peel and chop the onion, heat a little olive oil in a frying pan, let the onion just melt and turn pale yellow before putting in the meat. Fry gently, and if raw meat is used, moisten it with a little water or stock, or it will be dry. Add the crushed garlic. Season with salt only at this stage. When the meat is well cooked, stir in the chopped walnuts, the parsley, the dried mint and the spices, using only a very small sprinkling of cayenne. It is, of course, necessary at this stage to taste the meat. You may need to add more salt, or extra spice.

Core the apples but do not peel them. Still using the apple corer or a small spoon, excavate a little more of the apple flesh (this can be added to the stuffing) so that there is room for the meat mixture. Do not overdo this hollowing-out operation. If there is too much stuffing in proportion to the fruit, the dish will be stodgy.

Fill the apples with the meat, arrange them in a baking dish in which they can be served, and in which they fit nicely. Reheat the prepared sauce, pour about 6 tablespoons of it round the apples, add approximately 300 ml (½ pint) of boiling water. Cook uncovered on the centre shelf of a moderately hot oven (180°C/ 350°F/gas mark 4) for 30 minutes, then move the dish to the bottom shelf and leave it for another 15–20 minutes, or until the apples are very soft but not broken. If it is necessary to slow up the cooking, cover the dish at this stage and reduce the temperature.

It is traditional to serve rice with these stuffed apples. Personally, I prefer them on their own.

Allow 2 apples per person. Any not eaten can be reheated slowly, in a covered dish.

Notes

1. Although walnuts are very characteristic of Persian cooking, I have sometimes used pine nuts instead. They are best left whole, and a couple of tablespoons will be sufficient. Sometimes minced beef is used instead of lamb. I have, incidentally, halved the quantity of meat specified by Mr Haroutunian. He, or his chef, hollows out the apples almost completely. To me, this makes for too much meat and not enough fruit.

2. When fresh tomatoes are scarce and expensive the sauce can be made entirely with the tinned variety. Those who object to the tomato pips will find it very easy to sieve the sauce.

3. Although Persia is predominantly a Moslem country, and therefore officially a non-alcohol drinking one, it is also one of the oldest wine-producing countries in the world, so the inclusion of wine in traditional Persian dishes is not surprising. And not every Moslem adheres to the rules laid down by the Prophet.

4. A spoon and fork are the implements needed for eating these stuffed apples.

5. A recipe very similar to the one used by The Armenian Restaurant is given in Claudia Roden's *Book of Middle Eastern Food* (Penguin 1968), although Mrs Roden includes cooked yellow split peas in the stuffing and omits the walnuts. Her sauce is a sweet-sour one of wine vinegar, sugar and water, without tomatoes.

Unpublished, September 1973

OSSI BUCHI BENEDETTI

The following recipe for ossi buchi, a famous speciality of northern Italy, was sent to me, via Signora Fany Benedetti, by the lady who, for many years, supplied my shop with olive oil direct from her Tuscan property. Seldom have I tasted more delicious olive oil, and rarely has any reader or acquaintance given me a recipe which has so taken my fancy.

My own recipe for ossi buchi, published in my *Italian Food*, is the one more usually encountered in Italy. I wrote it and cooked it from versions noted down after I had eaten it in and round about Milan, said to be the native home of the dish, in 1951 and 1952. Signora Benedetti's formula seems to me altogether superior, lighter, and more interesting. Her recipe, given to me in a brief paragraph, and with perfect clarity to anyone already familiar with the dish, dispenses with onion, tomato and stock, and calls for garlic, parsley, spices, white wine, and lemon in the form of whole slices rather than simply the grated peel, as normally used in the better known version. I suspect that the Benedetti recipe must be an older one, perhaps from the days before the tomato became so commonly used in Italian cooking.

I recommend this recipe to anyone who can manage to lay hands on the right cut of veal, which is knuckle, sawn across the bone into slices approximately 3 cm (1¼ in) thick. (In Italy, where the veal used is much younger than any we get in England, the slices are cut thicker, as there is less meat to the bone, and it requires a shorter cooking time.)

You will need 4 slices of knuckle of veal sawn across into 3-cm (1¼-in) pieces, salt, freshly milled pepper, freshly grated nutmeg, powdered cinnamon. It is not feasible to suggest precise quantities of spices and seasonings, which must depend upon the taste of the cook – and in the case at least of cinnamon will vary according to the quality and freshness or otherwise of the ground spice; 2 cloves of garlic, 2–3 tablespoons of roughly chopped parsley (the flat leaf variety when obtainable), 6 thin slices of lemon with the rind, approximately 6 tablespoons of olive oil, 300–450 ml (½–¾ pint) of water, 150 ml (¼ pint) of dry white wine.

It is advisable, at any rate for a first attempt, not to cook more than 4 slices of ossi buchi (which means, literally, hollow bones) at a time. The meat takes up a lot of room in the pan, and the pieces must be cooked in one layer or the gradual reduction of the liquid as the meat cooks will not work with the quantities given.

To prepare the meat, rub each slice on both sides with salt, then add seasonings of freshly milled pepper, ground cinnamon and freshly grated nutmeg.

Peel, slice and crush a couple of cloves of garlic, have ready chopped 2 or 3 tablespoons of parsley, and prepare about half a dozen thin slices of lemon with the peel, and without the pips.

Immediately before the ossi buchi are to be cooked, sprinkle them lightly with flour.

In a 25-cm (10-in) sauté pan, deepish frying pan or skillet, warm enough olive oil to cover, generously, the bottom of the pan. In this brown the pieces of meat, gently and on each side. Now scatter in the garlic, parsley and lemon slices. Pour in enough cold water to reach just or barely to the top of the slices of meat. Cover the pan, lower the heat, and simmer gently for just about one hour.

By this time the meat, although not yet ready, should be tender enough to be easily pierced with a skewer. Into the pan pour a glass of dry white wine. Increase the heat just for a minute or two, so that the wine and juices bubble a little, then lower it again, and leave the meat to cook for approximately 30 minutes. Whether at this stage you cover the pan or leave it open depends upon the degree to which the liquid has already reduced. Bearing in mind that by the time the ossi buchi are quite tender there should not be so much sauce that the meat is swimming, but sufficient to ensure that it is not dry, the cook must make his own decision. So much depends upon the shape and weight of the pan as well as upon the degree of heat and the relative toughness or otherwise of the meat that it is impossible, and would be misleading, to give precise instructions.

By the time the meat is perfectly tender, the sauce should be reduced to barely more than a half-dozen tablespoonsful. Veal, of its nature, and especially knuckle or shin, produces a characteristically gelatinous and sticky quality in the sauce, a key point in this particular dish.

Transfer the ossi buchi to a heated serving dish, pour the sauce over them, and if you like, add a little extra freshly chopped parsley.

The special treat of ossi buchi is the marrow from the bones; a teaspoon or marrow scoop should be provided for each person – and bread on which the marrow can be spread.

In Lombard tradition, a risotto, saffron-flavoured, is always served with ossi buchi. This is a good combination, but a very filling one. A lighter and more delicate accompaniment is a dish of courgettes, grated and cooked in butter. A dish of chopped spinach, very freshly cooked, would be another good alternative.

Sufficient for 2 or 3, according to capacity; my own never runs to more than one slice, but the young and hungry would certainly be able to manage two.

Notes

To be sure of getting knuckle of veal, it is advisable to order from your butcher well in advance. It is no bad idea to take the extra pieces (the knuckle cuts into 7 or 8 pieces, the 4 in the centre being the best) and freeze them to use later for broth, to add to a pot-au-feu or to a chicken stock. Shin of veal from the front legs of the animal is often used in Italy as an alternative to knuckle. Again this is due to the difference in age and size of the calves. In England, it is best to use knuckle which, contrarily, is the name given by English butchers to the lower *hind* leg of the animal, while shin is the lower *foreleg*.

Care should be taken that the butcher does not cut the slices too thin, or they will buckle during the cooking, and emerge in shapeless and unattractive condition.

I have seen recipes in which a weighty cast-iron cocotte, or casserole, or in American usage Dutch oven, hermetically sealed, is recommended for the cooking of ossi buchi. This is exactly what is not wanted. Although, if absolutely necessary, ossi buchi *can* be transferred to the oven once the initial browning has been achieved and after the water is added, this method is less satisfactory than cooking over direct heat in that it fails to reduce the sauce slowly, steadily, and to the correct consistency, with this dish a point of prime importance. How much less satisfactory would be a hermetically sealed oven pot in which no evaporation takes place, is surely obvious.

Unpublished, 1972

PORK CHOPS, SPICED AND GRILLED

This is an effortless and delicious lunch or supper dish. It does however presuppose a supply of the home-made Italian spice (white peppercorns, juniper berries, nutmeg and cloves) for which the recipe is given on page 95.

Pork chops with the rind, about 2 cm (1 in) thick, salt, garlic, olive oil, Italian seasoning, wild thyme on the stalk, dry bay leaves.

The pork chops should be rather thick ones, with the rind left on – for the reasons given in the recipe for pork chops with green peppercorns on page 91.

Rub each chop on both sides with a cut clove of garlic, salt and olive oil. Then sprinkle them on each side with Italian seasoning – it really is not possible to give precise quantities, but allow something in the region of a quarter-teaspoonful for each chop.

Put the prepared chops in a shallow, fireproof dish, with the twigs of thyme and the bay leaves and one or two pieces of garlic.

Cook them under the grill, about 15 cm (6 in) away from the heat, for about 15 minutes, turning them from time to time with steak tongs.

Transfer the dish to a low oven, 170°C/325°F/gas mark 3 for about 7 minutes. Serve the chops in the dish in which they have cooked, so that they will be sizzling hot.

A simple salad is a better accompaniment than green vegetables, but potatoes cooked in the oven are always good with pork chops.

Notes
There seems to me no reason why this recipe should not also be used for lamb cutlets – the Italian seasoning is good with lamb – but they would take less time to cook.

Anyone who has the ingredients of the spice mixture in the kitchen cupboard can, it goes without saying, make up enough for each dish as needed; but it is not easy to pound cloves so the ready-ground variety would probably have to be used.

Unpublished, 1973

BACON IN BRIOCHE

Buy a 1–1.2 kg (2½ lb) piece of long back bacon (the leanest end), preferably Wiltshire mild-cured. Soak it in cold water to cover for 48 hours, changing the water at least twice.

To cook the bacon, wrap it in two sheets of foil, twisting the ends and folding in the edges so that no juices escape while the bacon is cooking.

Put the parcel on a rack in a baking tin half-filled with water. (This is to create steam which keeps the bacon moist.) Place low down in the oven, and bake at 150°C/300°F/gas mark 2 for approximately 2 hours, or ¼ hour to 500 g/1 lb, turning the parcel at half time.

Remove from the oven, leave for 30 minutes or so before unwrapping and peeling off the skin, which is easily done while the bacon is still warm.

When cool, spread the fat side of the bacon with a scant teacupful of the herb, spice and breadcrumb mixture described on page 181 of *Salt, Spices*, etc. Press well down, spreading it as thickly as you can. Press some of the mixture also into any cavities left where bones have been removed. Leave to set.

For the brioche dough, you will need 250 g (8 oz) of strong plain flour, salt, 15 g (½ oz) of bakers' yeast, 2 whole eggs, 4–6 tablespoons of very thick cream. (If possible, use Jersey cream bought a day or two in advance.)

With a little warm water, mix the yeast to a cream. Put the flour in a bowl with a teaspoon or two of salt. Add the yeast and the whole eggs and mix, using a wooden spoon. Add the cream (or if you prefer, 75–90 g/2½–3 oz of softened butter). Knead very lightly into a ball. Sprinkle with flour. With scissors make a deep cross cut in the dough. Cover it, and leave to rise in a warm place for an hour to an hour and a half. (The ideal temperature is about 21°C/70°F.) By this time the dough should have doubled in volume, and will be soft, springy and malleable. Break it down, and without kneading, re-shape it into a ball.

Brush an iron baking-sheet with melted butter or pork fat, and sprinkle it with flour. Put the ball of dough in the centre. With your fingers and knuckles press it out (if very soft, it may need extra sprinklings of flour) into a rectangle large enough to enclose your piece of bacon.

Put the bacon in the centre of the sheet of dough, gather up the edges, so that the bacon is completely enveloped. You should have a neat rectangular parcel (perhaps at the first try it may be rather ragged and untidy. No matter. After one or two more experiments it will all be very easy.)

The joined edges of the dough should be pressed together with your fingers dipped in cold water. This detail is quite important. If forgotten, the joins may break open during baking.

Heat the oven to 220°C/425°F/gas mark 7. Put the baking-sheet with the enwrapped bacon on top of the stove for 15 minutes while the oven heats up.

Finally, with the back of a knife make light scores in the shape of a diamond or criss-cross pattern on the dough. Bake on the centre shelf for 15 minutes, then lower the oven to 190°C/375°F/gas mark 5 and cook for another 10–15 minutes.

When you take the brioche from the oven, brush it over with thick cream. This gives a nice finish in the pastry, without making it too shiny.

Transfer the bacon in brioche to a board and leave it for a few minutes before carving, on the slant.

Notes

Larger pieces of bacon can, of course, be cooked in the same way, increasing the proportions of dough accordingly. Remember, though, that although bacon – or almost any meat – in brioche dough is very good cold on the day after it is cooked, the brioche soon goes hard and dry. So don't make a great deal more than you need for two meals.

Another point to bear in mind is that the bacon should be pretty well cooked before it is enclosed in its covering of dough. It will not cook very much more once it is insulated from the heat by the dough.

Ordinary white bread dough can be used instead of brioche dough – and it should be noted that the dough described above is a very simplified and very easily mixed version of a true brioche dough.

Unpublished, December 1971

A version of the recipe for a Spiced Herb Mixture to Spread on Baked Gammon to which Elizabeth refers the reader is given on page 96. JN

John Nott

The receipts collected by John Nott into his own very personal idea of dictionary form were those of the published books of the second Stuart age, let us say from approximately 1650 to 1715. Many were revised or slightly rewritten versions of receipts which had appeared in *The Compleat Cook* of 1655, and in Robert May's *The Accomplisht Cook* first published in 1660, the year of the Restoration. Others come from Sir Kenelm Digby's posthumously published collection entitled *The Closet of the Eminently Learned Sir Kenelme Digbie Kt. Opened*, 1669, and *A Perfect School of Instructions for the Officers of the Mouth*, 1682. This was a translation by Giles Rose, one of Charles II's master-cooks (brother, perhaps, of his head-gardener, John Rose) of *L'Escole parfaite des officiers de bouche* published in Paris in 1662 and again in 1682.

No doubt Nott drew on many other sources, including works

by his more immediate predecessors. There had recently been quite a spate of books written or compiled by men who had worked for rich noblemen and in the royal kitchens. Among the latter was Patrick Lamb, whose name was attached to a collection called, with brevity and authority, *Royal Cookery*. This was published in 1710, after Lamb's death. He had some right to the title, having spent fifty years in the palace kitchens at St James's and Whitehall, serving Charles II, James II, William III and Mary, and Queen Anne. Another royal cook, or rather, confectioner, whose little work was published in 1718,[1] was Mrs Mary Eales 'confectioner to her late Majesty Queen Anne'. Several other professionals, following the contemporary fashion of naming illustrious former employers on their title pages, had produced cookery or confectionery manuals.[2] On the whole they were repetitive and derivative, and Nott's most important contemporary source appears to have been *The Court and Country Cook*, published in 1702. This was the translation of the 1698 edition of François Massialot's famous *Cuisinier Roïal et Bourgeois* which had first appeared in Paris in 1691. Combined with the original work in this translation, by one J. K., was a version of Massialot's second book, dealing with preserves, confectionery, cordials, lemonades, syrups, and the distilling of the aromatic waters then fashionable at the court of Louis XIV. Known as *eaux d'Italie*, these were increasingly often frozen and served as part of the dessert, and at the open air collations and fêtes so beloved in French royal and aristocratic circles. Directions for freezing were given by Massialot, and taken up – at any rate in print – by English practitioners, including our John Nott.

In 1723, the very same year that Charles Rivington published the first edition of Nott's *Dictionary*, another of the ex-royal cooks, a man called R. Smith, published a work entitled *Court Cookery: or, The Compleat English Cook*, naming the Dukes of Buckingham and Ormond and the French Ambassador as having been among his exalted employers. This must have been annoying, to say the least, for John Nott who had contented himself with the comparatively modest announcement that he was 'Cook to his Grace the Duke of Bolton'. So here was a potential rival to Nott and his publisher, an author naming one of the very noblemen for whom Nott himself had worked. (The 2nd Duke of Ormond, undoubtedly the one concerned, had been implicated in the 1715 Jacobite plot. He was impeached for high treason and his estates confiscated. He then retired to France, so it must have been some years since Nott and Smith had worked for him. His daughter, Lady Mary Butler, had however married the 3rd Baron Ashburnham of Ashburnham in Sussex, so possibly it was on leaving Ormond's service that Nott moved to Lord Ashburnham's.)

Nott's omission of Ormond's name, and those of other exalted personages in whose kitchens he had worked was remedied when, in 1724, Rivington brought out the second edition of the book, and the string of imposing names on the title page henceforth gave it extra appeal. From the wording, it looks as though Nott had in the meantime either died or retired. 'Late cook' could have meant 'lately', or 'late' in the modern sense.

It is at any rate sufficiently clear from Nott's choice of receipts and from his instructions generally that he was already an elderly man when he compiled his *Dictionary*. His heyday would have been that age when great noblemen, city magnates and East India merchants were building new country mansions, laying out parks and gardens, creating artificial lakes and waterfalls, stocking new fish ponds fed by running water, planting fruit orchards and kitchen gardens, growing orange trees in heated orangeries, constructing ice wells such as had been common in Italy for a century or more. It was the period of scientific discovery, of the great Royal Society, of burgeoning knowledge in every field. It was also, as we are sharply reminded by some of the receipts, the period when smallpox and the plague regularly decimated the population and medicine was primitive to a degree now hard for us to envisage.

Given all the circumstances, Nott's *Dictionary* cannot but be of the greatest interest, particularly so to anyone who had been enchanted by the diaries, the travel journals and the memoirs of the time. Nott's employers were familiar figures in late Stuart society, some of them at least were known to John Evelyn (James Butler, 2nd Duke of Ormond, formerly Lord Ossory, was the son of that Thomas Butler, Earl of Ossory, who had been one of Evelyn's dearest friends).[3] Celia Fiennes of travel journal fame visited or wrote of their houses. She would have known all about the dishes Nott describes. So would John Evelyn. Over and over again in Evelyn's absorbing record we find references to the ingredients, the dinners, the feasts, the extraordinary arrangements of sweetmeats, preserves and fruit which made up what in Evelyn's day was still called the banquet or banquetting course, but which by the time John Nott put his book together was more usually called the dessert. It was still of course an elaborate affair, requiring much skill and taste on the part of the confectioners, pastrycooks, and often the ladies of the house, who made or ordered the different components and put them together in such charming displays. Nott's instructions concerning this art, given right at the end of his book, with a simple diagram, are clear and well written. They could almost be followed today.

As for the kind of houses in which John Nott worked, and indeed some of the duties of a cook of the time, they come most vividly to life in John Evelyn's writings. Here he is describing the grounds and gardens of one recently created by his friends, the 2nd Earl of Clarendon and his countess.

The date is 23 October 1685, the place Swallowfield in Berkshire. Evelyn has journeyed there by coach from London, stopping on the way for 'a plentifull dinner' at Mr Graham's Lodge at Bagshot. Arrived at Swallowfield, Evelyn finds the house is built in the ancient manner but 'the Gardens and Waters as elegant as it is possible and Lady Clarendon extraordinarily skilled in "the flowry part" of the garden'. His lordship had displayed great diligence in the planting of trees and 'there were delicious and rarest fruits', and an orchard of a thousand golden and other cider pippins. 'The Nurseries, Kitchin-garden, full of the most desirable plants; two very noble Orangeries well furnish'd; but above all, the Canale & fishponds, the One fed with a white, the other with a black-running water, fed by a swift & quick river: so well and plentifully stor'd with fish, that for Pike, Carp, Breame, & Tench; I had never seene anything approching it: We had Carps & Pike of size fit for the table of a Prince, every meale, & what added to the delight, the seeing hundreds taken in the drag, out of which the Cooke standing by, we pointed what we had most mind to, & had Carps every meale, that had been worth at London twenty shill a piece.'[4] (Pike also was expensive. It was sold by measurement. In 1691 six 28 in. pike, for example, cost the Earl of Bedford at Woburn 12s. apiece, while three 30 in. specimens were 15s. apiece.)[5]

This, then, was the kind of establishment in which our John Nott would have worked, the contemporary reliance of such households on fish from their own ponds being attested by his twenty-five receipts for pike – today it would be surprising to find more than three or four in a similar compendium – fourteen for carp, eleven for tench. Orchard fruit is equally well represented in Nott's work. There are no fewer than ten receipts for making cider, and a curious one for *Mure* which turns out to mean the *marc* or husks of the apples. For quinces, apricots and cherries there are respectively twenty-two, twenty-seven and twenty-five receipts. Those go back to the earliest Stuart days and are among the most delightful in the book. Here are all those solid marmalades, the preserves and the jellies so much loved by the English ever since the cultivation of fruit trees, the import of cheaper sugar from the colonies and the establishment of sugar-refineries in English ports had brought such delicacies within reach of a comparatively wide range of households – albeit always fairly wealthy ones. A 'marmalade of cherries sharp tasted' made with two quarts of redcurrant juice to 8 lbs of cherries is a lovely receipt, 'cherries booted', 'cherries in Ears' and 'cherries in Bunches' are all from the Massialot book. So are apricot ratafia and apricots again 'in ears', while 'codlins like mango' is a receipt reflecting the contemporary interest in home-made imitations of the pickles and chutneys brought home by returning East India merchants.

Ingredients new to England in the second half of the seventeenth century were chocolate and coffee, the former still used rather tentatively, in very small quantity to colour and flavour biscuits and creams, and more commonly as a hot drink. John Nott took his receipts for chocolate biscuits and creams from the translation of Massialot's book, published in 1702. On 10 September of that same year a Bedfordshire lady, Diana Astry, noted that for dinner at Henbury there were for 'the first corse a calve's head haished, carps stw'd, a chine of mutton & a venison pastey. The 2^d cors a couple of turkeys rosted, samon, tarts, a salver of sullabubs & jocklett crames, and harricock pye the 5th dish.'[6] Had the Henbury cook been studying the newly published book?

A harricock pye means an artichoke pie. At the time the word was very variously spelled, one of the most common ways being hartichock. The place of the pie in a final course sounds rather unusual, but the natural sweetness of a number of vegetables, including green peas, parsnips, skirrets, potatoes and carrots were well understood by our ancestors, who often cooked them with currants, dates, prunes and even candied fruit to give additional sweetness and served them as what John Nott calls 'intermesses', i.e. *entremets*. These sometimes appeared in between more substantial courses, sometimes as a last course immediately before the dessert proper. Many such dishes, some sweet, some savoury, some quite substantial are given by Nott, who also lists an artichoke pye in his dinner menu for October, along with 'Fruit in a Dish, Tarts and Custard'. He writes enthusiastically that 'artichokes are of very great use throughout the Year, for almost all sorts of Ragoos, Potages, and Side-dishes; so that you should provide good store of them which you may preserve'. He gives two methods of pickling and three of drying them, receipts which must have originated in Provence and Italy where, until quite recent times, artichokes were commonly dried for winter use.

That John Nott thought it relevant to include such receipts in his *Dictionary* and to explain how useful they were does seem to indicate that in the kitchen gardens of the house where he worked leaf artichokes were cultivated in plenty. Among those houses – most of them were in the south and south-western counties – was undoubtedly one called Hackwood near Basingstoke in Hampshire. It was one of the mansions owned by the Dukes of Bolton, and it was evidently the 3rd Duke, Charles Paulet, Marquis of Winchester, who succeeded to his father's title in 1722 for whom Nott was working when his book appeared in 1723. Hackwood was described by Celia Fiennes in 1691 as 'another good house and fine Parke of the Duke of Bolton's'.[7] Another great mansion seen by Celia Fiennes on a later journey, 1702 or 1703, was the Duke of Somerset's 'newly building' house at Marlborough (now the nucleus of Marlborough College). She was impressed with the layout of the grounds, watered with ditches and 'such a cannal which empts itself into a fish pond to keep fish in, then it empts itself into the river, there is a house built over the fish pond to keep the fish in.'[8]

Charles Seymour, 6th Duke of Somerset (1662–1748) who was then building his new house, can hardly have been an easy man to work for. Known as the Proud Duke, his habit was to send outriders ahead of him to clear the roads along which he intended to pass so that 'plebeians' should not see him. On one occasion a farmer, understandably exasperated by his Grace's high-handed ways, refused to be prevented from looking over his own hedge. In the spirit of a cat may look at a king, he held up his pig so that he too might see the Duke.[9] Another of Somerset's unlovable whims was to force his two daughters to stand guard over him while he took his afternoon nap. On waking one day to find that one of them had actually dared to sit down he immediately docked

£20,000 from her inheritance. Or so the story goes.[10] Given such capricious and autocratic employers it would hardly have been surprising if their servants moved from house to house with some rapidity, although how long Nott stayed with the various men on his title page we have no means of knowing, nor do we know where he worked when he entered the service of Lord Lansdowne, although there is a distinct possibility that it was yet another of the great West Country houses, Longleat in Wiltshire.

George Grenville or Granville (the family, descendants of the famous Sir Richard Grenville of the *Revenge*, appears never to have made up its collective mind how to spell the name), son of Bernard Grenville and grandson of that Sir Bevil Grenville who in 1642 was killed fighting for the royalist cause at Lansdowne, was in his youth a quite successful dramatist and poet. For a time also a successful politician and courtier, in 1711 Queen Anne created him Baron Lansdowne of Bideford. After the Queen's death in 1714, Lansdowne and his wife were involved in the same 1715 Jacobite plot which cost the Duke of Ormond his estates. Both the Lansdownes spent eighteen months in close imprisonment in the Tower, and on regaining their liberty retired to Longleat, recently inherited by the 2nd Viscount Weymouth, Lady Lansdowne's seven-year-old son by her first husband, Thomas Thynne.[11] There the Lansdownes stayed until 1722, when financial difficulties made it expedient for his lordship to remove himself to Paris, where he stayed for ten years.[12] He had been a lavish spender and by all accounts was an amiable and civilised man. John Nott must have found him a good employer. We may suppose him to have been less happy at Hackwood with his Grace of Bolton. Described in *The Dictionary of National Biography* as proud, vain, dissatisfied, 'troublesome at court, hated in the country and scandalous in his regiment' (he was a notorious buck and gallant), this nobleman can hardly have been the ideal master of Hackwood or indeed of anywhere else. As we have seen, by 1724 John Nott had left the Duke's employ.

Surmise though much of John Nott's career must remain, we do at least know the kind of houses he worked in. Given the way such establishments were then run, he would have had under-cooks, turnspits, scullions, kitchen apprentices to assist him. There would have been a steward in charge of the entire household, and a butler to look after the wines and beverages, the plate and linen. (The folding and pleating of starched napkins into elaborate and fantastical shapes was an important part of the butler's duties.) Employers who were sufficiently desirous of keeping in the fashion and rich enough to do so also employed a professional pastrycook and confectioner, or at any rate hired one for special occasions. This may explain why Nott, in spite of including Massialot's directions for freezing in his anthology, gives only the scantest of receipts for actually preparing the sherbet-type beverages, and sweetened creams which were turned into ices. We get cherry, redcurrant (under currant), and raspberry waters, but no creams at all.

It would be strange if among the men he worked for none could boast of an ice well in his grounds. The storage of ice or compacted snow and its use as an aid to food preservation and for the cooling of wines and beverages had after all been one of the important innovations in England in the second part of the seventeenth century. Charles II had had such wells or pits constructed in the grounds of St James's, Whitehall and Greenwich palaces very shortly after his return to the throne.[13] Before long, the King's example was widely copied. It was a milestone of great significance in the history of English domestic refrigeration, and even if John Nott had little first-hand experience of the confection of ices he must surely have been familiar with the use of ice for the cooling of wine and fresh fruit.

By the early years of the eighteenth century, the existence of ice wells was being taken for granted. In about 1702 Celia Fiennes refers to them as a matter of course. At the Epsom residence of a Mrs Rooth, formerly Lady Donegal, she records that in the grounds were 'two mounts, cut smoothe, between is a canall, these mounts are severall steps up under which are ice houses, they are a square flatt on the top fenced with banks round and seates beyond which is a summer house in a tree'.[14] Ice wells were usually surmounted by a roof of thatch, and the ice or compacted snow was closely packed in between layers of straw. Lady Donegal's ice houses sound like a more recent development.

A few years later, in 1709, Joseph Addison, writing in *The Tatler* under the pen name of Isaac Bickerstaff, gives a sardonic and somewhat ungracious description of a dinner given the previous summer by a friend who admires French cookery. Addison cares for none of the fancy dishes and is indignant that the noble sirloin of plain roast beef, of which he has more than one helping, is relegated to the sideboard. When at last the dessert comes on,

Addison is actually impressed. 'It was as extraordinary as any Thing that had come before it.' It looked, he says, 'like a very beautiful Winter-Place'. There were several 'Pyramids of Candy'd sweetmeats, that hung like Iceicles, with Fruits scattered up and down, and hid in an artificial kind of Frost. At the same time there were great quantities of Cream beaten up into a Snow,[15] and near them little Plates of Sugar-Plumbs, disposed like so many Heaps of Hail-Stones.' There was also a 'Multitude of Congelations', i.e. frozen things, and 'Jellies of various Colours'. Addison declines to spoil the effect of this pretty spectacle by eating anything, and is annoyed with his fellow guests who do. 'I could not but smile', he comments maliciously, 'to see several of them cooling their Mouths with Lumps of Ice which they just before been burning with Salts and Peppers.'[16] Not one's ideal guest. His 'Lumps of Ice', by the way, is no doubt a comment on the unsatisfactory nature of the ices of the time. As can be seen from the directions in Nott's book, the method of freezing them was very hit and miss. It must have resulted in either a rock-hard and glassy mass or in an imperfectly frozen slush. 'Send it quick to your table or it will melt againe' runs the final line of a late seventeenth- or early eighteenth-century receipt for Ice Creame in a MS. cookery book which belonged to Grace, Countess Granville[17] who was Lord Lansdowne of Bideford's first cousin and his exact contemporary in age. Interestingly, some of the receipts in her book are the very ones used by John Nott.

Here we must leave our cook and his book and turn to his publisher, Charles Rivington. When in 1723 he brought out Nott's *Dictionary*, he had already been a successful publisher since 1711, when he had acquired the very flourishing fifty-year-old business of Richard Chiswell, publisher of Dryden's poems and one of the associates who in 1685 issued the fourth folio of Shakespeare's works.

The books published by Rivington were of an educational and serious nature. Volumes of sermons, histories, legal and medical manuals – among the latter was Dr Ratcliffe's *Pharmacopoeia* published in 1716, and two books by Daniel Defoe, *The Complete English Tradesman in Familiar Letters* and *A Plan of the English Commerce* which both appeared in the 1720s – were the kind of works for which the Rivingtons, father and son, were known. Following John Nott's book came *A New Treatise on Liquors* by

James Sedgwick in 1725, and in the 1730s Philip Miller's important *Gardener's Dictionary*.

Later, the Rivingtons achieved an extraordinary commercial success with the publication in 1741-2 of Samuel Richardson's four-volume *Pamela*, famous as the first English novel, and throughout the eighteenth century the Rivington imprint was to be associated with some of the greatest names in the literature of the period, names such as Addison, Pope, Dr Johnson and Tobias Smollett.

Charles Rivington, it becomes clear, was not the man to publish flighty books. John Nott's *Dictionary* must have been considered by him to be a substantial and instructive work of reference and its author a respected personage. Publishers of cookery books do not of course necessarily know anything about cookery or its literature. Charles Rivington may simply have considered a cookery manual in dictionary form a sound financial proposition, and been impressed with John Nott's credentials, and the book did in fact achieve a respectable success. Oxford, in his *English Cookery Books to the Year 1850* (1913) notes that following the original edition there were two printings in 1724, three in 1726, four in 1733, after which demand for it appears to have ceased. Oxford, incidentally, seems to have been struck by Nott's opening description of practical jokes played at banquets in former times. This, in fact, was derived by Nott from Robert May's book of 1660, and was then already far from new. Something very similar had been laid on at a reception at Castel Sant' Angelo in Rome in 1593 to amuse the three sons of William, Duke of Bavaria. The young men were paying a formal visit to Pope Clement VIII and the whole affair was described in the 1593 edition of *Il Trinciante*, the famous treatise on carving by Vincenzo Cervio. I think John Nott regarded Robert May's description as of historical interest. So it was. And so indeed today is the whole book. In republishing it, Lawrence Rivington, Charles' direct descendant, is continuing in the family tradition – according to *The Guinness Book of Records*, the Rivingtons are the oldest publishing family in Great Britain. As his father, Septimus Rivington, wrote in 1919 in *The Publishing Family of Rivington*,[18] theirs was 'the oldest name connected with the bookselling and publishing business ... a considerable achievement for one family'. That over sixty years on it should still be in the same business is even more of an achievement.

References

1. *Mrs Mary Eales's Receipts.* Confectioner to her late Majesty Queen Anne. 1718. Reprinted twice in 1733, one of the reprints, according to Oxford (*see* 2 below), being entitled *The Compleat Confectioner.* Other editions appeared in 1747 and 1753.

2. *See* A. W. Oxford's *English Cookery Books to the Year 1850,* published 1913, and in facsimile by the Holland Press, London, 1977, for authors and titles given in date order.

3. *The Diary of John Evelyn.* Edited by E. S. de Beer. OUP, 1959. *See* index for many references to Thomas Butler, Earl of Ossory, and James Butler, Earl of Ossory, later 2nd Duke of Ormond. Also *The Dictionary of National Biography* and Cokayne's *Complete Peerage.*

4. *The Diary of John Evelyn.* pp. 829–31. The gardens of Swallowfield Park are now open to the public during the summer months.

5. Gladys Scott Thompson. *Life in a Noble Household 1641–1700.* The Bedford Historical Series, London, Jonathan Cape, 1937.

6. *The Recipe Book of Diana Astry c 1700.* Bedfordshire Historical Records Society No 37. 1957.

7. *The Journeys of Celia Fiennes.* Ed. and with an Introduction by Christopher Morris. Cresset Press, London, 1947.

8. ibid. For much detail of the social and domestic life of the time, *see also* Mark Girouard's *Life in the English Country House.* Yale University Press, New Haven and London, 1978.

9. *Cokayne's Complete Peerage.* Ed. Vicary Gibbs.

10. *Memoirs of the Kit Kat Club,* 1821.

11. Roger Granville. *History of the Granvilles.* Exeter, 1895.

12. *The Dictionary of National Biography.*

13. H. M. Colvin, *History of the King's Works.* Vol V. 1976. Edmund Waller's *A Poem on St James's Park As Lately Improved by His Majesty.* 1661. *The Times* 19.9.56. *The Harvest of Cold Months,* article by Elizabeth David published in *Petits Propos Culinaires* No. 3, 1979, Prospect Books.

14. *See* (7) above.

15. This referred to the charming dish of whipped cream and egg whites which had come to us long before via Italy. There can scarcely be a printed or family receipt book of the seventeenth century which does not contain at least one recipe for snow

cream or snow cheese. Nott has a version called 'Ice and Snow'.

16. *The Tatler*. Paper 148, March 18th to 21st, 1709.

17. I have written about Grace, Countess Granville and her receipt book in *Petits Propos Culinaires* No. 2. 1979. See note 13 above. Also in *The Herbal Review*, Spring 1980. Published by The Herb Society, 34 Boscobel Place, London, SW1.

18. Published by Rivingtons, 1919.

Introduction to the 1980 facsimile edition of John Nott's *Cooks and Confectioners Dictionary*, 1726

What to do with the Bird?

A nice thought, although perhaps an unworthy one, that when Christmas morning dawns, for four whole days there won't be any shopping to do. Or anyway no serious food buying. That means that for once the house won't be crammed with a lot of unnecessary food. And the surprising thing is that it is unlikely we'll be in any great danger of starving.

I suppose the question of what to cook with the bits of leftover turkey (good as it is cold, there does come a moment when it can't be faced again) or goose, ham and the rest will have to be pretty well planned beforehand, but this isn't really such a burden as everybody makes out. I don't believe, myself, in opening a whole lot of jars and bottles and tins to help out with the remains. I don't want a whole stack more oddments becoming problems in their turn. And on the whole, dishes made from already cooked birds and meat are very much more attractive if you treat them as if they were dishes in their own right. They only become squalid little horrors when you doll them up with a lot of ingredients without point or purpose.

So the only extra supplies I shall bother about are a few more eggs than usual, some cream in the refrigerator, the usual things like onions and carrots for soup stock, rice, a small supply of Parmesan or Gruyère cheese for grating, plenty of olive oil, lemons, and coffee, and a piece of pork to help out with a goose dish when the time comes. I suppose I might think about getting a tin of tunny fish or prawns to use in a salad, and perhaps a couple of refreshing honeydew melons from which either salads or dessert dishes can be made.

And if any of those marauding bands of persons who apparently roam the countryside calling themselves unexpected guests appear at my door – well, they'll have to make do with soup and an omelette and a glass of wine to help them on their way to their next victims. I think I'd feel less nervous anyway offering them this sort of food than I would if I'd made a lot of little surprises with names like Pantry Shelf Fishbits and Fantastic Belgian Meat Balls and Festa Turkey-Nut Logs. I didn't make them up, I swear I didn't, I read about them in a desperately sad American cookery book all about leftovers.

Now first here is a really worthwhile dish to make with some of the turkey meat; it's a dish I often make from a chicken cooked especially for the purpose, because the creamy, cheese-flavoured sauce with the chicken makes such a soothing, gentle combination of flavours and textures. That is to say, it does if the sauce really *is* creamy and if there is rather a lot of it in proportion to the chicken or turkey meat.

GRATIN OF TURKEY IN CREAM SAUCE

Ingredients for a dish for 3 or 4 people are about 375 g (¾ lb) of cooked turkey or chicken weighed when it has been taken from the bone and, for the sauce, 45 g (1½ oz) of butter, 2 tablespoons of flour, 300 ml (½ pint) of milk, 4 tablespoons each of stock from the bird and cream or, if there is no stock, 8 tablespoons of cream. Seasonings include nutmeg as well as salt and freshly milled pepper and 3 tablespoons of grated Parmesan or Gruyère, plus a little extra, with breadcrumbs, for the final cooking of the dish.

Melt the butter in a thick saucepan, put in the flour, stir it round, off the fire, until it forms a smooth paste; add a little of the warmed milk. Return to the fire and stir while you add the rest of the milk. When the sauce is smooth and thick add the stock, cream and seasonings; there should be a good measure of pepper and nutmeg but only a very little salt until after the cheese has been added. It may then be necessary to add more. At this stage put the saucepan into another large one containing water and let it cook in this bain-marie, stirring frequently, for a good 20 minutes. Now add the cheese and stir again until it has amalgamated with the sauce. Remove all skin and sinew from the turkey or chicken, cut it into thin strips, as much of a size as possible.

Cover the bottom of a shallow gratin dish with a thin layer of the sauce. Put in the turkey or chicken in one layer. Cover it completely with the rest of the sauce. Sprinkle with breadcrumbs and grated cheese and cook for about 15 minutes in a moderate oven (180°C/350°F/gas mark 4), and then transfer it to the grill for a minute or two and serve it when the top is just beginning to blister into golden bubbles. If you do this gratin in larger quantities, use a dish in proportion. It will not be good if it is squashed into too small a space.

TURKEY OR CHICKEN SALAD

The important point to remember about cold roast turkey is that a tendency to dryness has to be counteracted. A mayonnaise would seem to be the obvious answer, but in fact it is not in the least what one wants to eat so soon after all the heavy Christmas food. On the other hand, a salad made from a turkey and a vinaigrette dressing, augmented with hard-boiled eggs, appears to be altogether a more acceptable proposition. The ingredients may be precisely the same as those for a mayonnaise, but the effect is quite different.

For about 350 g (¾ lb) of cold turkey or chicken, freed of skin and bone and sliced into thin, even pieces, make the following sauce: chop 2 shallots with the well-rinsed leaves of a bunch (about 30 g/1 oz) of parsley and any other herbs you may happen to have, such as tarragon and a little lemon thyme; stir in a seasoning of salt and freshly milled pepper, 2 scant teaspoons of French mustard, 6 tablespoons of olive oil and the juice of a small lemon.

Beat all the ingredients well together and then mix the sauce with the pieces of turkey. Leave the whole mixture in a covered bowl until serving time. Then arrange the salad in a shallow dish with sliced hard-boiled egg all round and, should they be available, a few peeled prawns, seasoned with oil and lemon, on the top. They make an excellent combination with turkey and chicken. Such things as capers, pickled cucumber, strips of crisp raw celery or cubes of melon can also be added to the salad.

RILLETTES D'OIE

Although it is not orthodox to make this dish with cooked meats, a piece of roast goose mixed with uncooked fat pork makes excellent rillettes, and is a useful way of using up the Christmas goose, for the rillettes can be stored for a few days until this sort of food can once again be faced.

Suppose you have a leg of goose and perhaps a few good pieces of the carcass meat left, then buy 750 g–1 kg (1½–2 lb) of fresh belly of pork, and have the rind cut off. Remove the bones as well, and cut the meat and the goose roughly into 2.5-cm (1-in) square pieces. Put them into an oven pot, adding about 4 tablespoons of the fat saved when the goose was cooked. Pour in about 150 ml (¼ pint) of water, bury a bouquet of herbs and a crushed clove of garlic in the centre of the meat, season with a teaspoon of salt and a little pepper. Cover the pot and cook in a very slow oven (140°C/275°F/gas mark 1) for about 4 hours, until the meats are swimming in their own clear fat. Empty the whole contents of the pan into a sieve standing over a big bowl, and let the fat drip through. Slightly mash the meat, taste it for seasoning and add salt and pepper if necessary, then, with a fork in each hand, pull it into shreds. Pack these very lightly into glazed earthenware or china jars, leaving plenty of room for the fat. When this has cooled, pour it, leaving behind any sediment and juices, over the rillettes, completely filling the jars and covering the top. Put lids on the jars, or tie greaseproof paper over them. If they have to be stored in a refrigerator rather than a larder, take them out some hours before serving, for rillettes should be soft, rather like potted meat. Serve them as an hors d'oeuvre, with bread or toast, but butter will not be needed.

House & Garden, January 1959

CHICKEN VERONICA

Many years ago, when I was living in a tropical climate, I evolved this recipe to replace chicken mayonnaise for picnics and cold suppers. Prepared ahead of time, which they should be, dishes of chicken or fish and mayonnaise tend to acquire an oily and unappetising appearance in warm weather and especially after a long car journey. No matter what the circumstances or the temperature, the cream sauce in this Chicken Veronica retains all its pristine qualities for many hours.

A day or two in advance cook a nice fat boiling fowl of about 2 kg (4 lb) weight, with its giblets (but not the liver, keep that for an omelette, or as a *bonne bouche* for the cat) with 4 or 5 carrots, a couple of onions, a piece of celery, a clove of garlic, a faggot of parsley stalks, tarragon and a strip of lemon peel, 2 tablespoons of salt and water to cover.

The chicken will need about 2½–3 hours very gentle simmering and keep the pot covered but tilt the lid to allow the steam to escape. Should it be more convenient, the cooking can be done in a very slow oven. When the chicken is tender and the flesh beginning to come away from the drumsticks, take it out of the pot and leave it to cool. Strain the stock, measure off 150 ml (¼ pint) for the sauce, and keep the rest aside for a soup or for further cooking with fresh beef and shin of veal for a double consommé. Other ingredients for the sauce are: 300 ml (½ pint) of double cream, 4 tablespoons of rich sherry or Madeira and the yolks of 4 eggs.

Put the cream, the 150 ml (¼ pint) of chicken stock and the sherry into a wide and shallow saucepan such as a sauté pan. When this mixture is hot, pour a little of it on to the very well whisked egg yolks. Stir thoroughly. Return all to the first pan. Stir over very gentle heat until the sauce begins to thicken. In a wide pan this happens quite quickly, in a tall deep one it takes an eternity. But don't let the mixture overheat, and keep stirring all the time or the eggs will scramble. The finished sauce should be of the consistency of a home-made custard. Rectify the seasoning. You may need more salt, possibly lemon juice. You may even add a drop or two of Armagnac, Cognac or Calvados, perhaps a little more sherry. When you take the sauce from the heat, go on stirring it until it has cooled a little.

Carve the chicken into nice, even-sized pieces, not too big and not too small. Keep all skin and bone for strengthening the original stock when you cook it up again.

Arrange the chicken pieces in a shallow dish. Pour the sauce through a strainer over the chicken. If it looks rather liquid at this stage remember that it thickens as it cools. Before serving, sprinkle chopped parsley, tarragon or chives over the dish.

At Christmas time this recipe can be usefully applied to cold turkey.

Cooking with Le Creuset, 1969

RICE AND CUCUMBER SALAD

This makes just the right accompaniment to the chicken dish.

For 6 to 8 people put 500 g (1 lb) of good quality rice in an 8-litre (gallon-and-a-half) capacity saucepan nearly full of boiling salted water. Add half a lemon and when the water comes back to the boil float a couple of tablespoons of oil on the top. This will help prevent the water boiling over. The rice will be cooked in 12–18 minutes depending on the type of rice you are using. In any case, keep it on the firm side.

As soon as you have drained the rice in a colander, turn it into a big bowl. Immediately, add any necessary salt, approximately 6 tablespoons of oil, 2 teaspoons of tarragon vinegar, 2 shallots sliced into paper-thin rounds, and a good quantity of grated nutmeg. This latter seasoning makes the whole difference.

Have ready a cucumber, peeled, sliced in four lengthways, the seeds removed, the flesh cut into small cubes, and seasoned with salt. Mix these with the rice. Add also, if you like, a dozen or so black olives, a few cubes of raw celery, and a few shreds of raw green pepper (tinned red peppers are not to be recommended for this dish, they are too soft, too sweet, and too obtrusive). Mix all together very lightly and the salad is ready, except for a sprinkling of chives or parsley.

As a change from cucumber, try instead little cubes of green or yellow honeydew melon which goes well with both chicken and turkey.

Cooking with Le Creuset, 1969

CHICKEN BAKED WITH ITALIAN SPICE AND OLIVE OIL

For this extremely simple dish, you need a really good roasting chicken, free range if you can find one, of approximately 1.8 kg (3¼ lb) when dressed and drawn, 3–4 tablespoons of good olive oil, a half-teaspoon of the Italian spice described on page 95, and salt, plus foil or greaseproof paper for wrapping the chicken and a pastry brush for coating it with the olive oil while cooking.

Rub the cleaned chicken with salt and paint it with about half the olive oil, then rub in the spice.

Wrap the chicken in paper or foil, put it on its side in a shallow fireproof dish. Cook it on the centre shelf of a medium hot oven

(180°C/350°F/gas mark 4), for 30 minutes before unwrapping it, painting it again with olive oil, turning it over on to the other side, re-covering it with the paper, and this time leaving it for 20 minutes.

Now turn the chicken breast upwards, use the rest of the olive oil for brushing it over once more, and leave it, again covered, for the final 20 minutes.

Remove the paper or foil carefully so that the juices fall back into the baking dish. Heat them quickly, pour them into a small bowl or sauce boat and use them as the only sauce necessary with the chicken.

The taste of the spice and the olive oil make a delicate seasoning for the chicken which, given a properly reared bird, will be perfectly cooked, very moist, tender, and the legs still a little pink inside. It will be excellent as a cold dish. Leave it to cool naturally, and serve it with a very simple salad.

The small quantity of olive oil is all that is needed for keeping the chicken moist. All the basting considered necessary with poor quality birds is quite redundant when you are dealing with a good one. And as for that maddening thing called a bulb baster, I never have understood what anyone could possibly need it for.

Unpublished, 1970s

LEMON AND GARLIC SAUCE OR MARINADE FOR GRILLED CHICKEN

For this excellent Lebanese sauce, used for marinating chicken to be grilled over charcoal, the requirements are really good firm garlic, a juicy lemon, coarse salt, fruity olive oil.

For 1 small chicken or 500 g (1 lb) of pork fillet (tenderloin) you will need approximately 12 garlic cloves (15 g/½ oz when peeled), 1 lemon, 1 tablespoon of coarse salt, 2 tablespoons of olive oil.

Skin the cloves of garlic (fewer are needed if the cloves are large), pound them in a mortar with the salt, add the strained juice – say 3–4 tablespoons – of a lemon, then stir in the olive oil.

Turn the sauce into a clean bowl, keep it covered until you are ready to use it. All garlic sauces are at their best when the garlic is fresh, so do not make it too long in advance – and, above all, a

garlic press should not be used for this sauce. Garlic is obviously a potent ingredient. It should not be an acrid one, which it becomes when the juices only are extracted by the crushing action of the garlic press.

Marinate chicken legs or breasts for 2 hours. Legs will require 30–40 minutes to cook through, boned breasts 10–15 minutes. Cubes of pork fillet marinaded in the same mixture and grilled on skewers are perhaps even more successful than chicken. Grill for 20 minutes.

Twelve cloves of garlic may sound overpowering. Curiously enough, by the time the sauce has been, as it were, distributed among the pieces of meat or chicken, it is by no means too strong, and meat with a tendency to dryness is much benefited by the

combined flavours as well as by the action on it of the constituents
of the marinade.

Unpublished, 1970s

POULET ROBERT

This is a Norman chicken dish – one for a special treat for 2 or 3
people – and although it comes from only just across the Channel
it has a wonderfully unfamiliar flavour.

For a roasting chicken weighing approximately 1.2 kg (2½ lb),
the other ingredients are 45 g (1½ oz) butter, 2 tablespoons olive
oil, 1 onion, 60 g (2 oz) ham, a teaspoon of chopped tarragon or
celery leaves, 150 ml (¼ pint) of white table wine or medium dry
still cider, a teaspoon of strong yellow mustard, salt, freshly milled
pepper, and 4 tablespoons of Calvados. This last is the celebrated
and potent Norman spirit distilled from cider, but our own native
whisky can be used instead – it's a better substitute in this case
than cognac.

In a heavy cast-iron pot in which the chicken will fit neatly,
heat the butter and oil and in it melt the sliced onion with the
chopped ham. Add the neck, heart and gizzard and then the
chicken, seasoned inside with salt, pepper and the tarragon or
celery. Let it brown gently on both sides.

In a soup ladle or small saucepan warm the Calvados or whisky
and set light to it. Pour it blazing over the chicken, at the same
time turning up the heat and tilting the pot from side to side until
the flames have burned out. Then add the wine or cider. Let it
bubble for two or three minutes. Cover the pot with its lid.
Simmer steadily, not too fast, for 20 minutes. Turn the chicken
over. Cook another 20 minutes. Remove the chicken. Extract the
giblets. Let the remaining sauce boil fast while you quickly joint
the bird.

Finally, having stirred the mustard into the sauce, pour it with
all its delicious little bits of ham and onion, into a warmed serving
dish, which should be about as deep as an old-fashioned soup
plate – there isn't a lot of sauce but what there is has an intense
and rich flavour – and put the pieces of chicken on top. Scatter a
little parsley over it. The accompaniment to this dish should be
either 2 dessert apples, peeled, cubed and fried in butter; or plain
little new potatoes; or 250 g (½ lb) of small sliced mushrooms

cooked in butter. No green vegetable – but most decidedly a fresh crisp green salad.

If you have to keep the chicken waiting while a first course is being eaten, then place your dish, covered, over a saucepan of gently simmering water. This is a better system than putting it into the oven, where the sauce would go on cooking and the butter and liquid would separate, leaving rather a messy mixture.

From a pamphlet written for Le Creuset, late 1960s

BIANCO-MANGIARE

A kind of cold chicken pâté.

300–375 g (10–12 oz) cooked chicken, weighed without skin and
    bone
60 g (2 oz) almonds, skinned
2 eggs
150 ml (¼ pint) cream
2 tablespoons rosewater
3 tiny slices green ginger
salt, sugar
for decorating: pine nuts or split almonds

Almonds to be ground very fine.
Chicken in grinder with rosewater, ginger, sugar, very little salt.
Stir in almonds.
Beat in eggs. Fold in cream. Add more salt if necessary.
Turn into non-stick loaf tin. Cover with foil.
Cook in a bain-marie, 170°C/325°F/gas mark 3, below the centre,
    for 50 minutes.
Cool and put into the fridge.
Next day turn out. Stand the tin in a little cold water for a few
    minutes before inverting it on to the dish. After a sharp tap or
    two with a knife handle the pâté should slide out easily.
Stick toasted pine nuts or almond slivers upright all over, like a
    hedgehog.

This is a manuscript recipe, written in note form, for Elizabeth's friend Lesley O'Malley, probably in the 1970s. The information is indeed brief, but to the point; you are told when to add each ingredient, and how. Most importantly, you are told at what temperature and for how long to cook the bianco-mangiare. JN

DUCK BAKED IN CIDER

Rub a 3 kg (6 lb) duck thoroughly with about 125 g (¼ lb) of coarse salt; leave it with its salt in a deep dish for 24 hours, turning it once or twice and rubbing the salt well in. To cook it, wash off the salt with cold water.

In a deep baking dish or enamelled tin with a cover (such as a self-basting roasting pan) put a couple of carrots, an unpeeled onion, a clove of garlic, a bouquet of herbs, and the giblets but not the liver of the duck. Place the duck on top of the vegetables, pour over about 450 ml (¾ pint) of dry vintage cider, and then fill up with water barely to cover the duck. Put the lid on the pan, stand this pan in a tin of water, cook in a very slow oven (150°C/300°F/gas mark 2) for just about 2 hours.

If to be served hot, take the cover off the pan during the final 15 minutes cooking, so that the skin of the duck is baked a beautiful pale golden-brown. If to be served cold, which is perhaps even better, leave it to cool for half an hour or so in its cooking liquid before taking it out.

The flavour of this duck is so good that only the simplest of salads is required to go with it.

The stock, strained, with fat removed, makes a splendid basis for mushroom or lentil soup, or for onion soup.

Unpublished, 1960s

PARTRIDGES STEWED IN MILK

For 4 stewing partridges the other ingredients are 90 g (3 oz) of butter, 750 ml (1¼ pints) of milk, 600 ml (1 pint) of water, 3 level tablespoons of flour, seasonings.

Brown the birds gently in the butter in a heavy and fairly deep stewing pot. Over them pour 600 ml (1 pint) of the milk, hot, and the water, also hot. When the liquid reaches simmering point, cover the pot, transfer it to a very low oven (150°C/300°F/gas mark 2) and leave it for a minimum of 3½–4 hours. At this stage the birds should be tender, but as a matter of fact old partridges are often so incredibly tough that I have before now left them as long as 7 hours without them coming to the slightest harm.

To make the sauce, mix the flour and the rest of the milk (cold) to a smooth paste in a saucepan. Put it over very gentle heat and gradually add some of the hot liquid from the partridges, stirring all the time until the sauce is thick and smooth. To give the sauce an extra lift, a couple of tablespoons of brandy, Calvados or Armagnac could be added at this point. The sauce should not be too thick – just about the consistency of thick cream.

Discard any liquid remaining in the pot. Pour the sauce (through a strainer if by any chance it has turned lumpy) over the partridges and return the pot, covered, to the oven for at least another half hour. Serve with plain boiled potatoes and french beans.

This is simply the basic method of making the dish and small variations can be made by anyone with a bit of imagination.

With mushrooms or celery

250 g (½ lb) of mushrooms – sliced or quartered, cooked a minute or two in butter, well seasoned, and added to the sauce when it is thickened – make a big improvement. Alternatively, a couple of tablespoons of chopped celery or watercress or a seasoning of half a dozen crushed juniper berries.

Sunday Dispatch, 1950s

Alexis Soyer

Head chef in charge of a brigade of twelve undercooks in a Paris restaurant at the age of seventeen, Alexis Soyer came to England in 1831. In five years, working first under the aegis of his brother Philippe, chef to the Duke of Cambridge, subsequently in the kitchens of the Duke of Sutherland, the Marquess of Waterford, and for four years at Aston Hall, Oswestry, seat of a gentleman called Lloyd, he had made his mark among the London aristocracy and the landed gentry as a chef of great flair with a brilliant gift for organisation.

In 1837, still only twenty-five years old, Soyer was offered the post of chief cook at the recently constituted Reform Club. The offer carried with it the opportunity to have his say in the lay-out and furnishing of the kitchens in the great new Club house planned to replace the old premises in Pall Mall. The architect was to be Charles Barry, and Soyer was to collaborate with him on the overall design of the kitchen quarters, the stoves, the equipment. For the ambitious, inventive, hyperactive young Frenchman it was the chance of a lifetime.

Soyer's activities at the Reform are legendary. Within half a dozen years of the opening of the splendid new Club house in March 1841, he had made himself one of the three best known chefs in London. The Reform's kitchens were the most talked of, most visited in the country. Cooking was done on a variety of fuels. There were coal, charcoal, and gas stoves – the latter a great innovation. The meat and game larder was fitted with slate dresser tops and lead-lined ice drawers, the temperature maintained at 35 to 40 degrees Fahrenheit. The fish was kept fresh on a large marble slab with three-inch high slate sides, and cooled by a constant stream of iced water. The table in the principal kitchen was made of elm, in an ingenious twelve-sided design. In the centre of the table was a cast-iron steam closet in which delicate entrées could be kept hot. On either side, the two columns support-ing the kitchen ceiling passed through the table, and Soyer utilised them as supports for tin-lined copper condiment cases in which spices, salt, freshly chopped herbs, breadcrumbs and bottled fish sauces were kept. All seasonings were thus ready to hand for each cook working at the table without moving from his or her place. (Several of Soyer's assistant cooks were young women.)

Today's kitchen planners could do worse than make a study of Soyer's own descriptions of his kitchen furnishings and of the illustrations supplied in his famous book *The Gastronomic Regenerator*. His gift for publicity, on the other hand, and his almost manic pursuit of it, would be difficult to emulate. It far out-classed that of any present-day Bocuse. What he might have done given television promotions, colour supplement treatments, public cookery demonstrations, chat show appearances, news-paper interviews, is scarcely to be contemplated. As an organiser of fund-raising events and famine relief he could have made Bob Geldof look like the village vicar. Even in mid nineteenth-century England, everything Soyer did was instant news. Whatever novelty he produced, from a new bottled sauce to a pair of poultry dissectors, from a six-inch portable table cooker to a gas-fired apparatus for roasting a whole ox, every London newspaper, a good many provincial ones, and often a few Paris journals thrown in, had their say, and at length, about his latest doings. To *Punch* his whole career proved a god-sent gift.

When *The Gastronomic Regenerator*, a work of well over 700 pages, appeared in 1846, *The Times* compared the author's labours to those of a Prime Minister or a Lord Chancellor, invoking for good measure the great names of Sir Robert Peel and the famously versatile Lord Brougham. Soyer's book, it was revealed by *The Times*, had taken ten months to prepare, and during that time the great chef had furnished 25,000 dinners, 38 important banquets comprising 70,000 dishes, had besides provided daily for sixty Club servants, and received the visits of 15,000 strangers 'all too eager to inspect the renowned altar of a great Apician temple'.

Impressive figures indeed. But *The Times* reviewer was quoting them from Soyer's own foreword which he called *Description of the Composition of this Work*, in other words what would nowadays be the blurb printed on the dust-jacket. So the Thunderer's tongue, it is to be feared, was ever so slightly in its cheek when it remarked that there was nothing to admire more in Soyer than his matchless modesty. Modesty, and matchless at that, isn't the epithet that most immediately springs to mind in connection with Soyer. But reading the account of his life put together by his former secretaries, F. Volant and J. R. Warren, as a tribute following his death in 1858 and published in 1859, it becomes plain that, while modesty was not his strong suit – his achievements were after all something to boast about – he was at the same time an affectionate, endearing, much-loved, and rather touching character. I don't think, in spite of his undoubted administrative genius and his marvellously inventive mind, that he ever quite grew up. Certainly he never grew out of his love of theatrical exploits, absurd practical jokes, awful puns, dressing up. His whirlwind enthusiasms and financial fecklessness were characteristics which alternately aroused the protective instincts and the exasperation of his friends.

The little volume, which his secretaries called *Memoirs of Alexis Soyer*, and in which their subject's qualities and defects are very fairly assessed, must have been published in a small edition – surprisingly in view of Soyer's contemporary fame – and is now a collector's item of extreme rarity. The *Memoirs* make a valuable

addition to the story of the Reform Club's genie, the man who also volunteered to organise the almost non-existent cooking for the troops in the Crimea, who attempted to relieve the Irish during the famine, who could as easily superintend a 238-cover civic banquet in York in honour of the Prince Consort as a Christmas dinner for 22,000 of London's poor – once more the whole ox roasted by gas – or betake himself to Castle Howard to show off his dexterity with his famous little Magic Stove. Cooking on the supper table in the ballroom (the Queen was staying), Soyer produced, or appeared to produce, his well-known *oeufs au miroir* at the rate of six every two minutes.

Soyer's capacity to turn every event he organised or attended into a major theatrical show, and to get it into the news, was boundless. He could even use an upturned fallen column on the Acropolis as a table on which to set up his Magic Stove and cook a *déjeuner à la fourchette* (his own term) for half a dozen travelling companions on their way to the Crimea, and then write home to the *Illustrated London News* describing the event. The resulting illustration may be seen in *Soyer's Culinary Campaign*, his account of his Crimea activities, published in 1857.

If those who already possess a copy of the Helen Morris biography *Portrait of a Chef*, published in 1938, find that some of the stories in *Memoirs of Alexis Soyer* sound familiar, it is because they are. Mrs Morris lifted large chunks of the Volant/Warren book, sometimes word for word, and without the slightest mention of its existence. It was an odd omission, for her book was not in other ways dishonest and, although rather plodding, does provide detail and the hindsight of posterity naturally lacking in the little book written with such immediacy after its hero's sad death at the age of forty-eight. For reference, both volumes are needed. But poor Mrs Morris has been properly found out.

One of the great treats in the Volant and Warren book is their account, as participators in its creation, of the extravaganza at Gore House which Soyer christened his Universal Symposium. There he had organised kitchens producing foods of all nations, installed restaurants and refreshment rooms appropriate to all pockets. It was a palace of entertainment for the visitors to the Great Exhibition of 1851. Lady Blessington's one-time salons and boudoirs were transformed into pagodas, pavilions, kiosks, arctic grottoes filled with mirrors and real ice, crystal-ceilinged caverns. In the grounds were picnic tents and a gigantic banqueting pavilion. Fountains and statuary were everywhere. As a theatrical impresario Soyer was born out of his time. His proper element would have been the Hollywood of the great silent epics. At least when his Universal Symposium was demolished it was replaced by a building not inappropriate in scale and purpose. It was the Albert Hall.

Tatler, March 1986

Perfumed Toothpicks and
Table-hopping Birds

Bartolomeo Scappi's *Opera (Work)*, later subtitled *Del Arte Dal Cucinare* or *The Art of Cookery*, was first published in 1570. Scappi, who was probably of Bolognese origin, called himself Cuoco Secreto, personal or private cook, to Pope Pio V, who reigned from January 1566 until 1 May 1572. Pius V, formerly Cardinal Ghisleri of Bologna, was one of several grandees of the Church who had employed Scappi, among them that Cardinal Campeggio who with Wolsey had presided over the court which in 1529 heard Henry VIII's divorce suit against Catherine of Aragon.

By 1536 Campeggio was installed in a palazzo in Trastevere, across the Tiber from Rome, and there, in April of that year, he gave a magnificent dinner to the Emperor Charles V, a celebration of his Imperial Majesty's formal visit to Pope Paul III.

Although it was still Lent, neither the grandeur of the occasion nor the lavish arrays of food were affected. There was of course no meat, but every fishy delicacy to be found in Italy was produced for the Emperor, and caviar imported from the *mar maggior*, the Black Sea, appeared twice during the feast, once plain with lemon juice, once in pies. There were truffles stewed in oil and citron juice, five separate salads, asparagus, capers, small lettuces, borage flowers, rosemary flowers. Raw sweet fennel, which figures in almost every one of the meals recorded by Scappi, whatever the season, made two appearances.

In honour of the Emperor a good deal of gold was in evidence. Large prawns – I think they were the ones we know as scampi –

cooked in wine were presented with their tails and claws gilded and silvered, and for eating the sweetmeats and conserves in the two final services – there had already been ten, for just twelve persons – gold and silver forks replaced the ordinary ones which had been used throughout the meal. (In 1536 any kind of table fork was an extreme rarity.)

Perfumed toothpicks and small bunches of flowers with silvered and gilded stalks were then placed before each guest, there was music, singing, live birds let loose from within the folds of starched and intricately-folded damask napkins hopped or flew around, and Cardinal Campeggio's imperial entertainment had clearly been a triumphant success.

The memorable meals recorded by Scappi, fascinating though they are, fill only one of the six books into which his *Opera* is divided. Recipes are the mainstay of the work. With the exception of tomatoes, peppers and potatoes, which had not reached his cooking pots, Scappi covers almost everything edible, from anchovies and aubergines – he calls them *molignane* – to *zambaglione* (three versions) and *zazzeri*, otherwise strips of dried gourd skin, part-boiled then re-cooked in a sauce of almonds or walnuts and garlic. A pound of *zazzeri* – the Roman pound was then about 10½ ounces – made enough for five dishes. They don't sound very enticing, but they were certainly economical.

Some of Scappi's most attractive recipes are to be found in his final chapter, which deals with food for convalescents and the sick. Here are no fearsome brews of sparrows' brains and dung such as physicians of the day were given to inflicting on their patients, but straightforward consommés, almond broths, green herb omelettes, simple fruit tarts filled with melon, pears, bitter cherries, peaches, quinces.

Then there are two *zambaglione*, one much as we know it today except that chicken broth is added to the eggs, sugar, and wine – Scappi used sweet malmsey – along with a heavy flavouring of cinnamon. The second version is a broth made green with pounded mint, marjoram and parsley. Beaten eggs and acid green grapes or gooseberries are added, together with grated bread. The mixture is cooked until it thickens and it is served hot. The broth apart, it sounds a bit like a fancy modern stuffing for turkey.

It is scarcely possible in a short article to convey an idea of the riches to be found in Scappi's book or of its truly magisterial quality, but for those who have the necessary Italian– there has never been a translation – it provides a lifetime of absorbing and enriching reading.

Now for a little book as different as can be from Scappi. Small, French, confined to one subject only, it was in its minor way quite as definitive. Its title is *L'Art de bien faire les glaces d'office*, it was published in Paris in 1768 and its author, Emy, describes himself as *officier*, meaning in this context, confectioner. That is all we know of the writer of this delightful treatise on ices, although the evidence of his own writing shows him to have been thoroughly conversant with the history of artificial freezing as well as with its practice and the confection of the cream and fruit ices for which he gives appetising and well-balanced recipes.

The variety he describes is equally impressive. Orange flowers, violets, rose petals, almonds, walnuts, hazelnuts, chestnuts, pistachios, black truffles, saffron and rye bread went into Emy's ices, and so of course did coffee, chocolate, caramelised sugar, and aromatics such as vanilla, cinnamon and cloves. He even devised pineapple ices, the last word in novelty. That rare fruit, he considered, was better in ices than in its natural state.

I don't think any of today's Florentine, Roman or Sicilian ice-cream shops offers more tempting variety than did Emy writing just about one hundred years after Louis XIV, his court, and the Parisian public, had first been introduced to those frozen delights. Lucky the people who enjoyed his ices.

So far as I know, there was never another edition of Emy's book, but it is worth recording that when in the 1950s I paid a London bookseller £10 10s for my copy, I was told that nobody was interested in the subject. Tastes and times have changed. So have prices. In a recent catalogue sent to me by an antiquarian bookseller a copy of Emy was offered at £700, and I have seen another at £950. Perhaps it would pay some publisher to do a facsimile.

Eliza Acton's *Modern Cookery for Private Families*, published by Longmans in 1845, was initially an immense and deserved success. It ran into several editions – three in the year of publication – and is indeed a very great and original cookery book. Apart from Sir Kenelm Digby's entrancing, posthumous *Closet Opened* of 1669, Eliza Acton's must be the finest in the English language, but after the author's death in 1859, the publisher apparently forgot about her book.

Two years later, in 1861, young Mrs Beeton was not so neglectful. She helped herself to a number of Miss Acton's recipes, publishing them without acknowledgement and in an emasculated form. Miss Acton had expressed herself with some force on the subject of plagiarism – she had had good cause – but now she was dead, and Mrs Beeton's borrowings, to use a euphemism for a disreputable procedure, went unchecked and apparently unnoticed. *Modern Cookery* was available in an abbreviated form in a Penguin paperback, but secondhand copies of the original are infinitely preferable, and not difficult to come by, if rather expensive.

Coming to our own day, one book (of course there are many others) I regard as indispensable and would certainly take to a desert island is Tom Stobart's *Herbs, Spices and Flavourings*. Stobart was a photographer and a mountaineer, and had photographed the famous Everest expedition of 1953. He was also a most gifted writer, who turned what he claimed to be simply a work of reference into an original, irresistible book.

Daily Telegraph, 17 September 1988

The Baking of an English Loaf

A very exaggerated idea of the difficulty and trouble of bread making prevails amongst persons who are entirely ignorant of the process.
Eliza Acton: *The English Bread-Book*, 1857

Any human being possessed of sufficient gumption to track down a source of fresh yeast – it isn't all that rare – and collected enough to remember to buy at the same time a pound or two of plain flour, get it home, take a mixing bowl and a measuring jug from the cupboard, and read a few simple instructions can make a decent loaf of bread.

And if you cannot, after two or three attempts, make a *better* loaf than any to be bought in an English shop – and that goes for health-food and whole-food and crank-food and home-spun shops generally, just as much as for chain bakeries and provision stores and small independent bakers – then I am prepared to eat my hat, your hat, and almost anything else put before me, always with the absolute exception of a loaf of English commercial bread.

Please do not jump to conclusions. It is not my intention to make even a slight attempt to persuade you into baking your own bread. I am simply going to tell you how to set about it if you feel you must, and I find it comical as well as shameful that in this day and age anybody should be forced into so archaic an activity.

No Frenchwoman, at least no French townswoman, would dream of baking her own bread. In France, fresh loaves are baked twice daily by every baker and bought twice daily by every householder. If and when the French bakery system breaks down, there is, as every schoolchild knows, a revolution. Had Marie Antoinette been a French princess rather than a Hapsburg from Vienna, she could never have said, or have been credited with saying, that the people of France could make do with cake instead of bread.

As recently as the summer of 1965, the people of Paris rose up in revolt against the annual August closing of some sixty per cent of the city's bakeries. To Parisians, it had become a major grievance to be obliged to walk perhaps as far as a kilometre to find a baker who kept his business open during the summer exodus to the sea and the country. The Government was obliged to step in and decree that the bakers (not, mind you, the shoe-makers, the plumbers, the electricians, and the laundries, just the bakers) must stagger their holidays. A baker, in other words, has a public responsibility and cannot with impunity desert his post.

In France, a meal without good bread and plenty of it is simply not a meal. For that matter, a meal without bread isn't a meal anywhere in Europe except in England. And I mean England. I do not mean Scotland or Ireland, where it is still possible to buy real bread.

A certain school of English patriot is much given to the expression of belief in the creed that we have in England the finest ingredients in Europe and that 'British cuisine at its best is the best in the world'.

I find it amazing that any responsible person can presume to make such a claim when our basic necessities are so hard to come by, when a new-laid egg is as rare as a flawless ruby, when English butter is not nearly as well made as Dutch, Danish or Polish, when the best fresh vegetables available to Londoners and other city-dwellers are flown from Cyprus or Kenya or sent from Italy, Spain or Madeira, when our cheese is marketed by packaging factories, and when, manifestly, not one householder or one restaurateur in a thousand has grasped the elementary truth that the finest ingredients and the greatest cooking skills this side of Escoffier can combine to produce only a bleak and hollow sham of a meal, joyless and devoid of stimulus, if the customer or the guest is offered no more in the way of bread to go with his food than a skimpy little wedge of white winceyette placed with boarding-house gentility underneath a folded napkin upon a side-plate.

A good many readers of cookery articles must be bored to death with being told that one main dish, with a salad, cheese, and a loaf of crusty bread, makes an ample, balanced, nourishing, economical, easily-cooked and satisfying family meal. Well, so it does, if you can get it; in fact, the bread and the cheese would be a perfectly good meal without the so-called main dish. And the bleak truth is that mighty few of us can lay hands on either the cheese or the bread unless we happen to live within walking distance of a specialist cheese shop and a bakery which is not only independent and bakes its own bread but bakes it well and produces it for sale at an hour when the ordinary householder can go out and buy it.

I was driven to making my own bread because my local bakery, which does, in fact, produce quite acceptable French-type loaves, doesn't have them on sale until midday, at which time I, in common with most other women in my neighbourhood, am already busy at the stove preparing lunch and it is highly inconvenient to leave the house. And such is the demand for even remotely edible bread, that if I leave my shopping until the afternoon, nothing but wrapped and sliced factory loaves are left on the baker's shelves.

I repeat, I am not canvassing those who are prepared to put up with shop bread because they just have not the time or inclination to make it themselves; I am not preaching to those who buy shop bread because they actually like it; I am giving instructions purely as basic guidance to those who have already reached the conclusion that it is pretty ludicrous to spend three days planning menus to include shrimp-filled avocados, trout with almonds, fillet of beef in puff pastry, pineapple ice cream and no end of a palaver over the grinding and percolating of the coffee, if they cannot offer their guests a decent piece of bread. It should be added, in fairness, that in those households where home-made and well-made bread is on offer nobody needs to worry about all that prestige-type food. Have it by all means, if that's what you like, but if it's prestige you're after – or, to put it in a cruder way and since it isn't unknown to any of us occasionally to do the right things for the wrong reasons – what will most impress your friends and arouse the maximum envy in your rivals is the sight and the taste of fresh, authentic, un-cranky bread, with its slightly rough and open texture, plain unvarnished crust, and perceptibly salty bite.

This is the kind of bread which should be cut in good thick chunky slices straight from the loaf left upon the table for all to see and enjoy.

In fact, if I go into a friend's dining room and see no loaf on the table, I feel as uneasy as I do if there is no evidence of wine glasses or bottles. Now that I've been forced into making my own bread, I often take it with me. Nobody takes offence, any more than they did in the days of rationing when it was the custom to take one's own marge or butter, sugar and eggs, or egg, whenever invited out to a meal.

It's only a matter of time before the braver and angrier among us start taking our own bread to restaurants. After all, there are plenty of establishments to which we may take our own wine. I see nothing to prevent us taking our own bread as well. The restaurateurs can always increase their cover charges to include the loan of a bread knife – if they have one.

Flour for Bread

The ideal flours for English bread, and for all yeast doughs, are milled from hard wheat, whereas cake, short pastry and sauce flours are or should be soft-wheat flours. Hard flours have a high gluten content, which makes the dough more elastic and expansive. Soft flour tends to make rather flat bread. (French bread is mostly made from a softish flour because this is the type of wheat mainly grown in France. The French have adapted their bread techniques to their flour.) Nearly all the ordinary white flour sold by grocers in London and the southern area is soft household flour. In the Midlands and the North, where home-baked bread and yeast cakes are still made, the requisite flours are easier to come by.

Whole-wheat flour, stone-ground, 100%, 90% or 85%, whole

wheatmeal, can be bought from health food stores and the like. The first type, 100% wholemeal, is the whole grain of the wheat with nothing removed and nothing added. The 85% and 90% wheatmeal have husk and bran removed and make a lighter and finer loaf. Some wholefood addicts recommend these flours for pastry and sauces. I don't.

The difference between hard gluten flours and ordinary soft household flours becomes apparent as soon as you start handling the dough. The first almost immediately becomes springy and lithe, the latter tends to be sticky and puttyish, although it becomes harder with kneading.

Flours can be mixed. For example, to save continual journeys and the carrying of large parcels of flour bought from a special shop, a mixture of say 125 g (4 oz) of 100% whole wheatmeal flour and 375 g (12 oz) of ordinary soft household flour make a quite respectable pale brown loaf, although not such a good one as strong plain or bakers' white flour and 85% or 90% whole wheatmeal flour in the same proportions.

Some of the whole wheatmeal flours on sale in health food and crank shops make a heavy and pudding-like loaf. For that matter, much of the bread sold in these shops is inexpertly made, dry, heavy, calculated to put all but nut-food nuts right off home-made bread for life. Into the bargain, so-called home-made health food is extortionately expensive.

The Yeast

In spite of the disappearance of huge numbers of small independent bakeries, a few such shops are still to be found in most towns and suburbs. The bread they sell may not be up to much, but at least most of them will supply yeast if asked. If they won't, it is because, in the concise phrase used by Mr Clement Freud in an *Observer* cookery article, they are bloody-minded. Or it could be that, as in the case of one of my local Chelsea bakeries, the assistants have made their own bye-laws as to the times of day they will dispense yeast. Or it may depend entirely upon the attitude adopted by the customer.

My own experience is that yeast should be asked for not as a rare favour ('We don't *sell* yeast, we oblige with it,' I have been told by bakeresses) but as a commodity which it is to be taken for granted is sold by a baker as a publican sells beer and as a newsagent sells newspapers.

As opposed to brewers' yeast, which is liquid (and very bitter), bakers' yeast (formerly called German yeast, no doubt because it came from Holland) is compressed yeast. It looks like putty-coloured plasticine. Bakers who make their own bread on the premises will sell yeast – if they sell it at all – in small quantities, from 30 g (1 oz) upwards. Bakers' yeast is also now sold by some health and whole-food shops.

Yeast can be stored for several days in an airtight box in the refrigerator, so long as it is kept perfectly dry.

It should feel cool and plastic to the touch and smell sweet and alive. The fresher the yeast, the easier it is to make the dough and the better the resulting loaf.

15 g (½ oz) of bakers' yeast will aerate 500–750 g (1–1½ lb) of flour. For a 1.5 kg (3 lb) batch of dough, use 30 g (1 oz) of yeast.

Dough made with dried yeast in granules takes a lot longer to rise than dough made with bakers' yeast, and the resulting bread tends to be dry and uninteresting because it lacks the characteristic flavour and smell of yeast. In other words, I find dried yeast unsatisfactory, although many people swear that it's just as good and as easy to work with as bakers' yeast.*

The Equipment

1. A small self-sealing plastic box for the storage of yeast in the refrigerator.
2. Scales.
3. A cup for mixing the yeast and water.
4. A measuring jug.
5. A large mixing bowl or bread panshon (a wide earthenware bowl glazed inside) or large wooden bowl.
6. A flour-shaker or caster.
7. A plastic or rubber or wooden spatula or scraper.
8. A clean tea-cloth and a small thick towel.
9. Bread tins (1.2-litre/2-pint capacity for a loaf made with 500 g/ 1 lb of flour and 300 ml/½ pint of water). An attractive flat round loaf can be made in a shallow (5-cm/2-in) French cake tin. I make most of my bread in this type of tin, because I prefer the maximum

---

* I've now found out what goes wrong. Most people use too much dried yeast, and don't wait for it to re-activate properly. I've made plenty of excellent bread leavened with dried yeast. Just don't use too much, don't mix too much sugar with it – and give it time.

proportion of crust to crumb. An ordinary round 1 kg (2 lb) cake tin also makes an attractive loaf. A long narrow aluminium tin makes a beautiful loaf, easy for slicing and ideal for sandwiches. It is worth bearing in mind that English bread used to be baked in earthenware pans. If you have no suitable tins, perhaps you have a straightforward earthenware casserole or pie dish which will serve the purpose. Some people even use ordinary flowerpots, very well rubbed with fat and they make perfectly good loaves. At Easter, I make bread in the fish-shaped moulds traditional to Alsace and Germany.

10. A wire grid or cake cooling rack.

AN ENGLISH LOAF

My advice to beginners is to start with the basic recipe for a loaf made with 500 g (1 lb) of flour, 15 g (½ oz) of yeast and 300 ml (½ pint) of water, and baked in a 1.2-litre (2-pint) capacity tin. Only when it is made and cut and pronounced passable or a failure, read the remainder of these notes. Then make another loaf. If after two or three attempts things still don't seem quite right, try one of the variations. My recipe suits me and I know that it has suited quite a few complete beginners. That doesn't say it will suit everybody. No recipe ever suits everybody, and this is perhaps more true of bread making and baking than of any other branch of cookery, with the exception of meat roasting.

For a loaf of 85% or 90% whole wheat flour or plain white flour, preferably strong or bakers' flour, you need: 500 g (1 lb) plain white or wholemeal flour (or 350 g/12 oz to 125 g/4 oz wheatmeal), plus a little flour in a shaker or a bowl for sprinkling on the dough while kneading, 15 g (½ oz) bakers' yeast, 2 heaped teaspoons of coarse rock or sea salt (more if you like salty bread – I do), and use 30 g (1 oz) per 500 g (1 lb) flour, about 300 ml (½ pint) of tepid water, fat for greasing the bread tin.

Put the yeast into a teacup, make it into a cream with 2 or 3 tablespoons of cold or tepid water.

Take off your rings and put them in a safe place.*

---

* This recipe was originally written for my sister Diana Grey, whose tendency to mislay her engagement ring while cooking has caused many a household drama. In fact it is always wise, when working with dough which may be sticky, to remove any ring other than a plain band.

Put the flour into a big wide bowl, mix well, make a hole in the centre of the flour and pour in the yeast and water paste. Flick the flour over the yeast. Add the water, into which you have stirred the salt until it has dissolved. You may need a little more or a little less than the 300 ml (½ pint); this depends on the flour. Mix the dough. This can be done with your hands or with a spatula or long-handled wooden spoon. The mixture should come away fairly smoothly from the bowl, like pastry dough. At this stage, start kneading. (With a small batch of bread, you don't need a board; mixing and kneading can be done in the bowl.) Almost at once, you feel that the dough is beginning to acquire its proper elastic quality. If it is too soft and wet – that is, if you have added too much water – you can dry it by sprinkling it with more flour, but after you have made bread a few times, you won't need to do this because you will get to know just how much water your flour will absorb. Within a few seconds, the dough should be pliable enough to be rolled or folded over on itself in a roughly three-cornered fashion, then to be punched down again. If at this stage the dough is sticky, sprinkle it again with flour. Repeat the folding process three or four times.

Now form it into a large bun shape. Sprinkle it with flour, cover the bowl with a floured tea-cloth (the flour is to prevent the dough sticking to the cloth as it rises), and a small thick towel, folded.

In the winter, I leave my dough for its first rising for one to one and a half hours on top of the stove while the oven is on at 140°C/275°F/gas mark 1. When the weather is exceptionally cold, increase the oven heat a little.

The dough is sufficiently risen when it has just about doubled in volume.

Butter or grease a 1.2-litre (2-pint) capacity tin, warm it in the oven for a minute or two. Break down the risen dough. Knead it very thoroughly. Soon it will be like a piece of thick smooth cloth which you can pick up and smack down again on the table or into the bowl. This second kneading is more important than the first. The more you knock the dough about, the better it will be. The object is temporarily to check the action of the yeast. The second kneading for a pound of dough takes a maximum of three minutes. A big batch of dough obviously takes longer.

Advice to owners of electric mixers with dough-mixer attachment: do the kneading by hand until you get used to the process;

when you know how it should feel and look, you can make larger batches and use the mixer.

Put the dough into the prepared tin, sprinkling the top with flour (for a wholemeal or half-wholemeal loaf, use wholemeal rather than white flour for this operation – it makes a more attractive crust) and giving it roughly the shape of the tin, which at this stage looks a good deal too big for the amount of dough.

Cover the tin with the floured cloth and towel and return it to a warm place for the dough to rise for the second time. In about 45 minutes to an hour (on top of the stove with the oven alight), the dough should have risen to the top of the tin and is ready to bake.

The airing cupboard and a warm spot close to a boiler are alternatives, and in summer, particularly in steamy weather, the dough can be left uncovered on the kitchen table without benefit of extra heat.

By this time, have the oven turned on at 240°C/475°F/gas mark 9. Put the bread in the centre of the oven. After 15 minutes turn down the heat to 220°C/425°F/gas mark 7. Cook for another 25–30 minutes. By now the loaf is slightly shrunk in the tin. Turn it out of the tin upside down on to a wire rack on the kitchen table. With your knuckle, tap the underside of the loaf. If it sounds hollow, like a drum, it is cooked. If it feels soft, it is undercooked. Return it, upside down, to the oven and let it cook for another 10–15 minutes with the oven turned down to 200°C/400°F/gas mark 6. An alternative timing, and temperature, is about 50 minutes at 220°C/425°F/gas mark 7 throughout the whole baking. Where bread is concerned a little too long in the oven is preferable to an undercooked loaf.

Always let the bread cool on a wire rack or grid, so that air circulates round it.

When the loaf is cool, wrap it in a clean cloth or put it in a bread crock or enamelled bin. Plastic boxes soften the crust.

Variations on the Basic Bread Recipe: A Quickly Made Loaf

Once you know how to make bread, you find that there are many variations on the basic method. You can, for example, get up quite late in the morning and still bake a fresh loaf in time for lunch.

For this method, I used a slightly smaller tin than usual.

Procedure: measure out 250 g (½ lb) of strong plain flour and 125 g (4 oz) of 85% or 90% wheatmeal. Have your 15 g (½ oz) yeast ready, and make it into the usual cream with a little tepid water. Put 20 g (¼ oz) of pounded *gros sel* into your measuring jug. Cover it with a little *very hot* water so that it dissolves. Add enough tepid water to make up 250 ml (8 fl oz).

Stir the yeast into the flour in the usual way. Add the water, mix the dough very quickly, and do not knead very much.

Put the dough straight into the greased and floured tin. Sprinkle the top with flour, cover it and leave it on top of the stove to rise as usual, but turning your oven a little higher – say to 180°C/350°F/gas mark 4 – for about an hour (although the timing can vary from 45 minutes to 1½ hours according to outside climatic conditions), and the dough will have risen to the top of the tin. Turn the oven to 230°C/450°F/gas mark 8 and when it has been heating for 15 minutes, put the bread in to bake as usual.

Although the quantity of dough is less than for the basic recipe, the baking time is the same or even slightly longer, because a loaf made with only one turn of rising and very little kneading must be very thoroughly baked.

Bread made by this method may have a few holes in the texture. It will be very good while fresh, but will not keep so well as a loaf made by the orthodox method.

Quite often when I come home from my shop in the evening, I find it possible to make, by this method, a quick loaf for a late supper or for next day's sandwich lunch.

A Loaf Made by the Extra Slow Method

Sometimes it may be convenient to prolong rather than to hurry the rising of your bread dough. Nothing is easier.

Use the quantities and the mixing method given in the basic recipe, page 223. Instead of leaving the dough in a warm place to rise, put it in a well-covered bowl in a cool spot, for example, near an open window in an unheated room. There are those who advocate the refrigerator for a still slower method. The dough can now be left for 8 to 10 hours. When it is fully risen, it will be unusually light and spongy. It must be very thoroughly knocked down and kneaded for rather longer than usual before it is put, as in the basic method, into the ready-prepared tin to rise for the second time.

By the slowed-up method, the second raising of the dough will also take a little longer than usual. To speed matters – and also to improve the appearance of the loaf – two or three deep slanting cuts can be made in the dough. For this purpose, there is a special utensil called a Scotch scraper or dough-cutter – a wide-bladed curved-edge knife similar to the instrument used by butchers to scrape their meat-chopping blocks. Failing this, the crescent-shaped chopping knife, nowadays sold with a wooden chopping bowl in every kitchen utensil shop, will serve the purpose.

The rest of the preparations and the baking of this loaf are as for the basic method.

The slowed-up system produces an excellent, well-grown* loaf with good keeping qualities.

First published in *Queen*, 4 December 1968

The Baking of an English Loaf was subsequently published as a booklet by Elizabeth David in 1969, and reprinted several times. In 1973 Elizabeth signed the contract with Penguin Books for *Baking your Loaf*, intended as the second volume of ENGLISH COOKING, ANCIENT AND MODERN. This was the title we had conceived for what was to be her new series of quite short books on English food, which started with *Spices, Salt and Aromatics in the English Kitchen*. The book took three years to write, instead of the one originally envisaged, as she explored baking in great depth. Published in 1977 as *English Bread and Yeast Cookery*, the book sold out on publication as thousands of people took to bread making. Restaurants also improved the quality of the bread they offered and the appreciation of and demand for good bread had changed for ever in Britain.

JN

SALTED AND SPICED BREAD STRIPS OR RIBBONS

This is a very easy, light bread dough, and the system of dividing it into strips or ribbon shape before baking results in a most original form of roll, very convenient for a party, as it is quickly baked and needs no slicing at table.

To make about 3 dozen strips, quantities are 500 g (1 lb) of white flour (ordinary plain can be used), 15 g (½ oz or 1 scant

---

* The term used by bakers to denote a shapely, professional loaf.

tablespoon) of yeast, 450 ml (¾ pint) of milk, 30 g (1 oz) of butter, 2 teaspoons of salt. For adding to the dough after the first rising: 2 teaspoons of fennel seeds, cumin seeds or caraway seeds, whichever you prefer. For strewing over the ribbons before baking: extra salt, preferably in coarse crystal form, and a few more seeds, and for brushing the dough, a little milk.

Put the flour and salt into a bowl. Stir in the yeast, then the warm milk and butter. Mix to a fairly firm, smooth and flexible dough. Cover and leave to rise for about an hour, or until at least doubled in volume, and very puffy and light. Knock the dough down, knead it a little, working in the warmed seeds as you do so. Divide it into two equal portions. Press each of these out flat on a floured board or baking sheet (if you have a non-stick one, it is just the thing for this type of dough), then with a rolling pin, roll the dough into a rectangle, as neatly and evenly shaped as you can manage.

Repeat the process with the second portion of dough. If your rectangles of dough have been rolled out on a board, transfer them to a floured baking sheet. With a sharp knife, make one cut right through the centre of each rectangle, from one side to the other. Then, working from top to bottom cut long strips, about 2.5 cm (1 in) in width, so that the whole rectangle is literally cut to ribbons, but left in its original shape.

Brush the ribbons with milk, scatter a few more seeds over them, and add a good sprinkling of coarse salt (Maldon salt in flakes is especially successful for the purpose, but crystals of sea or rock salt will also serve very well.)

Leave the dough to recover its spring. This will take about 15–30 minutes.

Have the oven heated to 200°C/400°F/gas mark 6 and bake the ribbons on the centre shelf for 15 minutes, and for another 5 on the lowest shelf.

By the time the ribbons are cooked, they will have puffed up, expanded and almost re-joined themselves into one rectangle of bread; they are however easily broken apart, and can be piled lightly on to a dish or in a basket. They are delicious while still warm, with soft mild cheeses, and with rough red wine.

Notes
  1. Of the three seeds specified – fennel, cumin and caraway – my own preference is for fennel. Cumin comes second, caraway last (I think that it is the hardness of caraway seeds which I find

off-putting, rather than the flavour or the aroma.) Aniseed is a fourth possibility, and one which I have not yet explored. Poppy seeds or sesame seeds could be tried, although for me they are too sweet for this type of bread.

2. Delicious hot cheese sandwiches can be made with bread ribbons. Simply slit them and insert a finger of melting cheese such as Port Salut, Gruyère, or Bel Paese into each, heat them on the lowest shelf of a very moderate oven, 170°C/325°F/gas mark 3, for about 10 minutes.

3. This milk and butter dough is a particularly good-tempered one, and if you prefer to cook half the batch only and leave the rest for later on, simply break it down, knead it into a ball, leave it in its bowl, put this in a cool place, and the dough will be just as good several hours later.

Written for *English Bread and Yeast Cookery*, but not included

CHEESE AND DILL STICKS

A richer, puffier dough than the one used for salted and spiced ribbons, and a really excellent confection to offer with the white wine which so many of us now drink as an aperitif instead of spirits or vermouth.

For the first trial, make a small quantity as follows: 250 g (½ lb) strong plain flour, 2 teaspoons of salt, 7 g (¼ oz) of yeast, 125 g (4 oz) of butter, 6 tablespoons of cream, 3 teaspoons of dill seeds, 60–90 g (2–3 oz) of a soft melting cheese such as Bel Paese, Port Salut or Gruyère, a little extra cream for brushing the dough.

Put the flour and salt in a bowl, cream the yeast with a little water. Warm the butter until it is quite soft. Rub it into the flour. Add the creamed yeast, then mix to a light dough with the warmed cream. Form it into a ball, cover and leave to rise until it is light and puffy, and at least doubled in volume.

Strew a little flour on a non-stick baking sheet. Break down the dough, rather gently, scatter in two teaspoons of the dill seeds. Put the dough on the floured baking sheet, press it out into a rectangle roughly 23 × 18 cm (9 × 7 in), then with a rolling pin, roll it out quite evenly. On it strew the cheese, cut into tiny cubes. Fold the dough into three. Roll out and fold again, twice, rather as if for puff pastry or croissant dough, but very quickly and lightly, and without waiting to rest the dough between each turn.

Finally when you have rolled the dough out into a 23 × 18 cm (9 × 7 in) rectangle for the fourth time, make three lengthways cuts right through the dough, then ten to twelve cuts the other way. The cuts should go right through the dough.

Brush the surface with a little cream or milk, sprinkle the remaining teaspoonful of dill seeds on the top, cover with a light cloth and leave the dough to recover, for about 30 minutes.

Bake in the centre of the oven, 200°C/400°F/gas mark 6, for 15 minutes, and for another 10 minutes on the bottom shelf, at the same temperature. (If you intend reheating the sticks, take them out after the first 15 minutes, and reheat them on the bottom shelf when convenient.)

During the baking, the sticks join themselves together again but are still clearly defined so that it is a matter of seconds to divide them, making neat portions, all except the outside sticks having soft sides, with the cheese melting in the middle. This system of baking rolls, buns and so on so that they re-adhere as they rise in the oven is called 'baking crumby'.

These little sticks are very easy to make and most delicious. There will be about 3 dozen little sticks, but provided you have a large enough baking sheet and oven, it is perfectly simple to double the quantities of ingredients and divide the dough into two rectangles, or make one large one.

Written for *English Bread and Yeast Cookery*, but not included

FARINATA, ALSO CALLED *TORTA DI CECI OR FAÏNA ALLA GENOVESE*

Ingredients: 250 g (½ lb) chick pea flour, 1 tablespoon of salt, 800 ml of water (1½ pints less 2 or 3 tablespoons) olive oil, salt, pepper.

Put the chick pea flour in a bowl, add the water a little at a time, stirring well. When smooth and about the consistency of pancake batter, add the salt. Cover and leave for a minimum of 4 hours, or overnight if more convenient.

Into a shallow earthenware dish approximately 28 cm (11 in) in diameter pour enough olive oil to cover the surface rather amply. Stir the batter and pour it into the dish. Again stir it well, so that the oil and batter are well incorporated.

Bake the *farinata* in a hot oven (properly, it is cooked in a bread oven), 220°C/425°F/gas mark 7, for about 50 minutes, until the top is golden and crusty. Serve it hot, sprinkled with freshly milled pepper, and cut into lozenges. Normally, *farinata* is eaten as a snack rather than served at meals, although at San Remo where it is made very thin and sold in the great covered market, it is served as an entrée, accompanied by a salad of assorted small chicory leaves – an excellent combination.

Notes

1. Among other variations, the *farinata* of Oneglia is strewn with very finely sliced onions before it is consigned to the oven, and at Savona it is sprinkled with rosemary leaves and baked in an open, wood-fired oven, with the burning logs surrounding the pan – in much the same way as the traditional *sardenara* (the pizza of the San Remo area – *see* p. 233) is, or was, cooked.

2. The thickness of the *farinata* varies a good deal. Sometimes, as at San Remo, it is little thicker than a pancake; at Oneglia it is traditionally 2–3 cm (1–1¼ in) thick. Beyond that it becomes stodgy.

3. A variation of my own is to strew the *farinata* with a few fennel seeds before baking it – or stir them into the batter if you prefer. The Genoese are fond of fennel seeds as a flavouring, and remembering an excellent flat bread or galette – locally they call it a pizza – strewn with fennel, I borrowed the idea. To my mind, the fennel flavouring is a great improvement on rosemary.

4. To reheat *farinata* simply sprinkle it with olive oil and put it in a moderate oven for a few minutes, or cut it in wedges and either toast them, or cover each with a slice of cheese and bake them in a hot oven.

5. Across the Italian border, in the Niçois country, the equivalent of *farinata* or *faïna* is called *soca*. Traditionally it is cooked, like the San Remo version, on a round iron baking sheet with a shallow rim and in an open, wood-fired oven. In the markets it is kept hot on its own iron sheets over charcoal braziers and sold in small portions.

6. Yet another variation is the *panisse*, for which the chick pea flour is first cooked in water to a thick porridge, then poured into oiled saucers, left to set, turned out and fried golden in olive oil: like *soca*, *panisses*, familiar in the Niçois area, and called *panissa* or *paniccia* in Genoese, are sold in the markets and by street vendors.

7. Italian chick pea flour is not to be found in England, but the Indian equivalent, called gram flour or *besun*, is just the same. It is to be bought in Indian provision shops and sometimes wholefood stores. Indians will tell you that gram flour is ground from lentils; this is because they class the chick pea among the dhal or lentils.

Unpublished, 1970s

Variations of Pizza

A few weeks ago I read, in a catering trade magazine, an account of a pizza house recently opened in the university city of Oxford. Ingredients used for the fillings, it was reported, were ham and onions, ham and pineapple, ground beef, prawns, sardines and anchovies, hot salami and olives, mushrooms, onions and egg, and to conclude the list 'a superior Special which has everything'.

Oh dear. A pizza with everything is just what I don't want. Some people, of course, and I'm afraid this is a very English disease – perhaps in Denmark you don't suffer from it – tend to think that the more ingredients you can cram into any dish and the more oddly assorted they are the more interesting the result will be. Others regard the cheap and popular specialities of other countries simply as a means of using up left-overs. They equate cheapness with lack of balance. This results in such dishes as the Italian risotto, the pizza, and I regret to say the Scandinavian smorgasbord, being the ones people think about on the day they've just cleared the refrigerator and brought to light a saucer-ful of green peas, three mushrooms, a grilled sausage, and half a tin of sardines – not to mention, *pace* the Oxford operator reported above, a few pineapple chunks and a slice or two of salami.

It's a pity. Those who treat the pizza as a dustbin miss the joy of fresh hot dough, well-risen and spongy, with an onion and tomato mixture, aromatic and pungent, seeping into the air pockets to form one delicious whole. This is really the whole point of the pizza at its best: dough and filling should become one and indivisible, and when a miscellaneous collection of knobbly, unyielding things are piled on top of a piece of dough no fusion can take place. In the heat of the oven the bits and pieces become tough and rubbery and indigestible. It's not surprising that the pizza very often has a bad name as a stodgy and coarse dish for the undiscriminating. Once, though, that you have learned how to make it with a light dough and a simple basic sauce or filling you begin to see why it is such an excellent invention, and why it has achieved world-wide popularity. You quickly discover also what a world of difference there is in both cost and quality between the pizza you make yourself and the one you buy from the deep-freeze counter or eat in a pizza house.

A LIGURIAN PIZZA OR SARDENARA

For a 22–24-cm (8½–9½-in) pizza, the ingredients for the dough are 150 g (5 oz) of plain unbleached bread flour, 1 teaspoon of salt, 7 g (¼ oz) of yeast, 2–3 tablespoons of olive oil, 4–5 table-spoons of milk, 1 whole egg.

Warm the flour and salt. Mix the yeast to a cream with 2 tablespoons of the tepid milk. Break the egg into the centre of the flour. Pour in the creamed yeast and 2 tablespoons of olive oil. Mix to a light soft dough. If too dry add the rest of the milk and another tablespoon of oil. Form into a ball. Cover with a sheet of polythene and leave in a warm place to rise. Allow 2 hours.

For the filling: 500 g (1 lb) of ripe tomatoes or half and half fresh and Italian tinned tomatoes, 2 small onions, 2 cloves of garlic, seasonings of salt, sugar, freshly milled pepper, and dried oregano (the Italian version of dried marjoram), olive oil, a small tin (50 g/approx. 2 oz) of anchovy fillets in oil. Optionally, 8–10 small black olives. There is no cheese on this pizza.

Slice the peeled onions very thinly. Cook them very gently in 4 or 5 tablespoons of olive oil in a covered pan until they are pale yellow and quite soft. They must not frizzle or turn brown. Add the skinned and chopped tomatoes. Increase the heat. Add seasonings and the crushed cloves of garlic. Cook uncovered until most of the water from the tomatoes has evaporated and you have a fairly thick sauce.

When the dough is ready, that is when it has just about trebled in volume and is light and puffy, break it down, shape it into a ball, and pat it out into a 22-cm (8½-in) disc on a perfectly flat, oiled fireproof platter, or on a baking sheet.

Spread the warm sauce lightly on the dough, leaving a little uncovered round the outer edge. Make a lattice pattern with the anchovies, and if you are using the olives, stone them, cut them in halves, and add them to make a decorative pattern. Scatter a little more oregano and a little more olive oil over the filling and leave to rise for 15 to 20 minutes before putting it into the centre of the oven to bake. Temperature should be fairly hot, 220°C/425°F/gas mark 7, and the pizza will take from 20–25 minutes to cook.

There will be enough for 2 to 4, depending on appetite and what else you have for the meal.

Notes

1. If you like the pizza can be cooked in a 24-cm (9½-in) removable-base tart tin.

2. Unless you can get the right kind of olives, very small and black, it is best to omit them. The large, brownish, rather acrid ones are useless for a pizza. In Provence, the country people use olives so small that they don't even bother to stone them.

3. There is no cheese in a Ligurian pizza, nor in a Provençal one, and personally I find these versions much the best. Those who prefer the Neapolitan style, with mozzarella, will find that it is advisable to add the cheese (about 125 g/4 oz cut into slices) only half way through the cooking. In this way, it doesn't get quite so tough and rubbery.

A PIZZA IN THE ROMAN WAY

In the pizzeria where I used often to eat when I spent a winter in Rome twenty-five years ago, by far the best pizza was spread only with onions stewed in olive oil and seasoned with oregano. The Romans themselves claim this as the only true pizza, and dismiss the tomato and mozzarella version of Naples as a fanciful upstart.

To make the Roman onion pizza all you need, then, is dough as for Ligurian pizza (page 233), about 750 g (1½ lb) of onion cut into fine rings, stewed slowly, slowly, in fruity olive oil until quite soft and yellow. Season with salt and a good sprinkling of oregano. Spread on the prepared and well-risen dough. Add a little extra oil and bake as above.

A PROVENÇAL PISSALADIÈRE

This used to be spread with a brined fish product called *pissala*, peculiar to the Mediterranean coast between Nice and Marseille. It is now a thing of the past, and the pissaladière is made mainly with stewed onions and anchovies. There is also a version in which a tomato sauce figures. This one is excellent.

It is made as follows: spread the dough (made as for Ligurian pizza, page 233), with a mixture of 6 tablespoons of the onion and tomato sauce (also made as for the Ligurian version), the contents of a 60-g (2-oz) tin of anchovy fillets and 2 cloves of garlic pounded up together, almost to a paste. Bake as before. This anchovy filling is my own favourite.

A PIZZA IN THE ARMENIAN MANNER

The Armenians claim that they invented the pizza, and that theirs is of far older origin than the Italian and Provençal versions. Very possibly they are right. After all, leavened dough and the domed bread ovens still used for pizza-baking in Italy are both believed to have come to southern Europe from Asia Minor, and to this day the typical, traditional bread of the Middle Eastern world is a flat loaf which forms a pocket in which the basis of a splendid portable meal – olives, white cheese, mint, coriander leaves and raw tomatoes – can be enclosed. Sometimes meat, charcoal-grilled on skewers, is slid off the skewers into the pocket of bread.

It isn't so far from there to the disc of dough which is the basis of the pizza, the Armenian variation being made with minced meat. I use lamb or pork, and spread it on top of the dough, in the Italian fashion – and a portable meal it still is.

Mix double quantities of dough (recipe as for Ligurian pizza, page 233), with 250 g (8 oz) of flour, 15 g (½ oz) of yeast, 3 tablespoons of olive oil, 8–10 tablespoons of milk, 2 teaspoons of salt and 1 large egg.

For the filling: 200 g (7 oz) of raw or cooked minced lamb or pork, 1 small onion, 2 or 3 cloves of garlic, a small tin of peeled tomatoes, salt, olive oil, and seasonings of ground cinnamon, cumin seeds, cloves, pepper and dried mint. The ground seeds of a plant called sumac are also a typical aromatic of the Levantine pizza filling; it is one that is hard to come by in Europe, but even without it the dish is still a winner. Many variations can be made on the spicing and seasoning.

For cooking this pizza you will need a 28–30-cm (11–12-in) flat earthenware platter or baking sheet.

To cook the filling: melt the chopped onion in olive oil. Add the meat and let it brown gently; put in the peeled and crushed garlic cloves, a level teaspoon each of cinnamon and ground cumin, a half-teaspoonful of ground cloves, and the same of freshly ground black peppercorns. Add the tomatoes from the tin, cover the pan, simmer gently until the juice from the tomatoes has evaporated and the whole mixture is fairly thick. Taste it for seasoning. It should be well spiced, and may need a little more pepper and perhaps extra cumin. A little sugar may be needed, and at this stage a teaspoonful of dried mint is also added.

When the dough is well-risen and light, pat it out on the oiled platter, spread it with the filling, leave it to rise again, and bake it as for the Ligurian pizza.

Notes

This Armenian variation of the pizza is one for which a left-over ingredient, in this case cold meat from a roast joint, can be used without detriment to the finished dish. In fact, it provides one of the best ways I know of using up cold lamb. (It is important, though, that the mixture be fairly moist, or it will dry up during baking.) But I wouldn't try adding pineapple and ham, or mushrooms and prawns. You have to know where to stop.

A GENOESE PIZZA

A *pizza genovese* is really more bread than pizza. The embellishments are incorporated into the dough rather than spread over it. The traditional version is made with cracklings, the delicious little pieces of frizzled pork fat left after the rendering down of lard when the pig is killed. It is eaten as an accompaniment to a soup or a meat stew rather than as a dish on its own, and a good variation can be made with little pieces of bacon and the fennel seeds so beloved in Italian cooking.

Simply make the basic pizza dough (page 233), and when it is risen and light, incorporate 125 g (4 oz) of bacon, cooked and cut into very small pieces. Add a tablespoon of fennel seeds (or aniseeds), work the dough as for bread, form it into a nice plump round about 15 cm (6 in) in diameter, sprinkle it with oil, and bake it as described for the Ligurian pizza. Cut it into wedges and serve it hot.

Søndags B-T, Denmark, 1976

Banketting Stuffe

The flowers we have this month are single anemones,
stock gilliflowers, single wall-flowers, primroses,
snowdrops, black hellebore, winter aconite, polyanthus;
and in the hot-beds the narcissus and the hyacinth.

The Complete English Gardener, Samuel Cooke, Gardener at Overton, in Wiltshire. London: Printed for J. Cooke, at Shakespear's-Head, in Pater-noster-Row. *c.*1780.

That little list of December flowers in the garden at Overton in the eighteenth century reminds me of the delightful directions for garnishing a trifle by Esther Copley in her *Housekeepers Guide* of 1834. The recipe is a long one, calling for all the ingredients usual at the period – Naples or sponge biscuits, ratafia drops or miniature macaroons, white wine, brandy, split almonds, jam, a pint of rich thick custard, a pint and a half of whipped cream, a scattering of non-pareils (we now call them hundreds and thousands). Having built up the edifice 'stick here and there a light delicate flower. Be careful to choose only such as are innocent: violets, heart's-ease, polyanthus, primrose, cowslip, geranium, myrtle, virburnum, jessamine, stock gilliflower, and small roses. These will afford variety, and some of them be in season at most times of the year.'

I wonder if the ladies of Overton used some of the innocent flowers, the aconite, the primroses, the polyanthus, grown by Samuel Cooke the gardener to decorate the creams and trifles and custards which surely figured among their desserts at the festive season. How ravishing those eighteenth-century tables must have looked when the crystallised fruit, the oranges and raisins, the spun sugar confections, the trays of syllabubs, the pyramids of jellies, the dishes of little almond cakes shaped into knots and rings and bows, the marchpanes spiked with candied fruit, the curd tarts and all the sweetmeats were spread. No doubt many such delicacies were made in their own stillrooms by the ladies of the household. Others were bought from professional confectioners. Long experience and a specialist's skill were needed – as indeed they still are – to produce the candied and crystallised flowers and fruit, the lemon and orange and citron peel, the sugared almonds, and the gilded marchpane sweetmeats in perfection. Even a great establishment like Woburn, seat of the Earls of Bedford, did not run to a specialist in the art of sugar confectionery. In *Life in a Noble Household* 1641–1700,[1] Gladys Scott-Thompson recounts how anyone visiting Paris was commissioned to bring or send back sweetmeats and even *confiture*, which was more likely to have been a paste of quinces or other fruit than what we know as jam. In 1671 fifty shillings' worth of *confiture* was sent over to the Earl from a Parisian confectioner called Monsieur de Villar, who also supplied candied oranges, lemons, apricots and cherries. For the festive season of 1673/74 the Earl[2] spent nearly £5.00 on sweetmeats from a M. Etienne Emery, known to the Woburn household simply as 'Monsieur'. Monsieur's bill for about 24 lb of candied fruit, chocolate-covered almonds, sugar cakes and marchpanes for that Christmas and New Year gives us some idea of the prices of those luxuries during the second half of the seventeenth century.

Monsieur's bill for sweetmeats.

	£	s.	d.
December 1673.			
4 pounds of machepain biscuit tartlets and conserve.		16	0
5 pounds and 6 ounces of all sorts of sweetmeats.	1	7	0
4 pounds of oranges and lemons.		16	0
January 1673/4.			
2 pounds of sweetmeats.		10	0
2 pounds and halve oranges and lemons and zingo roots.		10	0
1 pound of biscuit.		4	0
1 pound and halve of pistaches.		7	6
2 pounds and a quarter of chocolate amandes.		9	0
	£4	19	6

A point which we don't now always grasp when reading of the meals of the seventeenth century is that in those days, the dessert of sweetmeats and marchpanes, fresh and candied fruits, little cakes and biscuits, was known as the bankett or banquet course, and laid out in a room quite apart from the dining hall where the main meal was served. Sometimes there was even a separate building for the banquet room, perhaps in the garden, after the manner of a summer house, or even on the roof. There the party would proceed after dinner, to find the tables spread with 'banketting stuffe' as the Elizabethans and early Jacobeans had called the dessert. There would be sweet and spiced wines, the candles would be lit, the musicians would play, and if the banquet room was large enough, there would be dancing. *Danser, chanter, vin et espices et torches à allumer*, as the enchanting *Ménagier de Paris*[3] had put it over three centuries earlier.

It was from Italian sources that the English had first learned of the art of sugar confectionery, our early recipes being based on those given in a translation of the French version of an Italian work first published in 1557 by a certain Girolamo Ruscelli, otherwise known as Alexis of Piedmont. This was one of those *Books of Secretes* popular in the sixteenth century, the secrets being at that time mainly medical and cosmetic, and written more for the benefit of professional apothecaries, alchemists and physicians than for the amateur household practitioner. Given, however, the Elizabethan passion for novelty and for knowledge of every kind (the translation appeared in 1558, the year of Elizabeth's accession), it was inevitable that such publications should find their way into many educated households, and the 'secrets' be frequently copied out into the recipe books kept by almost every family cultivated enough to read and write.

So it was that the handful of confectionery recipes contained in *The Secretes of the Reverende Maister Alexis of Piedmont*, translated out of French into English by Wyllyam Warde in 1558, reappear in several little household compilations which found their way into print later in the century. It was a period when sugar was fast replacing honey as the main sweetening and preserving agent for fruit. Everybody wanted to know how to manage sugar, which required different techniques from the old ones used for honey. Alexis of Piedmont dealt with both, which makes his confectionery recipes – there were only a dozen of them – particularly interesting to us, as no doubt also to his original readers.

There were directions for clarifying both honey and sugar, for candying citrons, for candying peaches after the Spanish fashion, for making the conserve or confiture 'of quinces as they dooe in Valence, which also the Genovoyes dooe use'. (This was the French *cotignac* or Italian *cotognata*, the solid quince conserve for which the Genoese were particularly renowned. Under various names such as chardequince or quince meat it had long been familiar as an imported luxury in royal and rich households. It was now being made with sugar instead of honey.) There were methods of conserving melon, pumpkin and marrow rinds in honey, and others for candying green walnuts with spices, cherries preserved in honey, and orange peels also in honey.

Most interesting of all perhaps, to the original readers of the book, were the instructions for making a 'paste of sugre, whereof a man maye make all maner of fruites, and other fyne thynges, with theyr forme, as platters, dishes, glasses, cuppes, and such like thynges, wherewith you may furnish a table; and when you have doen, eate them up. A pleasant thing for them that sit at table.' The recipe is a detailed one for a sugar paste stiffened with gum tragacanth, but still pliable enough to be shaped into 'what things you will' and 'with suche fine knackes as maye serve a table, taking heede that there stand no hote thing nigh unto it. At the end of the banket they may eat al and breake the platters, dishes, glasses, cuppes, and all thinges: for this paste is verie delicate and savourous.'

This was just the kind of fantasy to catch the imagination of the Elizabethans. The pastry cooks must have set to work with great excitement, learning how to model those dishes, glasses and cups in sugar paste, for the amazement and amusement of the ladies and gentlemen who were to banquet off them, and for the pleasure, at the end of it all, of breaking and eating the plates and glasses – always provided that these hadn't already melted in the heat of the candles and the flambeaux.

There was yet another way of devising pretty confections with the sugar plates[4] and dishes, of 'moore finesse' than just straightforward sugar imitations of glass or earthenware. This was to make almond and sugar tarts, 'of like sorte that march paines be made of'. These were to be sandwiched between two sugar paste dishes. In this way there would be a double surprise for the company.

There was no end to the edible pyramids you could build up in this way. From such modest beginnings grew the art of the sugar confectioner, an art which in the Italy of the mid-seventeenth century had already soared to such ambitious heights that the most eminent artists, woodcarvers and sculptors were involved in the design and execution of the ornamental *trionfi*,[5] the triumphs or centrepieces in sugar work made to adorn the feasts given by popes and prelates, princes and noblemen of Rome, Florence, Naples, Mantua, Milan. From Italy this extraordinary art form spread to France, to find its apotheosis in the extravaganza designed by Anthonin Carême, the nineteenth-century chef who is said to have declared that architecture was nothing more than an offshoot of the pastrycook's art.

In less grandiose vein here is one of Alexis' banketting sweetmeats, in shape an early version of Naples biscuits or sponge fingers, but in content more like spice or pepper cakes. The directions give several interesting insights into the techniques of the period.

To make little morsels as they use in Naples, an exquisite thinge, for they be very savourous, do comforte the stomacke, and make a sweet breath.

Take thre pound of fine sugre, yn flower of male vi. pound, of Sinamom thre onces, Nutmegs, ginger, pepper, of eche of them halfe an once, but let the quantitie of the pepper be greater than of the residue, raw white honny, not clarified, three onces. Firste make a round cyrcle with the saide flowre, in the middle whereof, you shal put the sugre, and upon it a pound of Muskt Rose water, bray and breake well all these things with your handes, so longe, untill you feele no more sugre. This done, you shall put in the saide spices, and than the hony, mixinge well all together with your hande.

After this mengle it againe among the flowre, and kepe some of it to flower the tile or other thinges that you must bake it upon. And when all is well broughte and made into past, you shall cut the little morsels in sunder with your handes, making each of them thre onces weight, or there aboute, than turne and make them in to the fourme of a fyshe, dressinge them with youre instrument meete for the same purpose. Than heate your oven and laye them upon little tiles of copper or earth, makinge first upon the tiles a good thicke bed of floure, you must bake them the mouth of the oven open, keping evermore a fire at one of the sides of the mouth of the oven, ye must also touche them often times, to se if they be baked ynoughe, and whether they hange sure, and holde together betwene youre fingers: You may also bake them in the fire in ovens of copper covered, suche as tartes be made in, then when you have taken them out you must gilt them.

The Secrets of the Reverende Maister Alexis of Piedmont: Translated out of French into English by Wyllyam Warde. Imprynted at London by John Kingstone for Nicholas Inglande, dwellinge in Poules Churchyarde. Anno 1558, Mensa Novemb.

References
1. The Bedford Historical Series viii, London, Cape 1940.
2. William Russell, the 5th Earl and first Duke.
3. *Le Ménagier de Paris, Traité de morale et d'économie domestique composé vers 1393 par un bourgeois parisien*: Published for the first time by La Société des Bibliophiles françois 1847. p. 108.
4. Flat sugar discs or lozenges, variously coloured, had been known certainly since the fourteenth century but it was only in the mid-sixteenth century that sugar refining became common in Europe, making sugar both more accessible and more possible to work into complex confections. Printed instructions in English were also now accessible for the first time, Alexis however had almost certainly copied them from an earlier Italian work, probably *Deficio di Ricette*, or *Edifice of Receipts*, published in Venice in 1541.
5. Georgina Masson: *Food as Fine Art*, Apollo, May 1966, and Bartolomeo Stefani, *L'Arte di Ben Cucinare*, 2nd edition, Mantua 1671.

Petits Propos Culinaires No 3, November 1979

Caramel Desserts

Caramel creams, caramel ices, caramel soufflés and mousses, caramelised apples are all delicious light puddings, simple enough to make. Once you know how to cook the sugar for the caramel, there are plenty of variations to be made on the original recipes. Why anybody should think it difficult to caramelise sugar is hard to understand, yet I've heard many people say that a caramel cream for example is 'far too much of a nuisance'; and one must believe that they find it so, or would there be such a ready sale for packets of caramel custard and bottles of ready-made caramel syrup?

CARAMELISED SUGAR

For coating a mould of 1-litre (1¾-pint) capacity, use 6 tablespoons each of white sugar and water. The saucepan is quite a crucial point. On no account use a tinned or enamelled one. The sugar reaches a very high temperature, higher than that of the melting point of tin, so a tinned saucepan will be ruined, while an enamelled one will certainly craze and probably burn. If you have a heavy copper pan lined with stainless steel that would do. I use a small – ½-litre (1-pint) capacity – cast aluminium saucepan, but the professional sugar-boiling pan is made of untinned copper and has a pouring spout.

Put the sugar and water in your saucepan, set it over steady heat. Keep a sharp watch. There is no need to stir, but the quantities are so small that the transformation from sugar and water to caramel happens very quickly. The sugar bubbles, turns pale gold then rapidly goes through several changes of colour until, in a minute or two, it looks like bright, clear butterscotch. This is the moment to snatch the pan from the heat – a few seconds longer and the caramel turns black and bitter. Throw a few drops of cold water into the pan to arrest the bubbling, pour the caramel at once into your mould, tilting and turning this so that as much as possible of the sides as well as the bottom are coated with the caramel, which sets almost instantly.

APPLE CARAMEL (1)

This is a lovely dessert, not expensive and certainly not difficult to make. Quantities given are for 4 servings.

Apart from the caramel made as above, ingredients are 6 apples – say 750 g (1½ lb) – 6 tablespoons of sugar, a vanilla bean, 3 whole eggs.

The mould I use is the kind known as a charlotte mould, made of heavy, tinned steel, with plain, sloping sides. The capacity is 1 litre (1¾ pints), the diameter at the top 14 cm (5½ in), the depth 8.5 cm (3½ in). It has its own cover. Alternatives would be a cake mould or a porcelain soufflé dish.

To make the apple mixture: peel, core and slice the apples. Put them in a wide saucepan with the vanilla bean, the sugar and just enough water to moisten them, say 4 to 6 tablespoons. Cover the pan and let them cook fairly quickly until they are quite soft and transparent. Don't overdo the cooking. Half the charm of this pudding is the cool, fresh taste of the apples. This will disappear if they are stewed to a viscous mass.

Have the caramelised mould ready. (It can be prepared while the apples are cooking, or it can be done well in advance if it happens to suit you.)

Extract the vanilla bean from the apples, turn these into a big bowl, beat them to a purée – there is no necessity to put them through a sieve. Quickly whisk in the very well beaten eggs. These must be thoroughly amalgamated with the apple purée and the whole mixture vigorously whisked. Turn it into the caramel-coated mould, place this, covered with a plate or saucepan lid if it has no cover of its own, in a baking dish filled with water. Ideally, the water should come nearly to the top of the mould.

Cook the pudding low down in the oven, and at a low temperature, 150°C/300°F/gas mark 2, for just about one hour, or until the top is firmly set, but still a little soft to the touch.

Leave the mould in its baking tin for 15 minutes. Then transfer it to the refrigerator.

Turn out the pudding only shortly before you intend to serve it and replace the mould over it to prevent it from spreading. Fresh cream can be offered with apple caramel but is by no means necessary – on the contrary, the apple and egg mixture is itself rather like a creamy and delicate custard, and the coating of liquidised caramel on the top and running down the sides gives it the necessary interest. Cream or a sauce is really a mistake, but what makes a wonderful combination is a glass of sweet Sauternes or other dessert wine, well chilled.

Notes

1. The capacity of the mould is important. The apple and egg mixture should fill it almost to the top. If too large a mould is used the pudding will flop when it is turned out.

2. Covering the mould is important.

3. Cooking the apples as soon as they are sliced is important. If they are left until they start turning brown, the appearance – if not the flavour – of the pudding is spoiled.

4. The quality of the apples is important. I use a mixture of sweet and sharp, say 4 Cox's orange pippins to 2 Granny Smiths, or 1 large Bramley cooking apple. In the latter case reduce the amount of water used for cooking the apples or the mixture will be too wet. When this happens the pudding collapses when you turn it out.

APPLE CARAMEL (2)

This is a variation of the first recipe. The ingredients are the same, the method and the effect rather different.

Instead of using the caramel to line the mould, it is poured over the cooked and chilled apple custard. As the pudding is served from the mould in which it is cooked, choose a glass or porcelain soufflé dish rather than a metal mould. The capacity should be the same – 1 litre (1¾ pints) – but a wider, shallower shape is preferable.

Prepare and cook the apples as described above. Beat in the

eggs, turn into the mould, poach the mixture as in the first recipe. Leave in the refrigerator overnight, or for several hours.

Make the caramel with 6 tablespoons each of sugar and water, just as for coating a mould. Pour it sizzling over the whole surface of the ice-cold apple custard. It will set instantly, forming a thin, brittle covering, as though a clear amber-coloured glass plate had been set over the apple cream.

Cover the dish until it is time to serve it. This should be within a couple of hours, before the caramel turns soft.

APRICOT CARAMEL

This is made in the same way as apple caramel.

Ingredients for the apricot custard are 350 g (12 oz) of dried apricots, 4 whole eggs, 2 tablespoons of honey and the juice of half a lemon.

The caramel is made and the 14-cm (5½-in) charlotte mould coated as explained above.

Soak the apricots for a couple of hours in just enough water to cover them. Cook them in the same water, and without sugar, in a covered casserole in a slow oven for about one hour or until they are swollen and very soft, and all but a spoonful or two of the water evaporated.

Put the apricots into the blender bowl or goblet. Add the honey, the lemon juice and the eggs. Spin to a thick purée. While still warm pour it into the prepared mould. Cover and cook as for the apple caramel, but for a little longer, say an extra 10 minutes.

Serve well chilled with fresh pouring cream.

Note
Dried apricots make a thicker, more solid mixture than apples, so the apricot caramel has a very different consistency, something like that of a soft, moist cake. It holds its shape well.

CRÈME RENVERSÉE AU CARAMEL

This is the beloved crème caramel of French household and restaurant cooking. Under the name of *flan* it is also the favourite pudding of Spain. Even in very humble Spanish restaurants it is rare, or so I have found, to come across a *flan* not made with good fresh milk and eggs.

For a crème caramel to serve 4 people, use a charlotte mould of 1-litre (1¾-pint) capacity, as described above for the apple caramel.

Make the caramel with the same quantities – 6 tablespoons each of sugar and water – and coat the mould.

Ingredients for the custard are 600 ml (1 pint) of rich milk, 2 whole eggs and 3 yolks, 60 g (2 oz) of sugar, a half vanilla bean *or* a bay leaf *or* a strip of lemon peel.

To make the custard put the milk, sugar and chosen flavouring (it's hard to choose. On the whole I prefer the bay leaf which gives out a subtle scent of bitter almond) into a 1½- or 2-litre (3–4-pint) saucepan. Bring the milk very slowly to simmering point.

Whisk the eggs in a bowl big enough to hold the milk as well; having extracted the bay leaf, vanilla bean or lemon peel, pour in the hot milk, whisking vigorously, or use an electric blender if you prefer.

Strain the egg and milk mixture into the mould. Cover it. Stand it in a deep baking tin filled with hot water. Transfer it to the lower shelf of the oven. Cook at 150°C/300°F/gas mark 2 for 1½ hours – a little less, a little more. The cream should be firm but still very slightly trembly. Leave the mould in its baking tin for 15 minutes before transferring it to the refrigerator.

Turn out the crème caramel only shortly before you intend to serve it.

Note
See also the notes to apple caramel. The proportions of whole egg and yolks are only important to crème caramel.

Søndags B-T, Denmark, May 1976

Crème brûlée

The hors-d'oeuvre course of a grand dinner is hardly the place you would expect to find mention of a crème brûlée. Yet in seventeenth-century France, at any rate in the inner circles of Louis XIV's opulent court, that charming custard pudding did figure among the dishes which constituted the hors-d'oeuvre.

It must be explained, though, that in those days hors-d'oeuvre were not at all what they became two centuries later, a selection of cold dishes served as a preliminary to the midday meal, nor were they at all the same manner of dish. Rather they were a mixture of sweet and savoury morsels, light vegetable dishes, veal loaves, sweetbreads, pigeons with fennel or basil, pigs' trotters, fritters and the like, plus confections such as orange creams and blanc-manges of almonds, chicken and rice flour. These delicacies seem to have been an extension of, and on occasion interchangeable with, the *entremets* which followed the roasts of poultry and game, and which concluded the second service of the meal proper. In other words the hors-d'oeuvre were extra titbits and, as the term implies, outside the main business of the dinner. They were evidently provided at grand banquets to keep the company amused and to give them something to peck at during the long interval between courses, so were left on the table until the next service was brought on.

To many people the hors-d'oeuvre and the *entremets* must have been the best parts of those staggeringly tedious three-hour banquets, still conceived very much in the pattern of medieval and early Renaissance feasts, although no doubt the ingredients and the cooking were by now somewhat more refined.

In his influential *Cuisinier Roïal et Bourgeois*, 1691, Massialot gives accounts of several ceremonial dinners held during the previous year, his book being right up to the minute in informing the public what the royal family of France and their immediate entourage were served at banquets.

The dessert fruits and conserves which made up the Third Service were not included in Massialot's book, being the concern of the confectioner rather than of the cook. The creams, the custards, and the fruit tarts, however, were the responsibility of the kitchen proper – or so Massialot asserts – and he duly provides receipts. 'There is Cream of Almond, Cream of Pistachios, Crème brûlée, Crackling Creams, fried creams, and Italian creams, and still many others'.

Most of Massialot's creams are based on custards made with milk, eggs and the chosen flavourings. Here is the 1702 English translation of his receipt for crème brûlée. It was possibly on this receipt that many subsequent English versions were based, although the idea of burnt cream can hardly have been new since it had been known in Italy for about two hundred years. As was also the case with French and Italian milk-based ices, English cooks went one better, and replaced the milk with cream.

BURNT CREAM

Take four or five Yolks of Eggs, according to the bigness of your Dish or Plate; and beat them well in a stew-pan, with as much Flower as you can take up between your Fingers; pouring in Milk by degrees to the quantity of about a Quart:[1] then put into it a small Stick of Cinnamon, with some green Lemmon-peel cut small and likewise some candy'd Orange-peel may also be minc'd as that of Lemmon, and then 'tis call'd *Burnt Cream with Orange*. To render it more delicious, pounded Pistachoes or Almonds may be added, with a little Orange-flower-water. Then set your Cream upon the Furnace, and stir it continually, taking care that it do not stick to the bottom. When it is well boil'd, set a Dish or Plate upon a Furnace, and having pour'd the Cream into it, let it boil again, till you perceive it to stick to the side of the Dish. Then it being set aside, and well sugar'd on the top, besides the Sugar that is put into it; take the Fire-shovel heated red-hot, to give it a fine Gold-colour. To garnish it make use of *Feuillantins* small *Fleurons* or *Meringues*, or other cut Pastry-works of crackling crust. Ice your Cream if you please, or else let it be serv'd up otherwise, always among the Intermesses.'

The Court and Country Cook

[1] In Massialot's own text a *chopine* is 16 oz or half the Paris pint, and one English pint (600 ml), not a quart.

The English translation is not very faithful to Massialot. Apart from the discrepancy in the quantity of milk noted above, the translator changed a direction to draw the dish of thickened custard to the back of the stove into 'set it aside' and rendered 'if not, serve it without that' – ie without the icing, as 'let it be serv'd up otherwise'. No doubt the translator was baffled as to how you would ice your cream when it is already covered with a glaze of burnt sugar. I think that when Massialot said 'ice your cream' he simply meant you could sprinkle it with very finely powdered sugar, the equivalent of today's confectioners' sugar. Or did he meant set it on ice?

Recipes for Burnt Cream began to appear in English cookery books and manuscripts during the first half of the eighteenth century.

TO MAKE BURNT CREAM

This is an unusual version in that the Cream is served hot. It comes from the ms. receipt book of a Mrs Machen of Bloxworth, near Bere Regis, dated 1710 to *c*1750 and was published in *Dorset Dishes of the 18th Century*, ed. J. Stevens Cox, 1961.

'Take the yolks of four Eggs, one spoonfull of flower, a little orange flower water, beat it together, then put in a pint of cream and as much Sugar as will sweeten it, stir it together, put in a stick of Cinnamon, and set it on a gentle fire, keeping it stirring till tis pretty thick, then pour it in the dish you serve it up in let it stand till it is as thick as a custard, then sift Duble refin'd Sugar over it, and hold a red hott Sallimander over it till tis burnt pretty Black, servie it up hott.'

The Burnt Cream recipe in Mrs Rundell's *New System of Domestic Cookery*, first published 1806 is as follows:

Boil a pint (475 ml – being the 16-fl oz pint) of cream with a stick of cinnamon, and some lemon peel; take it off the fire, and pour it very slowly into the yolks of four eggs, stirring till half-cold; sweeten, and take out the spice, etc., pour it into the dish; when cold, strew white powdered sugar over, and brown it with a salamander.

Burnt Cream now disappears from the cookery books for nearly a century. Of the popular household cookery books published during the Victorian era none gives the old recipe. Mrs Rundell's *New System* was, however, still in circulation. Pirated from John Murray by no fewer than five other publishers, it was reprinted for the sixty-eighth time as late as 1867. Possibly it was via Mrs Rundell or simply as a handed-down tradition that Burnt Cream survived. Emanating, at any rate, from an Aberdeenshire country house, the recipe was offered, so the story goes, by a Victorian undergraduate of Trinity to the college cook, who turned it down. In due course the undergraduate, becoming a Fellow of his old college, came up again with his recipe which this time was accepted, and on its way to fame. According to Miss Eleanor Jenkinson, sister of Frances Jenkinson (1889–1923), who in 1908

Crème brûlée

published the story and a version of the recipe in her *Ocklye Cookery Book* (a collector's item, this little book of Edwardian family recipes), the year of the crème brûlée was 1879.

College cooks, it seems, won't divulge recipes (except perhaps to each other) but Miss Jenkinson's differs from Mrs Rundell's only in that the cream and egg mixture is neither sweetened nor flavoured but is returned to the fire to thicken very slightly after the boiling cream has been poured over, and stirred with, the beaten egg yolks. The crust of pounded sugar, spread over the cooled cream and browned with the red hot salamander, should make a hard surface 3 mm (⅛ in) thick and like light brown ice. Miss Jenkinson's plain unsweetened cream seems to me the best of all the recipes.

Assurances of modern cookery books and of several people I know that a perfectly good Burnt Cream can be produced with the aid of an ordinary domestic gas or electric grill are made presumably in good faith but perhaps without first-hand experience of the dish as it should be. Twice in recent months I have eaten it in restaurants. On neither occasion did it come within a hammer's throw of being the semi-liquid cream, calm, undisturbed and covered with the brittle caramel which together made up the potent charm of the dish as I remember it from my early youth in a household wherein dwelled a cook who must have been a dab hand with a salamander, for several of her party puddings were variations on Burnt Cream. Sometimes the caramel concealed an ice, once and most memorably, a frozen gooseberry fool.

My own experience of making crème brûlée by burning the sugar under a gas or electric grill is that the former works well perhaps once out of ten tries and the latter once out of seven. Neither seems quite high enough a percentage for a dish so expensive and of which so much is expected. What happens is that either the sugar, subjected to too prolonged a heating, runs down into the cream, ruining it with toffeeish gobs, or else the caramel blackens, turns to stickjaw, or is otherwise quite unlike Miss Jenkinson's 'light brown ice' and the 'glass-plate' so graphically described by Elizabeth Raffald in her *Experienced English Housekeeper* of 1769.

Compiled from an unpublished article and a *Spectator* article of
23 August 1963

In Pescod Time . . . I went to gather Strawberries

Speaking for myself, I seldom have enough strawberries to do adventurous dishes with them. Strawberry sorbets, fools and ices are so delicious that it seems unnecessary to look further, but so many people now go on pick-it-yourself fruit expeditions that I think the following collection of old, unusual and beautiful strawberry recipes will be of interest, at any rate to those who don't feel like consigning the whole load they've so painstakingly gathered straight to the deep freeze.

My title, by the way, comes from a poem called *The Sheepheards slumber* published in *England's Helicon* in 1600, over the name of Ignotus, said to have been a pseudonym used by Sir Walter Raleigh. That may well be wishful thinking, but at least the tenuous connection makes it appropriate that I should start with Sir Walter's recipe for strawberry cordial.

A CORDIAL WATER OF SIR WALTER RALEIGH

Take a Gallon of Strawberries, and put them into a pint of *Aqua vitae*, let them stand so for four or five days, strain them gently out, and sweeten the water as you please with fine Sugar; or else with perfume.

A Queen's Delight: or, The Art of Preserving, Conserving and Candying; As also A right Knowledge of making Perfumes, and Distilling the most Excellent Waters. Never before Published. Printed by R. Wood for Nath. Brooks, at the Angel in Cornhill, 1658.

Notes

Sir Walter Raleigh's strawberry cordial is a recipe worth following up, although 4.5 litres (8 pints) of strawberries to 600 ml (1 pint) of spirit does seem rather a lot. I tried it one year, using vodka and allowing 600 ml (1 pint) to 1 kg (2 lb) of fruit. After two or three days of steeping the strawberries had given all their colour and scent to the vodka. Having strained them out, it was necessary to filter the vodka, using a coffee paper filter and a glass jug. The filtering was a very slow process, but the result was good, although I think I was wrong in not adding any sugar. A little would have been an improvement.

I think we can accept that the receipt for the cordial really did come from Raleigh, or at any rate that it could have done so. We know that during his imprisonment in the Tower Sir Walter had access to a still and other apparatus necessary for the concoction of cordial spirits, that he availed himself of this welcome diversion and that he communicated the receipts and the 'virtues' of various of his inventions to companions who were with him in the Tower.[1] The 'virtues' of cordials were regarded as medical rather than as purely stimulant. Spirit of strawberries for example was 'excellent good to purifie and cleanse the blood; it preserveth from, and also cureth the yellow Jaundies, and deoppilateth the obstruction of the Spleen; it keepeth the body in a sweet temperateness, and refresheth the spirits. The dose is a spoonful at a time when need requireth any of those helps for the aforesaid diseases.'[2]

References
1. *Home Life under the Stuarts 1603–1649*. Elizabeth Godfrey, London 1925. p. 231. *A Choice Manual, or Rare Secrets in Physick and Chirurgery: Collected and practised by the Right Honourable the Countess of Kent, late deceased*. Nineteenth edition 1687. (First published 1653) Opp. p. 190.
2. *A Choice Manual*, p. 195.

COMPOSTA DI FRAGOLE AL LATTE DI MANDORLE
Compote of strawberries with almond milk

I adapted the recipe for this lovely dish from one given in a book published in Turin in 1846, when that city was still the royal capital of the House of Savoy.

For 500 g (1 lb) of strawberries, make the almond milk with 200 g (7 oz) of shelled almonds – preferably bought in their skins– 3 or 4 bitter almonds (or about 4 drops of pure extract of almonds) 200 ml (7 fl oz) of water. Sugar.

Blanch the almonds, slip them out of their skins, put them to steep in cold water for a couple of hours. Pound them to a paste, adding a few drops of water, or rosewater if you have it, to prevent the almonds oiling. Mix very thoroughly with the water. (The blender can be used for these operations.)

The mixture now has to be wrung twice through a finely woven cloth. This isn't really as daunting as it sounds, but it does take a little time. What should – and does – eventually emerge is a smooth white milk. The residue of almonds is kept for some other dish. Almonds are far too expensive to waste. (A saving can be made – a saving of time too – by simply stirring a couple of tablespoons of very finely ground almonds into 300 ml (10 fl oz) of thin cream. Leave an hour or two and strain.)

Hull the strawberries. Arrange them in a glass or white china compote dish or bowl, (or, perhaps easier to serve, individual goblets or bowls), strew them with sugar. Just before serving – on no account in advance – pour the almond milk over and round the fruit.

Francesco Chapusot. *La Cucina sana, economica ed elegante, secondo le stagioni.* Torino 1846.

Notes

Chapusot was a former head chef to the English ambassador to the Court of Savoy. In spite of his French surname he seems to have been a true Piedmontese by birth, although Piedmont and particularly its capital are close enough to France to seem in some respects very Frenchified. Chapusot's work, published in four slender volumes, each one giving recipes and menus for one season of the year – the strawberry and almond milk compote appears in the Spring volume – represents a school of cooking which is indeed rather franco-italian, although in an unusually delicate way. The ambassadorial style is also unexpectedly restrained, the illustrations of decorative and decorated dishes light and curiously graceful, the menus quite simple for the period. One of them, in which the strawberry and almond milk compote figures, is quoted below. All in all, Chapusot seems to have fulfilled the promise in his title of 'healthy, economical and elegant cooking according to the season'.

The strawberry and almond milk dish figures in a menu for a *pranzo di cacciatore*, a shooting lunch. The other dishes, in the order given, are fried spring chickens with small onions, cold roast beef, timbale of tunny fish, asparagus in salad, and scrambled eggs with ham. Not entirely a cold picnic, so presumably the lunch was to take place in a hunting lodge, with somebody to fry the chickens and make the scrambled eggs, a dish for which few chefs would think it necessary or worthwhile to give a recipe. Chapusot does.

CRÈME DE FRAISES

'Take about one half-setier (250 g/8 oz) of hulled strawberries, washed and drained, which you pound in a mortar, boil three half-setiers (750 ml/1¼ pints) of cream with a half-setier (250 ml/8 fl oz) of milk and some sugar, let them boil and reduce by half, leave to cook a little and put in your strawberries, so mix them together; dilute also a piece of rennet the size of a coffee bean and put it to the cream when it is no more than tepid, at once pass all through a tammy and turn it into a compotier which may be put straight upon the coals without breaking, so put your compotier upon a few hot coals, cover it with a cover and some hot coals on the top; when it has set you are to put it in a cool place or on ice until you serve it.

[Menon] *La Cuisinière Bourgeoise de l'office* etc. Nouvelle Edition. p. 381. A Bruxelles chez François Foppens, Imprimeur-Libraire, 1781. (First published 1745).

Note
I find this strawberry cream or rather strawberry junket a recipe of great interest, foreshadowing as it does the fruit-flavoured yogurts so commercially successful today. It is also a most unusual recipe for the period. But the technique of warming the cream with heat below and above is one we have lost with the disappearance of charcoal and coal burning stoves, and consequently of the utensils with special covers upon which hot coals were placed. It was this top heat which was so important to the successful cooking of a great many creams, open flans, custards and so on. The oven doesn't replace the old *tourtière*, or *testo* as it was called in Italy. So having put the rennet to the tepid strawberry cream I would simply transfer it to a warm place and leave it, as for any other junket, until set. Then into the refrigerator.

TO MAKE SNOW CREAM

Take a large deep dish, strew the bottom with fine sugar beat to powder; then fill it with strawberries; take some sprigs of rosemary, stick a large one in the middle, and several roundabout to resemble a tree; then take 1.2 litres (2 pints) of the thickest cream you can get, and the whites of eight or ten eggs; then whisk it up for half an hour, till you have made the froth very strong; let it stand ten minutes, and with a proper thing take off the froth, throw it over your tree and cover your dish well with it; If you do it well, it makes a grand pile in a dessert.

The Court and Country Confectioner: or the Housekeepers Guide: a new edition. By Mr. Borella, now head confectioner to the Spanish Ambassador in England. London. 1772.

Notes
Mr Borella's charming snow cream is a survival from the seventeenth century, when rosemary sprigs were frequently used in the manner he describes.

Petits Propos Culinaires, No 5, May 1980

SEVILLE ORANGE CREAM

2 Seville oranges, 300 ml (½ pint) double cream, yolks of 4 eggs, 4 tablespoons caster sugar, 2 tablespoons of Grand Marnier.

Pare the orange rind very thinly, boil it for 10 minutes, strain, and pound it to a paste. Add the Grand Marnier, the juice of the oranges, the sugar and the egg yolks, and beat for 10 minutes. Very gradually add the boiling cream and beat until cold. Pour into cups or wine glasses, and serve with a biscuit. Enough for 4.

Those who possess an electric blender will find it works beautifully for this recipe, both for reducing the peel to paste and for blending the other ingredients.

Entertaining with Grand Marnier booklet, n.d.

APRICOT MOUSSE WITH GRAND MARNIER

250 g (½ lb) dried apricots, 90 g (3 oz) sugar, the whites of 4 or 5 eggs, 2 tablespoons Grand Marnier.

Soak the apricots overnight, put them in a pan with the water and simmer until tender. Drain off the liquid, sieve the apricots. Add the sugar and the Grand Marnier. When the purée is quite cool, fold in the very stiffly beaten egg whites, turn rapidly into a soufflé dish, which should be completely filled. Put the dish in a pan of water, and steam on top of the stove for about 35 minutes. Now transfer the mousse, still in its pan of water, to a very slow oven (150°C/300°F/gas mark 2) for another 20 minutes, until the top is pale golden and firm to the touch.

Can be eaten hot or cold, but if the latter, then turn off the oven, but leave the mousse at the bottom, or in the plate drawer, to cool gradually. If exposed at once to the cold air it will collapse.

Entertaining with Grand Marnier booklet, n.d.

SPICED PRUNES

To make this excellent and useful dessert it is essential to use whole spices. Ground ones won't do at all.

For 500 g (1 lb) of large prunes the spices needed are: two 5-cm (2-in) pieces of cinnamon or cassia bark, 2 level teaspoons of coriander seeds, 2 blades of mace, 4 whole cloves.

Put the prunes and spices in a bowl or earthenware casserole. Just cover them with cold water. Leave overnight. Next day cook the prunes, in an uncovered casserole, in a low oven or over very moderate direct heat until they are swollen but not mushy. About half the cooking water will have evaporated. Take out the fruit and remove the stones.

Heat up the remaining juice with the spices, until it is slightly syrupy. Pour it through a strainer over the prunes.

To be eaten cold, with cream or yogurt, or with the cabbage dish on page 79.

Notes

1. Cassia is a variant of cinnamon. The two are very easily distinguished. Cinnamon quills are long, smooth and curled, cassia bark is rough and comes in large chips. Although often held to be inferior to cinnamon there are those – among them some Pakistani cooks – who consider cassia the better of the two. It is indeed cassia bark which appears to be most often used in tandoori restaurant cooking, at any rate in London. Confusion arises

however because Pakistani spice sellers and cooks insist that cassia bark *is* cinnamon.

2. Mace is the beautiful orange lacy covering of the nutmeg. When dried it turns pale tawny in colour and is very hard. It is marketed in broken pieces called blades. These give out a wonderful aroma when cooking. Unfortunately, most people buy mace in powder form and so have no notion whatever of its true character. In this dish of spiced prunes there is no substitute for whole mace.

3. An alternative way of using spiced prunes is to leave them in the turned-out oven after they are cooked. By the time the oven is cold, the prunes have soaked up nearly all the juice. They are fat and swollen. Serve them just as they are, without stoning them, as an after-dinner sweetmeat.

Unpublished, January 1979

GATNABOR
Armenian rice dessert

Cook 90 g (3 oz) of round-grained rice in 600 ml (1 pint) of milk, with a couple of strips of thinly pared lemon rind, and 60 g (2 oz) of sultanas. After about 25 minutes of very slow cooking (in a large, heavy, uncovered saucepan) the rice should be soft and nearly all the milk absorbed.

Stir in 90 g (3 oz) of white sugar, 2 tablespoons of rosewater, and 600 ml (1 pint) of fresh creamy milk.

Put in the refrigerator to cool. Before serving, extract the lemon peel, and add 60 g (2 oz) of toasted and split almonds, and a small glassful of Bacardi rum. Serve very chilled.

This recipe comes from the Armenian Restaurant in Kensington Church Street, London W8. It is a very delicious dessert, and is perhaps at its best when served in individual glasses or bowls, filled well beforehand and left in the refrigerator. The rice should be at the bottom of the bowls covered by the thin milk, while the toasted almonds rise to the top.

The rum is not, I think, strictly necessary. And failing rosewater, orange flower water can be substituted, or alternatively put a half vanilla pod to cook with the rice.

Unpublished, early 1970s

BUDINO DI RICOTTA
Ricotta pudding

A new version of the recipe in *Italian Food*. This is really more like a light soft cake than a pudding. In fact it is the very nicest and most delicate cheesecake filling without the pastry.

Ingredients are: 400 g (14 oz) of ricotta, 1 heaped tablespoon of flour, 4 whole eggs, 4 tablespoons of sugar, a pinch of salt, 1 tablespoon of candied orange or lemon peel, the grated zest of a small lemon, 3 tablespoons of rum, 2 teaspoons of powdered cinnamon.

Press the ricotta through a fine stainless steel wire or nylon sieve. (This operation will only take a minute or two.) Stir in the flour, 1 whole egg, 3 tablespoons of sugar, the salt, lemon zest, candied peel, and 1 teaspoon of cinnamon. Separate the remaining three eggs. Beat the yolks with the rum. Incorporate the ricotta mixture. Have ready a plain cake tin of 1.5-litre (2½-pint) capacity, preferably a non-stick one, buttered and floured. Set the oven to moderate, 180°C/350°F/gas mark 4.

Now whisk the egg whites until they stand in soft peaks. Quickly fold them into the main mixture. Give the tin a light tap

against the table to eliminate air pockets. Bake the cake for 45–50 minutes, just below the centre of the oven. The mixture rises quite a bit (hence the seemingly overlarge tin) but should turn only a very pale gold, not brown. Cream cheese batters burn easily, so take a look after the first 25 minutes of cooking, and if necessary reduce the oven heat. When the cake is just beginning to come away from the sides of the tin it is done. Leave it to cool before turning it out on to a plate or flat dish. Eat cold. Just before serving, sprinkle the top with the reserved sugar and cinnamon, mixed together. Enough for 4 to 6.

Notes

1. As the cake cools it sinks considerably. This is normal, but to ensure that it sinks *evenly* keep it in a warm place while cooling.

2. Instead of candied peel I prefer a mixture of candied angelica and fresh grated orange peel. Or try crystallised ginger or ginger in syrup. Quite unorthodox but interesting.

3. There are many variations of *budino di ricotta*. The above recipe is based on one given by Ada Boni in *La Cucina Romana*, 1st edition Rome 1947.

Unpublished, 1970s

TOURTE À LA CITROUILLE

A new version of the recipe in *French Country Cooking*. This is an interesting dish, a bit of a curiosity. I find the combination of yellow pumpkin and black prunes beautiful as well as unexpectedly good.

500 g (1 lb) peeled, de-seeded pumpkin, 60 g (2 oz) sugar, 150 ml (5 fl oz) fresh cream, 20 prunes, soaked, cooked and stoned, 60 g (2 oz) butter. *For the pastry*: 125 g (4 oz) plain flour, 60 g (2 oz) butter, a pinch of salt.

Make a shortcrust with the flour, butter, a pinch of salt and enough iced water to make a soft dough. Roll into a ball and leave to rest for 2 hours.

Cook the pumpkin, cut into chunks, in the butter. When reduced almost to a purée add the sugar and the cream, then the prunes.

Roll out the pastry to fit a 18-cm (7-in) removable-base pie tin. Line the buttered and floured tin with the pastry. Put in the filling, strew with a little extra sugar. Bake in the centre of a fairly hot oven, 220°C/425°F/gas mark 7, for 15 minutes, then at 190°C/375°F/gas mark 5 for 20–25 minutes.

A variation is to use the flesh of a yellow or green honeydew melon instead of pumpkin. Melon doesn't reduce to a creamy purée as pumpkin does and you need only 350 g (¾ lb), so with one average-sized melon two pies could be made.

Unpublished, early 1970s

LEMON AND BROWN SUGAR CAKE

As an alternative to the rich and leaden fruit cake of Victorian tradition I think this one might prove popular. It has a most refreshing flavour and attractive texture. There is nothing in the least troublesome about it, even to a reluctant cake maker like myself.

Ingredients are 250 g (½ lb) of plain white flour, 125 g (¼ lb) of butter, 125 g (¼ lb) of Demerara cane sugar, 125 g (¼ lb) of seedless raisins, the grated peel and strained juice of one large lemon, 125 ml (4 fl oz) of warm milk, 2 eggs, 1 level teaspoon of bicarbonate of soda. To bake the cake, a 17–18 cm (6½–7 in) round English cake tin, 8 cm (3 in) deep. (I use a non-stick tin.)

Crumble the softened butter into the flour until all is in fine crumbs. Add the grated lemon peel, the sugar, and the raisins. Sift in the bicarbonate. Beat the eggs in the warm milk. Add the strained lemon juice. Quickly incorporate this into the main mixture and pour into the tin. Give the tin a tap or two against the side of the table to eliminate air pockets. Transfer immediately to the preheated oven, 190°C/375°F/gas mark 5. Bake for about 50 minutes until the cake is well risen and a skewer inserted right to the bottom of the cake comes out quite clean. Leave to cool for a few minutes before turning it out of the tin.

Notes

1. The Demerara sugar is important. Barbados is too treacly for this cake.

2. The raisins I have been using of recent years are the little reddish ones, seedless, from Afghanistan. They need no soaking, no treatment at all. Just add them straight into the cake mixture. They are to be found in wholefood shops.

3. It is important to put the cake into the oven as soon as you have added the eggs, milk, and lemon juice mixture. This is because the lemon juice and bicarbonate start reacting directly they come into contact. If the cake is kept waiting, the rising action of the acid and the alkali is partially lost and the cake will rise badly.

4. Under the name of Shooting Cake, the recipe on which mine is based appeared in *Ulster Fare*, a little book published by the Ulster Women's Institute in 1944. I was struck by the composition of the cake – the Demerara sugar, the lemon juice replacing the acid or cream of tartar necessary to activate the bicarbonate and the grated peel instead of the more usual spices.

Unpublished, December 1978

MADELEINES

Madeleines are among the lightest and most beguiling of all French *petits fours* or small cakes. At one time they were made in a variety of sizes and in decorative moulds of different shapes. Nowadays, the name is mainly associated with the scallop shell shape characteristic, originally, of the madeleines of Commercy in Lorraine. These were the madeleines immortalised by Proust. Whatever small mould is used, the French madeleine mixture is extremely simple to cook. (French madeleines are not to be confused with the English coconut-decorated castle-pudding shaped cakes of the same name.)

To make 20–24 madeleines (the number will depend upon the dimensions of the moulds, which vary quite a bit) ingredients are 125 g (4 oz) each of plain flour, butter and sugar; 2 eggs; a teaspoonful of baking powder; 2 of orange flower water or fresh lemon juice; the grated zest of half a lemon; a pinch of salt.

Have the oven turned on to 200°C/400°F/gas mark 6.

Put the flour in a bowl. Sprinkle in the baking powder and salt. Add the sugar and grated lemon rind. Separate the eggs. Stir the yolks into the flour mixture. Add the orange flower water or lemon juice.

Put the butter in a small saucepan or bowl over very low heat until it has softened. Do not let it melt or oil. Keeping back a tablespoon or so for coating the moulds, stir the butter into the main mixture. With a pastry brush dipped in the reserved butter, paint the moulds. (These can be bought in sheets of six or twelve.) Now whisk the egg whites to a stiff snow. Amalgamate them swiftly with the cake batter.

Using a dessertspoon, put the mixture into the moulds. Each mould should be half filled, no more. This is the only difficult moment in the cooking of the madeleines – difficult because it is so hard to believe that the little spoonful of the mixture lying rather sadly in the mould will rise, swell and take on the beautiful shape and markings of the shell mould. At this moment faith is essential; should the moulds be overfilled, the mixture will spread sideways; the result will be a failure.

As soon as the moulds are filled, put them into the oven, on the centre shelf, and preferably on an iron baking sheet. In 14–15 minutes the madeleines should be cooked.

While they are baking, butter and fill a second sheet of moulds with the rest of the mixture. If you have only one sheet, you have to wait until the first batch is cooked. For the cook this slows up the proceedings, but the short wait does not affect the mixture.

When, after the prescribed 14 minutes, you see that the cakes have risen and are a very pale gold, remove them from the oven. Let them rest for just a few seconds before turning them out – using a small palette knife – on to a cooling rack. The underside of the madeleines should be a delicate golden sand colour. As soon as they are cool they are ready to eat, and at their best. They can, however, be reheated, extremely gently and for a few minutes only.

Madeleinettes

These are, fairly obviously, miniature versions of madeleines. The quantities given yield something like 80 madeleinettes, cooked on sheets of 20 moulds and for about 12 instead of 14 minutes.

Note
The lemon zest in the madeleine mixture is unorthodox. I find that it enhances the flavour. Leave it out if you prefer to adhere to tradition.

Unpublished, 1969 and 1971

ALMOND SABLES TO SERVE WITH ICES

150 g (5 oz) of plain white flour, 90 g (3 oz) of icing or caster sugar, 75 g (2½ oz) of almonds, 125 g (4 oz) of butter, 2 egg yolks, lemon juice.

Sift the flour into a mixing bowl. Throw the almonds into a small saucepan of boiling water, remove from the heat, leave for a minute or so before taking out the almonds with a perforated spoon. Skin them quickly, put them on a fireproof plate, dry them in a very low oven for 5 to 7 minutes. Don't leave them long enough to take colour. Put them with the sugar in a food chopper or processor and grind them until powdery. Shake them through a wire sieve into the flour.

With your fingertips rub in the softened butter, as lightly as possible, keeping aside a tablespoon or so for brushing the baking sheet. When the butter, flour, sugar and almond mixture is all in

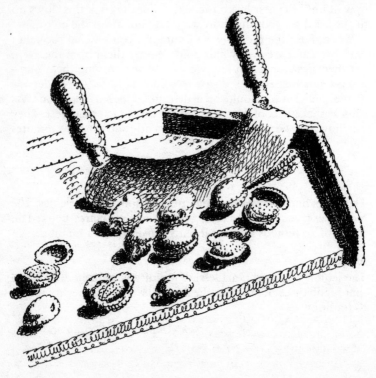

fine crumbs, beat the two egg yolks with a tablespoon of lemon juice and quickly, using a fork, beat them into the pastry mixture.

Roll the dough out lightly on a floured board, gather it up into a ball, leave it to rest, covered with a cloth or wrapped in greaseproof paper, in a cool place for about an hour.

Now roll out the pastry again, not more than 5 mm (¼ in) thick. Cut out small rounds, ovals, diamonds, transferring them as you go to the buttered baking sheet or, better, to a non-stick one. Gather the trimmings into a ball.

Heat the oven to 190°C/375°F/gas mark 5 and put the sablés in to bake when they have rested for about 10 minutes after cutting. They will take 7–8 minutes to bake and should be scarcely browned.

While the first batch is baking, roll out the trimmings, cut out and bake more sablés, repeating the process until all the dough is used up. Yield should be about 3 dozen.

Unpublished, late 1970s

Hunt the Ice Cream

First editions are fascinating to collectors of every category of book, no doubt with good reasons. When it comes to cookery books, however, it is a fearful mistake to pay large sums for first editions and neglect later ones, and this applies particularly to works which have had a long life. In my view – and I don't expect booksellers to agree with me – first editions of such books as Robert May's *Accomplisht Cook* of 1660, Hannah Glasse's *Art of Cookery Made Plain and Easy* 1747, and Mrs Rundell's *New System of Domestic Cookery* 1806 wouldn't be anything like as interesting to serious students of cookery as later ones, in which the authors themselves have made revisions, corrected errors, added new recipes, brought cooking methods up to date, and incorporated recently introduced ingredients.

It is of course – or would be – agreeable to own first editions and to be in a position to make comparisons, study an author's development and changing tastes over a period of time, establish at what moment certain types of recipe started appearing in print, and discover from them small landmarks in social history; but first editions *can* be studied in the great libraries, and furthermore in later and less rare editions the evidence of change is often contained in a new Author's Preface, Introduction or publisher's puff, and is there for anyone who reads their books attentively.

To take *The Art of Cookery Made Plain and Easy*, no cookery book of the eighteenth century provides a better example of the importance of studying successive editions and of the traps lying in wait for anyone who assumes that the earliest editions are more interesting than later ones.

Between 1747 and 1765 nine editions of the Glasse book were published and after the author's death in 1770, many more, pirated by different publishers. The earliest edition I have, or have seen, is the fourth, dated 1751. It was in this edition that the full page engraved advertisement for 'Hannah Glasse, habit maker to Her Royal Highness the Princess of Wales' appeared. It was the first time that the book was openly acknowledged as Mrs Glasse's, her signature, H. Glasse, being printed in facsimile under the title *The Art of Cookery* on page one of the text, although the title page proper still carries the earlier legend: 'By a lady'. It was also in 1751 that a four-page Appendix appeared, apparently for the first time.

Among the handful of 1751 additions in the Appendix were the well-known directions for dressing a turtle the West India way, and a recipe for raspberry ice cream. This is not quite the earliest so far found in an English cookery book,[1] but it precedes the apricot ice cream given by Elizabeth Raffald in *The Experienced English Housekeeper* of 1769 by eighteen years. It is unfortunate that Mr Eric Quayle, author of a recently published picture book (*Old Cookery Books, An Illustrated History*) asserts categorically that Mrs Raffald's was the first ice cream recipe published in an English cookery book. How did he come to miss the Glasse recipe? For that matter how did the O.E.D. miss it?

It is of course difficult to win with Hannah Glasse. Anyone who consulted only very late editions of *The Art of Cookery* might well get the impression that Mrs Glasse had plagiarised Mrs Raffald, for in a posthumous edition of 1784 Mrs Glasse's own raspberry ice cream was replaced with Mrs Raffald's apricot one. Interestingly, in her *Compleat Confectioner*, undated but 'judged by Oxford to be *c.*1760,[2] Mrs Glasse elaborated on her original directions, but did not, I think, borrow or lift from anyone. Not that I am for a moment suggesting that Mrs Glasse was innocent of plagiarism. In *The Art of Cookery* she made very free with the work of her predecessors, as did nearly all other cookery book compilers of her period, and for that matter of any other. In the instance of the ice cream, however, and also of the

The lower part of the frontispiece of Emy's L'Art de bien faire les glaces d'office 1768. (The upper part, too faint to reproduce, shows two ethereal beings reclining on a cloud and awaiting the ice cream which the cherubs are confecting for them.)

many recipes in the lengthy Appendix mentioned above, it is plain to me that she is reporting at first hand, and sometimes with an original and charming turn of phrase.

In the matter of containers for the freezing of her ices, Mrs Glasse used two pewter 'basons', the inner one with a close cover. In this the prepared cream was put. It was then set in the larger one and surrounded with ice and a handful of salt. After three quarters of an hour she uncovered the inner container, stirred the cream, covered it again and left it to freeze for a further half hour. After that, 'turn it into your plate'. That was her 1751 method. In the *Compleat Confectioner* she repeats it, but adds that 'your basons should be three cornered, that four colours may lie in one plate; one colour should be yellow, another green, another red, and a fourth white'. In both recipes she tells her readers that the basons are made at the pewterer's, adding the further note that 'some make their ice cream in tin pans, and mix three pennyworth of saltpetre and two pennyworth of roach allum, both beat fine, with the ice, as also three pennyworth of bay salt; lay it around the pan as above, cover it with a coarse cloth, and let it stand two hours'.

The mention of saltpetre is interesting. It was used to help reduce the temperature, but what the function of the roach or rock alum was I don't know. No doubt someone conversant with physics and chemistry can enlighten me. As to the basons of the original recipe, it occurs to me that by basons Hannah Glasse meant the tall pewter cylinders such as were in use in France for freezing ice creams. They are depicted in the frontispiece of Emy's *L'Art de bien faire les glaces d'office*, 1768, and I remember years ago seeing a splendid collection of them in the pousada at Elvas in Portugal. The 'three-cornered basons' are a little more difficult. I think that very likely they were deep wedge-shaped boxes or moulds with handled covers. When turned out on to a dish four differently coloured ices would form a complete circle, like a cake. An engraving of one such box appears on Plate 6 of Gilliers' famous *Le Cannameliste Français*, first (1751) edition, and is shown on the previous page with one other mould for the freezing of cream which flanks it on the Plate.

Those interested by the way, in knowing more of Mrs Glasse, her origins and career, should consult the original detective work done by Madeleine Hope Dodds, a Northumbrian local historian. The curious story was first told by her in an article called *The Rival*

Cooks, published in 1938 in *Archeologia Aeliana*, the journal of the Northumberland Archaeological Society. A summary of this, written by Mr Norman Brampton, was published in the Wine and Food Society *Quarterly*, no. 114, summer 1962, and a good account, interestingly illustrated and further researched, is given by Anne Willan in her *Great Cooks and Their Recipes. From Taillevent to Escoffier*, a correctly-documented book, although her publishers have made it difficult, owing to fancy production, to read the recipes Miss Willan quotes. Sources of the illustrations also take some ferreting out, but at least they are given. Mr Quayle, on the other hand, does caption most of his illustrations with their sources. There are, however, omissions, and these, together with many preposterous historical blunders other than the one concerning the ice cream, reduce the credibility of the book almost to vanishing point. Why for example are we not told the provenance of the semi-caricature captioned 'The redoubtable Mrs Hannah Glasse'? Authors who claim to write history and fail to cite sources can hardly expect to be taken seriously.

References
1. See Nathaniel Bailey's *Dictionarium domesticum*, 1736, cited by C. Anne Wilson in her admirable book *Food and Drink in Britain*, Constable 1973 and Penguin Books 1976.
2. The B.M. Catalogue puts it at 1770. The second edition is dated 1772.

THREE EARLY ENGLISH ICE CREAM RECIPES
1. FROM NATHANIEL BAILEY'S *DICTIONARIUM DOMESTICUM*, 1736.

To make ICE CREAM

Fill tin icing pots with any sorts of cream you please, either plain or sweetened, or you may fruit it; shut the pots very close; you must allow three pounds of ice to a pot, breaking the ice very small; laying some great pieces at the bottom and top.

Lay some straw in the bottom of a pail, then lay in the ice, putting in amongst it a pound of bay salt; set in your pots of cream, and lay the ice and salt between every pot, so that they may not touch; but the ice must be lai'd round them on every side; and let a good quantity be laid on top; cover the pail with straw, set it in a cellar, where no sun or light comes, and it will be frozen in four hours time; but you may let it stand longer; and take it out just as you use it; if you hold it in your hand and it will slip out.

If you would freeze any sort of fruit, as cherries, currants, raspberries, strawberries, etc. fill the tin pots with the fruit; but as hollow as you can; put lemonade to them, made with spring water, and lemon juice sweetened; put enough in the pots to make the fruit hang together and set them in ice as you do the cream.

2. FROM HANNAH GLASSE'S *ART OF COOKERY MADE PLAIN AND EASY*, 4TH EDITION, 1751.

To make ICE CREAM

Take two Pewter Basons, one larger than the other; the inward one must have a close Cover, into which you are to put your Cream, and mix it with Raspberries, or whatever you like best, to give it a Flavour and a Colour. Sweeten it to your Palate; then cover it close, and set it into the larger Bason. Fill it with Ice, and a Handful of Salt; let it stand in this Ice three Quarters of an Hour, then uncover it, and stir the Cream well together; cover it close again, and let it stand half an Hour longer, after that turn it into your Plate. These things are made at the Pewterers.

Note

Hannah Glasse, *The Art of Cookery Made Plain and Easy*, the Fourth Edition, with Additions 1751, p. 332. Although announced as Additions on the title page, the section of seven extra recipes is actually headed *Appendix*. In the 1758, sixth edition, they were re-titled *Additions*, and confusingly sub-titled *As Printed in the Fifth Edition*. This time the seven recipes had increased to ten, so presumably the three extra ones had appeared in the fifth, 1755 edition, which I have not seen. The sixth edition also has a new *Appendix* running to 45 pages.

3. FROM ELIZABETH RAFFALD'S *THE EXPERIENCED ENGLISH HOUSEKEEPER*, 1769.

To make ICE CREAM

Pare, stone, and scald twelve ripe apricots, beat them fine in a marble mortar, put to them six ounces of double refined sugar, a pint of scalding cream, work it through a hair sieve, put it into a tin that has a close cover, set it in a tub of ice broken small, and a large quantity of salt put amongst it, when you see your cream grow thick round the edges of your tin, stir it, and set it in again till it grows quite thick, when your cream is all froze up, take it out of your tin, and put it into the mould you intend it to be turned out of, then put on the lid, and have ready another tub with ice and salt in as before, put your mould in the middle, and lay your ice under and over it, let it stand four or five hours, dip your tin in warm water when you turn it out; if it be summer, you must not turn it out till the moment you want it: you may use any sort of fruit if you have not apricots, only observe to work it fine.

Note

The text has been copied from the eighth edition of 1782, p. 249. I understand that it does not differ from the text of the first edition. It is the fourth of forty recipes in Chapter X, devoted to Creams, Custards and Cheesecakes; and is the only ice cream in the collection.

Petits Propos Culinaires No. 1, 1979

Making Ice Cream

Some of the most delicious ice creams I have ever eaten were the ones made by Suleiman, my Sudanese cook in Cairo. He used an ancient ice bucket borrowed from goodness knows where. It made a fearful clatter, as of tons of coal being flung into the kitchen, as he whirled the handle round. It was of no consequence, because the old ice pail, in common with much other scarce kitchen equipment, went the rounds in war-time Cairo and nearly everybody was familiar with this characteristic background noise at dinner-parties. We knew it heralded the appearance of some confection as delectable as any that ever came from Gunters of Berkeley Square or Florians in Venice, in the days when ice creams really were ice creams, and a special treat for parties and holidays rather than something you buy along with the groceries and detergents from the shop on the corner.

Ice creams, real ones that is, are made with several different basic mixtures, of which the two main ones are either pure thick uncooked cream, fruit pulp and sugar syrup, or a custard made from milk or cream and egg yolks plus fruit pulp or some basic flavouring. These latter tend to freeze to a better consistency than those made of raw cream, but when fresh uncooked fruit such as strawberries and raspberries is being used the eggs, I find, detract rather from the flavour of the fruit. On the other hand, as a basis for flavourings such as lemon or coffee the rich custard is ideal. There is, of course, a big difference in price between milk and single cream; the advantage of the cream is that it makes a better-textured ice and that it cooks to a custard with the eggs in a very short time, much quicker and more efficiently than milk. In any case, if you are using milk, use rich full cream milk.

When made of the right ingredients and presented in their simplest form, unadorned with such things as chocolate and fudge sauces or fussed up with extra fruit, cake and the like, ice creams make an excellently digestive and welcome finish even to the heaviest meal.

Refrigerator ices have never, I think, entirely the consistency or professional finish of those made in the old-fashioned bucket, but if they are carefully made they can nevertheless be most delicious, and a revelation to anyone who has never known any but commercial ice creams.

IMPORTANT POINTS ABOUT REFRIGERATOR ICES ARE:

1. Turn the dial to maximum freezing point well before you put the ice mixture, which should already be well chilled, in to freeze. The quicker ice creams are frozen the better the consistency.

2. Cover the filled ice trays with foil; this protective covering does much to eliminate the risk of ice crystals forming in the cream.

3. While it is not strictly necessary to stir the ice during freezing, it will emerge with a more even consistency, and also freeze quicker, if you do.

4. The easiest and best-looking way to serve refrigerator ice creams is to have a long narrow flat dish on to which you can turn out the ice direct from the trays without breaking it up. Then cut it into portions for serving. If you have a refrigerator with a large enough ice-chamber to hold a deeper container than the ice trays, then you can make an ice of a rather better shape – using, for example, a decorative old-fashioned ice-pudding mould or a cake tin. But the container must be of metal or plastic. China or earthenware will not work.

5. If the weather is exceptionally hot, allow rather longer freezing time than is given in the recipes below. Also, one needs to be fairly well acquainted with the vagaries of one's own refrigerator. In some the freezing process takes longer than in others.

6. Refrigerator ices tend to melt rather quickly, so should only be taken from the ice-chamber shortly before serving. On the other hand a good ice should never be rock hard. It should be creamy round the edges just beginning to melt, so, if necessary give it a few minutes out of the fridge to soften a little before serving.

7. Home-made refrigerator ice creams can be refrozen quite successfully. Commercial ones cannot.

8. I have heard people say that they find it impossible to make ices for dinner-parties because that is just the time when the ice cubes are needed for drinks. But even if you have no thermos container, all you have to do is to transfer the ice cubes to a bowl and, at the low freezing temperature to which the fridge is turned to freeze the ice cream, they will keep perfectly intact for hours.

9. The recipes below are calculated for either 300-ml, 600-ml or 1.2-litre (½-pint, 1-pint or 2-pint) ice trays. Since it is advisable to have your trays all but full for the freezing process, the quantities should be adjusted to suit the capacity of your own ice trays.

Nowadays most people who make ice cream regularly have an ice cream maker. All of the recipes in this chapter can be made successfully in such a machine, following the manufacturer's instructions. I have included Elizabeth's notes on how to freeze ices in ice trays for those who don't have a machine. They work well.   JN

LEMON ICE CREAM

450 ml (¾ pint) of single cream or milk, the yolks of 3 large or 4 small eggs, 125 g (4 oz) of soft white sugar, the juice and grated peel of 1 large lemon.

Grate the peel of the lemon into the cream or milk. Pour over the egg yolks beaten with the sugar. Stir over low heat until you have a thin custard. Strain through a fine sieve and stir until half cooled.

When quite cold add the strained juice of half the lemon.

Turn into the ice tray, cover with foil, and freeze at maximum freezing point for 2½ to 3 hours. Enough for 4, and a most refreshing and lovely ice.

COFFEE ICE CREAM

This is a luxury ice cream: expense, time, trouble, but immensely good, and delicate in flavour.

600 ml (1 pint) of single cream, 150 ml (5 fl oz) of double cream, 125 g (4 oz) freshly roasted coffee beans, the yolks of 3 eggs, 90 g (3 oz) pale brown sugar, a strip of lemon peel, a pinch of salt, 1 tablespoon of white sugar.

Crack the coffee beans very slightly with a pestle in a marble mortar. Put them in a saucepan with the single cream, the lemon peel, brown sugar and well-beaten egg yolks, and salt. Cook over very gentle heat, stirring until the mixture thickens, then, off the fire, continue stirring until the mixture has partially cooked. Strain through a fine sieve.

Immediately before freezing, fold in the double cream, lightly whipped with the white sugar. Turn into the freezing tray of the refrigerator, which should already be turned to maximum freezing point, cover and place in the freezing compartment. It will take about 3 hours to freeze; and whether or not you need to turn it sides to middle once or twice during the process depends upon your refrigerator. Enough for 4.

RASPBERRY ICE CREAM

An ice cream with a most intense and beautiful fresh raspberry flavour.

500 g (1 lb) raspberries, 125 g (4 oz) red currants, 125 g (4 oz) sugar, 150 ml (¼ pint) of water, the juice of half a lemon, 150 ml (5 fl oz) of double cream.

Pick the raspberries over very carefully and discard any that are the slightest bit mouldy. This is essential, for even one mouldy one may spoil the taste of the whole mixture. Pick the red currants from the stalks. Press all the fruit through a nylon or stainless steel sieve (a wire sieve discolours the fruit).

Make a syrup from the sugar and water by boiling them together for 5 minutes. When it is quite cold, and not before, add this syrup to the fruit pulp. Squeeze in the lemon juice.

Immediately before freezing, whip the cream very lightly, just until it is heavy and thick, and fold it into the fruit.

Turn into the ice tray, cover with foil and freeze at maximum freezing point for 2½ to 3 hours. Enough for 4.

House & Garden, July 1959

APRICOT ICE CREAM

625 g (1¼ lb) of ripe apricots, 250 ml (8 fl oz) of water, 90 g (3 oz) of sugar, the juice of half a large lemon, 300 ml (½ pint) of double cream. Optionally, add 2 or 3 tablespoons of apricot brandy.

Wipe the apricots – there will be 20 to 24 apricots – with a soft cloth, put them in an ovenproof dish with the water. No sugar at this stage. Cover the pot. Cook the apricots in a low oven, 170°C/325°F/gas mark 3, for about 35 minutes or until they are soft. When cool, strain off the juice into a saucepan. Add the sugar, and boil to a thin syrup.

Stone the apricots, keeping aside a few of the stones. Purée the fruit. Pour the cooled syrup into the purée. Add the lemon juice. Crack 3 or 4 apricot stones, extract the kernels and crush them to powder. Stir this into the purée, then press the purée through a fine stainless steel or nylon sieve. Chill it thoroughly in the refrigerator.

Before freezing, taste for sweetness, adding more lemon juice if necessary. Turn into a metal or plastic container of about 1-litre (1¾-pint) capacity and transfer to the freezer.

After 2½ hours or so, turn the half-frozen ice into the food processor or high-power blender or beater and beat until the ice crystals have disappeared. If you have no suitable electric machine, use a big bowl and a heavy whisk or fork. Add the cream and the apricot brandy, and taste again for sweetness. Re-pack the cream into the container and return to the freezer.

In approximately 3 hours the ice should be frozen to about the right consistency for serving. An extra refinement is to give the ice a second rapid breakdown in the blender or food processor a short while – about 10 minutes – before serving. This restores the thick creamy texture of a good ice cream, and it can now be turned into a dish ready for serving, and returned to the freezer for a quarter of an hour. Alternatively, the second breakdown can be performed while the ice cream is still only two-thirds frozen. It is then turned into a simple or fancy mould and returned to the freezer until set.

Notes

1. To crack the apricot stones I have found that an ancient, common, metal nutcracker of the most basic design is also the most effective.

2. An alternative to using the apricot kernels is to crush up one or two Italian *amaretti di Saronno*, the little macaroons wrapped in crackly tissue paper, which are in fact made with apricot kernels, not with bitter almonds as was generally assumed until the listing of ingredients in packed confectionery became compulsory. Not that the *Saronno* people have anything to conceal. They tell me that their *amaretti* have always been made with apricot kernels.

Unpublished, 1960s

ALMOND ICE CREAM

This is a very delicate ice. The mixture can also be used as a basis for several fruit ices such as strawberry, orange, raspberry.

60 g (2 oz) of almonds, 90 g (3 oz) of sugar, 450 ml (¾ pint) of milk, 3 egg yolks, 150 ml (5 fl oz) of double cream, 2 tablespoons of Kirsch.

First skin the almonds. The best way to do this is to drop them in a small saucepan of boiling water, remove from the heat at once, and with a perforated spoon extract about half the almonds. Peel off the skins, then repeat the process with the remainder. Put the skinned almonds on a fireproof plate or dish in a very slow oven. Leave them for about 7 minutes, just long enough to dry them, but not to toast or colour them. Pound them to powder in a mortar or grind them in a food chopper. (Unless the almonds are very dry, this process will be difficult.)

Bring the milk and sugar to the boil, stirring all the time. Stir in the pounded almonds. Have the egg yolks ready beaten in the liquidiser or a bowl, pour the hot almond and milk mixture over them, give the whole lot a rapid whirl, return to the saucepan and cook gently, again stirring all the time, until the custard begins to thicken. Immediately take it from the heat, give it another whirl in the liquidiser or beat it in a chilled bowl, strain it through a fine sieve, chill it in the refrigerator.

Before freezing, stir in the cream and the Kirsch.

Notes

1. Don't let the custard cook much beyond the stage when it begins to thicken. Completely cooked egg yolks don't expand during the freezing process.

2. If you are using a sweet Kirsch liqueur rather than the white alcohol version, reduce the sugar in the custard by 15 g (½ oz).

3. Instead of Kirsch, a few drops of genuine bitter almond essence may be used, but be sure that the essence is the true one. The synthetic version won't do.

STRAWBERRY AND ALMOND ICE CREAM

To the almond ice mixture on page 277, add a purée made from
250 g (½ lb) of hulled strawberries plus an extra 30 g (1 oz) of
sugar and the juice of half an orange. This makes a most delicious
and subtle ice.

ORANGE AND ALMOND ICE CREAM

Grate the zest of one orange and the strained juice of two into the
almond ice cream mixture on page 277.

Add 2 tablespoons of orange flower water. An extra 150 ml
(5 fl oz) of cream, and 2 tablespoons of Cointreau or Grand
Marnier instead of Kirsch transform this ice into a very special
one. A scoop of strawberry and almond and one of orange and
almond make one of those blends of flavours from the golden age
of ices.

Unpublished, 1970s

LEMON AND GRAND MARNIER ICE CREAM

2 large lemons, 90 g (3 oz) icing sugar, 150 ml (5 fl oz) double
cream, Grand Marnier.

Put the thinly peeled rind of the lemons with the icing sugar in
125 ml (4 fl oz) of water, and simmer gently for 20 minutes. Leave
this syrup to cool, strain and add to it the juice of the lemons.
When quite cold, add it gradually to the whipped cream, stirring
gently until the whole mixture is smooth.

Pour into the ice-tray, cover with paper and freeze at maximum
freezing-point of the refrigerator for about 3 hours, taking it out
to stir it twice, after the first half-hour, and again after another
hour. Half an hour before serving, stir in a good liqueur glass of
Grand Marnier (the contents of a miniature bottle) and put back
in the freezing compartment. Being an orange-flavoured liqueur,
the Grand Marnier mixes well with the lemon, supplying the right
rich flavour against the sharp background of the lemon.

The amounts given will fill a 500-ml (18-fl oz) ice-tray. Should
the quantities have to be altered to go in smaller or larger trays,
alter them all in proportion. The amount of sugar in refrigerator-
made ice cream is important. Made in the above manner, there

will be no little ice particles, and the result is a soft, light ice cream, but it melts quickly, so leave it in the ice-tray until the moment comes to serve it.

Instead of the customary wafers to go with the ice, serve miniature, very fresh brown bread sandwiches with a filling of chopped walnuts, and a drop of Grand Marnier beaten into the butter with which the sandwiches are spread.

Entertaining with Grand Marnier booklet, n.d.

ORANGE ICE CREAM

The cream ices I make nowadays are nearly all based on *natillas*, the Spanish custard made with far fewer eggs to milk than the usual French, Italian and English equivalents. The Spanish version makes a lighter and more delicate ice cream and, the proportions and method once mastered, there is really no limit to the variations of flavouring which may be made. Using citrus fruit peels and juice, spices (cinnamon is particularly good), preserved ginger, honey, orange flower water and pounded macaroons or *amaretti*, I have based many delicious and refreshing ices on the *natillas* formula.

First the custard: ingredients for 1 litre (about 1¾ pints) of mixture are 750 ml (1¼ pints) of milk, 2 whole eggs and 2 yolks, 60 g (2 oz) of sugar, a piece of cinnamon bark or a teaspoon of ground cinnamon, a strip of orange peel. Additional ingredients are 200 ml (7 fl oz) of cream, orange or tangerine peel, and perhaps more cinnamon.

Put the milk, strip of orange peel, cinnamon and sugar in a heavy saucepan of 1.75-litre (3-pint) capacity. Bring to simmering point.

Have the eggs ready and well beaten in a bowl, or whirled in the blender. Over them strain the hot milk mixture and beat or whirl the mixture again. Return it to the rinsed pan.

Cook the *natillas* over very gentle heat, whisking continuously until the custard starts to thicken. Remove the saucepan from the heat and either continue whisking until the custard is cool or give it another whirl in the blender. Chill in the refrigerator.

Now the ice cream: immediately before freezing, whirl the custard once more in the blender, adding the 200 ml (7 fl oz) of cream and a little extra cinnamon and finely grated orange or tangerine peel.

Notes

1. If you do not have a sufficiently heavy, flat saucepan, cook the custard in a porringer or a *bain marie* improvised from a bowl and a pan of water. Be wary of using enamelled saucepans for milk or custards.

2. Note that the small proportion of sugar in the custard makes for much better results than the larger quantity usually called for in custards.

Unpublished, no date

MINT ICE CREAM

150 ml (¼ pint) water, 125 g (4 oz) sugar, a handful of fresh mint leaves, juice of 1 lemon, 150 ml (5 fl oz) of double cream.

Stir water and sugar over low heat till sugar dissolves. Bring to the boil, then cool for a few moments. Wash mint and put in blender with the syrup. Blend till mint is fine. Add lemon juice. Strain into an ice tray. Cool, then freeze till firm(ish).

Turn into a bowl and mash with fork. Fold into the lightly whipped cream, pour back into ice tray and freeze again until firm.

Unpublished, 1960s

GINGER CREAM ICE

Ingredients for the *natillas* or custard are as for the orange ice cream on page 279, except that the orange peel and cinnamon bark are not necessary. Additional ingredients are 4 tablespoons of finely chopped ginger in syrup, 4 of ginger syrup, 2 of lemon juice, approximately 150 ml (5 fl oz) of cream.

Make the custard as above. When it is well chilled, return it to the blender. Stir in all the additional ingredients and taste. You may need a little more ginger flavouring or a little extra lemon juice.

Give the mixture a quick whirl and freeze it.

Unpublished, 1970s

CHOCOLATE CREAM ICE 1

There are many ways of making chocolate ice. This one is rich but not heavy.

Ingredients are 200 g (7 oz) of very good bitter chocolate, 600 ml (1 pint) of creamy milk, 2 whole eggs, a half cup or 6 tablespoons of strong, unsweetened black coffee, 150 ml (5 fl oz) of cream, optional; 2 to 3 tablespoons of brandy, whisky or rum.

Break up the chocolate and put it in a bowl with the coffee in a low oven or over hot water. Meanwhile bring the milk to simmering point, and pour it over the eggs beaten preferably in the blender goblet or mixer bowl. As soon as the chocolate has melted stir it smooth, blend it with the milk and egg mixture and cook it over very low heat until it is just beginning to thicken. Because of the setting capacity of chocolate the mixture need be no more than just barely thickened. Chill it thoroughly, and immediately before freezing give it another whirl in the blender, adding the cream and brandy, whisky or rum.

Note that no extra sugar is added to the chocolate, which is already sweetened.

Plain, fresh, thin pouring cream is good with this lovely ice, and very simple, plain biscuits or slices of brioche are called for.

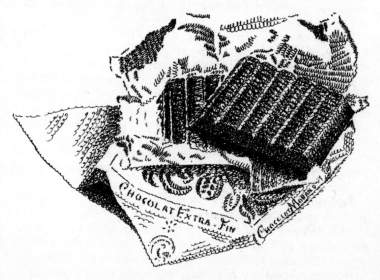

CHOCOLATE CREAM ICE 2

If you have a source of plain *unsweetened* cooking chocolate, allow 125 g (4 oz) plus 90 g (3 oz) of sugar, preferably brown. Other ingredients are as above.

Grate the chocolate, mix it with the sugar and black coffee or plain water. When it is melted and stirred smooth blend it with the hot milk and egg mixture as above. When chilled taste for sweetness.

Since there is no vanilla, true or false, in unsweetened cooking chocolate, one is free to choose one's own flavouring. I prefer cinnamon to vanilla. It's difficult to say how much because freshly ground cinnamon is much stronger and more aromatic than the powder which has been in a jar in a spice rack for a couple of years or more. So, if your cinnamon is freshly ground, 2 level teaspoons should be enough to flavour 125 g (4 oz) of chocolate, and if it is not fresh you may have to use twice as much, but cooking brings out the aroma so add it while you stir the chocolate, eggs and milk to a custard. And taste.

Alternative flavourings for chocolate ices are ginger, particularly successful in the form of the stem preserved in syrup. Some of the syrup can be used instead of sugar to sweeten the chocolate and a couple of tablespoons of the stems, finely chopped added before freezing.

For a true vanilla-flavoured chocolate ice, pound or grind a little piece of vanilla bean to powder and stir a half teaspoon of this into the milk before you set it on the stove to simmer. Or for a less powerful flavouring put a whole vanilla bean in the milk while it is heating up and remove it before combining the milk with the eggs, chocolate and sugar.

Orange and chocolate make another attractive combination. Grated fresh orange peel or ground dried tangerine or Seville orange peels can be used. So can candied orange peel, and the orange-based liqueurs such as Grand Marnier and Cointreau. But use liqueurs very sparingly. They are very sweet.

The coffee to be used when melting chocolate for creams, mousses and ices can be made either from one of the dried granulated Nescafé or other brands or from beans freshly ground and brewed, but Nescafé in granules freshly made is preferable to stewed stale watery real coffee. The coffee-flavoured liqueur Tia Maria can be used in very small quantity to give an extra fillip to a chocolate ice. But, again, the caution that it be sparingly used. Too much will make the ice cloying.

Both unpublished, 1970s

BROWN BREAD ICE CREAM

In one form or another, recipes for brown bread ices have been appearing in print since about the mid-eighteenth century. An early one was given by Emy, the French confectioner who published his elegant little book *L'Art de bien faire les glaces d'office* in 1768. His recipe called for rye bread, still in those days common in France and still perhaps the best for brown bread ice, although today it is more usually made with wholemeal.

Popularised in England early in the nineteenth century perhaps by Gunters, the famous Berkeley Square confectioners who did the catering for fashionable balls and receptions, brown bread ice also became a speciality of the Winchester College shop, and was much loved by the scholars of that famous school. Some twenty-five years ago, remembering the delicious brown bread ice sold by Gunters in the nineteen thirties – they delivered it by the bucketful for outdoor parties – I evolved my own version based on the recipe given by Alfred Jarrin, an early Gunter specialist, in *The Italian Confectioner* which first appeared in 1820, and published it in a magazine. About a year later I was gratified to hear from a courteous reader that my ice, made by her Italian cook, had been joyously received by her husband, an ex-Winchester scholar. The recipe I now use, slightly modified since those days, is as follows:

For 600 ml (1 pint) of double cream, the other ingredients are 180 g (6 oz) of crustless wholemeal or dark rye bread, 200–250 g (7–8 oz) of sugar.

First whisk the cream and 60 g (2 oz) of the sugar until it just starts to thicken. Do this by hand, in a chilled bowl. Take care not to overdo the whisking. Turn the cream into a metal or plastic box and set it to freeze.

Pull the bread into small pieces, put them on a baking sheet in a low oven. Let them toast until crisp, then crush them into coarse crumbs. This should be done by hand. A food grinder or chopper tends to make the crumbs too uniform and too fine, the crunchy and uneven texture of hand-pounded breadcrumbs being important to the success of the ice.

With the remaining sugar and the same amount of water make a thick syrup. Pour this, warm, over the breadcrumbs.

When the cream has frozen just enough to be firm, turn it out into a chilled bowl, whisk it for a few seconds, fold in the bread and syrup mixture. Before returning the cream to the freezer, taste it for sweetness. If too sweet add a little extra cream. Take care not to serve the ice in an over-frozen condition. The crunchy crumbs contrasting with the soft smooth cream are the attributes which constitute the appeal of this very simple mixture.

Notes

1. On no account flavour brown bread ice with vanilla. And don't think it's unimportant to freeze the cream before adding the breadcrumbs. When the bread is mixed directly into the unfrozen cream a rather pasty mass results.

2. Variations can be made using a mixture of pumpernickel and wholemeal bread. The pumpernickel is sweet so the mixture needs slightly less sugar. Granary bread, equally rather sweet because of its malted wheat content, can also be used. In the original Alfred Jarrin recipe, the bread was cut into small dice – before toasting in the oven – rather than made into crumbs, and it goes without saying that any number of other minor variations can be devised.

RYE BREAD ICE CREAM

This is the eighteenth-century French recipe given by Emy. It is very different from the later Gunter version of brown bread ice.

First you prepare a plain basic cream mixture with a pint (approx 1 litre) of cream (at that time the Paris pint was 32 oz, the equivalent of 2 pints U.S. today), 4 egg yolks, and about a quarter pound (125 g) of sugar. (The proportions are odd. They would surely need adjustment.) You are to cook this with extreme care or it will curdle, so even if it takes an hour of stirring 'you are to persevere until the cream has thickened' when you add a piece of crustless rye bread reduced to crumbs. Let these amalgamate with the custard, push all through the tammy, using a wooden spoon. Leave to cool, stirring from time to time to prevent the formation of a skin. Freeze as for all the ices. In other words, in a pewter cylinder set in a tub of ice and salt.

To an eighteenth-century confectioner the making and freezing of ice creams was hard manual labour. Emy's directions include the alternate scraping down of the frozen cream as it formed on the inner walls of the freezing pot, and the vigorous turning and shaking of the heavy cylinder for the space of a quarter of an hour at a stretch until at a given moment he was required to do the scraping and mixing with the right hand and the turning of the pot, simultaneously, with the left. Practice, says Emy, will make you adept. He himself was certainly an experienced and skilled man at ice making. His ices would have been as good as any that could at that time be produced. His directions for freezing, embodying many acute observations on the effects of the weather on the whole process and on the proportions of salt to ice required for the freezing of different categories of confection, whether *neiges* or *fromages glacés*, whether rich or plain and so on, leave me in no doubt that Emy was a practitioner of unusual gifts as well as a highly literate writer.

Both unpublished, *c.*1984

Pomegranates Pink

Fifteen years ago in Murcia, Valencia and Alicante, the three Levantine provinces of Spain, there were some hundred establishments dealing in pomegranates and pomegranate syrup, the grenadine known to almost every barman in Europe. How many of these pomegranate dealers still flourish I don't know, but what struck me at the time was the extraordinary contrast between the important commercial value of pomegranates and the total indifference of the village people – at any rate those of the village in Alicante province where I was then staying and have often stayed since – to this beautiful fruit hanging so heavily on the splendid trees. Nobody seemed to bother even to pick them.

How curious that the Persian Arabs who originally occupied Spain and Sicily and contributed so much to Spanish and Italian cooking appear to have bequeathed to Europe no lasting legacy concerning the kitchen uses of the pomegranate. In middle-eastern countries it is still much used, a salt as well as a sweet pomegranate juice often appearing as a seasoning or condiment, chiefly in conjunction with fat or rich foods such as duck, liver, and eggs cooked in oil or butter. The sharp juice acts as a corrective, as do lemon juice, vinegar, and verjuice, the fermented juice of a particular variety of acid grape which figured so largely in medieval European cooking.

The cooks of fifteenth- and sixteenth-century Spain were certainly familiar with the kitchen uses of the pomegranate, for both seeds and juice appear frequently in their recipes, just as they do in English, Italian and French cookery books of the same period, and even though pomegranates were comparative rarities in England and France, a good deal was known of them. A century later, much more.

In mid seventeenth-century France, for example, one Pierre de Lune, well known as cook and head steward in various households, among them those of Hercule de Rohan, duc de Montbazon, and the duchesse d'Orléans, wrote a cookery book called *Le Cuisinier*, published in 1656, chez Pierre David, Paris. From the many dishes and recipes *à l'espagnole* which appear in the book, it has been deduced that Pierre de Lune was of Spanish origin. It seems possible, although it does not necessarily follow. In grand French – and English – households the cooking of the period was still much influenced by the old Spanish and Italian methods, re-introduced and renewed by cooks brought in the trains of ambassadors and noblemen, through royal marriages, and via Jewish refugees from the Spanish Inquisition. There was also quite a cross-traffic in the translation of cookery books, Italian into French and English, French into English and Italian, and Spanish into Italian and vice versa. Cooking in the great houses of Europe in those days must have been as international as in a twentieth-century Hilton Hotel.

Pierre de Lune's recipes certainly have a very cosmopolitan flavour, some showing a distinct Arab influence in the use of sweetmeats, spices, clove-studded lemons, and notably of pomegranate seeds as a decorative element in his dishes, much as in English cooking clusters of shining little red barberries were scattered on every other dish. Against the gleam of pewter or silver platters they must have looked uncommonly pretty. Pomegranate seeds likewise.

One of Pierre de Lune's most charming recipes is called *oeufs à la germaine et à la romaine*. This dish, with its somewhat mysterious name, consists of eighteen egg yolks beaten together with cinnamon, salt and orange flower water, a quarter at a time being

made into a kind of flat galette or omelette, each one strewn with
little pieces of candied lemon peel, apricots, and pistachio nuts,
plus a crumbled macaroon, a little cream, and 'scented water'.
The fourth and final layer of this elegant confection is garnished
with pomegranate seeds and cinnamon of Florence.

Another of Pierre de Lune's egg recipes, 'a yellow rock of eggs'
distinctly bears the stamp of the Spanish confectioner's lavish
hand with egg yolks (tons of them still go into Spanish sweets and
turrons). For the yellow rock you make a syrup of sugar and
white wine. To this you put a couple of dozen egg yolks and cook
them until they come away from the pan. 'When they are cooked
put to them a little muskified orange flower water and the juice
of a lemon, and pass them through a canvas cloth on to the dish
you wish to serve them on. Garnish with pomegranate seeds and
lemon rind dipped in *sucre cuit*,' meaning, I think, a heavy sugar
syrup. The name of the dish is descriptive enough, and anybody
who has tried some of the incredibly rich Spanish – and Portuguese
– sweetmeats and desserts will have a good idea of how it tasted.

De Lune's recipes are wonderfully rich, strange and decorative.
A leveret pie *à l'Anglaise* is made in an oval shape, or fashioned
in the form of a hare. The leveret is larded, seasoned with salt,
pepper, nutmeg, cinnamon and pounded bacon or salt pork.
Separately you make a composition of lemon peel, Levantine
dates and Brignolles prunes, all sliced and cooked in white wine
with sugar, cinnamon, pepper, green citron peel. This seems to
have been the equivalent of an English caudle, although eggless,
for when the cooked pie, iced with sugar and orange flower
water, was ready, you were to remove the cover and pour in the
composition. In serving, the juice of a lemon and pomegranate
seeds were to be added – presumably strewn over the carved-up
and replaced cover.

Another pie, *à la Portuguaise* this time, has a filling of breast
of guinea fowl and bone marrow. The usual spices, dried and
candied fruit, sliced pistachio nuts and bacon are added, the pie
crust being made of puff pastry in the shape of two dolphins, tail
to tail. For the cooked and iced pie you were to make an *aigre
doux* of lemon juice and sugar, to be poured in as in the leveret
pie. Again, *en servant garnissez de grains de Grenade*.

Lovely stuff, all this. Not much in it though for the modern
cook, although someone may like to try a modified version of
the *germaine et romaine* dish. My own small contribution to

pomegranate cooking for times when consignments of Israeli or
Spanish pomegranates turn up, are a sorbet and an ice cream,
both much experimented in Spain, experiments observed with
amazement by my host's two young village maids.

POMEGRANATE WATER ICE OR SNOW

You need 600 ml (1 pint) of fresh pomegranate juice – in Spain I
found the pomegranates so rich in juice that four yielded enough
– plus 300 ml (½ pint) of red wine, the juice of one large orange,
and a thick syrup made from 180 g (6 oz) of sugar boiled with a
half tumbler – 90–120 ml (3–4 fl oz) – of water. Combine all the
ingredients – you don't cook anything except the sugar syrup –
and freeze.

The name for this came from Gilliers' *Le Cannameliste Français*, 1751. Gilliers was confectioner and distiller to Stanislas,
King of Poland, last Duke of Bar and Lorraine, father-in-law of
Louis XV. His pomegranate water ice was called *Neige de Grenade*. The flavour is fine and fresh, the colours very rich deep garnet
and carnation, varying and interestingly striated. Serve it in heavy
but clear glass goblets.

POMEGRANATE ICE CREAM

Make a custard with 300 ml (10 fl oz) of cream thickened with
three egg yolks and sweetened with 125 g (4 oz) of sugar. When
cooled, add to the custard the fresh juice of two large pomegranates. When frozen this ice comes out a mysterious pale cedar-pink
colour, and has a subtle flavour not easily identifiable.

Abigail Books, Catalogue, Winter 1979

STRAWBERRY GRANITA

Now that we can buy strawberries nearly all the year round, a
strawberry sorbet would seem to be the best basic one to know.
Mine is the Italian version. It contains orange juice, which brings
out the flavour of the strawberries in a remarkable way, giving
the mixture an intensity and concentration of scent not otherwise
to be achieved with any but the finest strawberries fresh from the
garden.

Quantities are 1 kg (2 lb) of strawberries, the juice of half a lemon and of half an orange, 250 g (8 oz) white sugar, 150 ml (¼ pint) of water.

Hull the strawberries, purée them in the blender, press them through a stainless steel or nylon sieve (wire discolours the fruit). Add the strained orange and lemon juice.

Boil the sugar and water for about 7 minutes to make a thin syrup (to make a sorbet of greater density boil the syrup for 10 minutes or until it is beginning to thicken) and leave it to cool before adding it to the strawberry pulp.

Chill the mixture before turning it into the refrigerator trays to freeze, which will take 2–2½ hours at the normal ice-making temperature. Keep the trays tightly covered with foil during the freezing process, and transfer them from the ice compartment to the less cold part of the refrigerator for about 10 minutes before dividing up the ice and serving it.

As the name implies, this type of water ice should be slightly grainy, no more than just barely frozen. The quantities given should be enough for 6 to 8 helpings. Serve with French boudoir biscuits or sponge fingers.

STRAWBERRY AND CREAM SORBET

According to Escoffier, a fruit juice ice with added whipped cream is still a sorbet. It is the basic egg-thickened custard mixture which turns an ice into an ice cream. Whatever its name, this type of ice is very light and delicious. Make the mixture as for the *granita*, boiling the syrup rather longer to increase its density.

For 1 kg (2 lb) of strawberries allow 150 ml (5 fl oz) of double cream. Whip it very lightly, fold it swiftly into the chilled fruit and syrup mixture, freeze it in the covered ice trays, at the *maximum* freezing temperature, for 2–2½ hours. It should not be necessary, given the foil covering, to stir the ice.

RASPBERRY AND REDCURRANT GRANITA

In this mixture is concentrated the very essence of summer itself. Make it quickly while the season lasts and eat it freshly made. It does store in the deep-freeze, but with long keeping the strength of flavour goes out of it.

Proportions and method are the same as for the strawberry

granita except that the orange is replaced by the freshly pressed juice of 125 g (¼ lb) of redcurrants per 500 g (1 lb) of raspberries.

LEMON AND ORANGE SORBET

4 oranges, 1 large lemon, 125 g (4 oz) of sugar, 150 ml (¼ pint) of water, whites of 3 eggs, 125–150 ml (4–5 fl oz) double cream.

Grate the zest of one orange and of the lemon into the sugar and water. Boil to a thin syrup. Strain when cool and mix it with the strained juice of the fruit. Chill and then freeze as for the strawberry *granita*.

Turn the frozen mixture into a bowl. With a fork break it into a snow. Quickly mix and fold in the egg whites whisked to a stiff froth. Now add the cream. Return the sorbet to the ice trays, cover them. Freeze, with the refrigerator turned to *maximum* freezing temperature, for about 1 hour.

LEMON AND RUM SORBET

While I would not monkey about adding liqueurs or frills to soft fruit ices, a lemon sorbet, however good, can stand a little dressing up. A spoonful or two of white rum, for example, poured over each sorbet as it is about to be served, makes it more interesting. Never add liqueurs or spirits to a water ice mixture before it is frozen or it may not freeze at all.

THE EDWARDIAN SORBET

'The sorbet is served in small cut glasses for this purpose. They are sent into the room on a silver tray, and on the service table are placed each on a small plate with its corresponding teaspoon, before serving them to the guests.

'As soon as the sorbet is served, the butler or a waiter hands round a large box of Russian cigarettes, and a second one passes a lighted spirit lamp or a small candle.'

The Modern Caterer's Encyclopaedia by J. Rey, published by Carmona and Baker, *c.*1907.

Nova, 1965

MULBERRY WATER ICE

Sir Harry Luke, author of *The Tenth Muse*, one of the most civilised and original of modern cookery books, claims that the mulberry, his favourite berry fruit, makes the best of all water ices.

Made according to the same method as the strawberry *granita* on page 288, but omitting the orange juice, a mulberry ice is indeed both delicious and beautiful.

Unpublished, n.d.

MANGO SORBET

To make 1 litre (1¾ pints) of this delicious ice you need 4 or 5 fine ripe mangoes, a thin syrup made with 60 g (2 oz) of sugar to 150 ml (¼ pint) of water, 150 ml (5 fl oz) of cream, about 2 tablespoons of lemon juice.

Peel the mangoes and slice all the flesh into a bowl, scraping as much as possible from the stones. Purée it in the blender. There should be 650–700 g (22–24 oz) of fruit pulp. Add the cold sugar syrup and the lemon juice. Immediately before freezing blend in the cream.

MANGO SORBET 2

As above, omitting the cream and using one extra mango to make up the quantity. A little more lemon juice will also be needed.

Unpublished, 1970s

PERSIMMON SORBET

4 or 5 very ripe persimmons, 125 g (4 oz) of sugar, 150 ml (¼ pint) of water, the juice of a half a small sweet orange, 150 ml (5 fl oz) of double cream.

Having peeled away and discarded the skin of the persimmons, turn the pulp into the blender and purée until smooth. There should be 600 ml (1 pint) of purée. Boil the sugar and water for about 5 minutes, to make a thin syrup. Chill this in the refrigerator, and when quite cold amalgamate it with the persimmon purée. Add the strained orange juice. Immediately before freezing give the mixture another whirl in the blender, adding the cream. Turn into the freezer.

These quantities make a little under a litre (approximately 1½ pints) of sorbet. A very delicious and pretty one, too.

Unpublished, 1970s

LOGANBERRY SORBET

500 g (1 lb) of loganberries, 125 g (4 oz) of sugar, 250 ml (8 fl oz) of water, the juice of 1 orange.

Boil the sugar and water to a thin syrup. Put the fruit into the processor bowl or blender goblet, pour in the warm syrup and purée the fruit. Press the purée through a fine sieve to eliminate the pips. Add the strained orange juice and chill.

Loganberries tend to be very acid, hence the rather larger than usual allowance of sugar for the syrup. Before freezing, check the sweetness and if necessary add a little more sugar, or a little cream to soften the taste.

Freeze the sorbet. There should be altogether 600 ml (1 pint) of sorbet.

Unpublished, 1970s

QUINCE AND HONEY SORBET

This is quite a trouble to make, but worth it to addicts of the strange flavour and wonderful perfume of quinces.

First bake 6 medium-sized ripe unpeeled quinces in a covered pot in a low oven (140°C/280°F/gas mark 1) until they are soft. Add no water. This preliminary cooking will take about 1–1½ hours.

Peel, slice and core the fruit, putting the parings and cores into a saucepan but discarding any bruised or damaged parts of the fruit.

Cover the cores and peel with cold water – about 1.2 litres (2 pints). Boil hard for a few minutes, until the water is well-flavoured and coloured with the quince parings. Strain through a fine sieve into a large bowl or jug. Return this quince water – there will be 750 ml (1¼ pints) – to the saucepan. Add the sliced fruit – there should be approximately 500 g (1 lb) – and let it boil for about 10 minutes until quite soft. Now add 8 tablespoons of honey and boil until the juice has turned to a light syrup which just drops from the spoon.

Purée the whole mixture in the blender, and chill in the refrigerator. Immediately before freezing give the purée another quick whirl in the blender, adding 300 ml (10 fl oz) of whipping or double cream.

The quantities given will yield about 1.2 litres (2 pints) of mixture, too much for freezing all at once in a small-scale electric sorbetière, but since it is hardly worth cooking fewer than 6 quinces at a time, the best course is to divide the prepared purée into two parts, adding cream only to the amount to be frozen. The rest of the purée will keep for a few days in the refrigerator. Again, add the cream only immediately before freezing.

Note
Instead of double cream try using buttermilk, or half and half fresh home-made yogurt and cream. The flavour of quince is powerful enough to stand up to the acidity of buttermilk and yogurt.

Unpublished, 1970s

The Madeira Era

'I was born saturated in Madeira,' writes Noël Cossart in his recently published, wholly absorbing *Madeira: The Island Vineyard* (Christie's Wine Publications). He is to be envied. He is also to be congratulated. His book is as rich with the lore of his subject as is his mother's *bolo de mel*, the true cake of Madeira (good though it may be, the English one is an impostor) with candied citron, spices, almonds, walnuts, butter, and sugar cane honey, otherwise molasses or black treacle. The dough is yeast-leavened, and so in a sense is the book. Wherever you open it some fresh aspect of the subject becomes apparent. Crumb and crust are both uncommonly interesting and varied. Each chapter encapsulates a special story, a facet or a phase in the production of the wines of the island, their properties, their almost miraculous longevity – a century and a half of life is not in the least uncommon for a great single vintage of one of the island's extraordinary wines. A lifetime's knowledge of Madeira's history, its people, industries, agriculture, customs, architecture, fauna, flora, climate, above all his fifty years' active experience of wine-making in the island, are shared by Mr Cossart with his readers in a delightfully easy manner and perfectly unpretentious language.

Madeira is the wine the world owes to the foresight of Prince Henry the Navigator (1394–1460), who in the first half of the fifteenth century decreed that malmsey vines, first brought from Crete to the Iberian peninsula, should be planted in the volcanic soil of the Atlantic island which was in his special care. So spectacularly did they flourish and so good was the wine made from. their grapes that by 1588 the Portuguese Diego Lopes, calling at Madeira on his way to India, could declare that the island's malvasia wine 'is the best in the universe, and is taken to India and many parts of the world'.

European wines made from the malmsey or malvasia grape had long been known for their excellence. In renaissance Italy they were imported from Candia in Crete, and the vine, which had come originally from Monemvasia in the Peloponnesus, was planted in Romagna, Tuscany and the Campania. The rich *Greco* wines it yielded soon became the most prized in the peninsula. In England the native malmseys of Greece and Crete had been in demand ever since the crusading armies encountered them on their voyages to the Holy Land. 'Wyne Greke' was drunk at the ceremonial feasts of Plantagenet and Tudor kings, noblemen, princes of the Church. Malmsey gave its name to a richly spiced and brightly coloured confection of dates, pine kernels, wine, sugar and shredded chicken or pheasant called Mawmenee, recorded in 1390 by Richard II's cooks – and has there been an English schoolboy for hundreds of years who has not heard of Shakespeare's false, fleeting, perjured Clarence and the improbable legend of how he met his death in a butt of malmsey wine?

How fortunate it must have seemed to those European travellers, colonists and adventurers, who in the seventeenth century flocked to India and the Far East, when they found the noble wine of their homelands so conveniently available out there in the mid-Atlantic. They bought the best for consumption during the onward voyage, more for storage when the ships arrived at their destination. Beyond Madeira no wine was to be found. So it was that malmsey, and later other noble wines of Madeira made from grapes called Sercial, Verdelho, Bual, Terrantez, Moscatel, became those common to the colonists of the vast Portuguese empire which reached from the Azores to India and Brazil; to the Dutch in India, Malaysia and the Moluccas; and to the British in Bengal, Madras, Bombay, the trading posts of China (in Canton the British traded Madeira for ginseng), the West Indian sugar plantations, the colonies of North America. Danish traders, who had their own East India Company, took a taste for Madeira back to Scandinavia, and today Denmark and Sweden are among the best markets for fine wines from the island. Early in this century Russia was absorbing 12 per cent of Madeira's wine production, Germany 40 per cent, France 25 per cent. The French also consumed quantities of wines boldly labelled *Madère d'Origine* and *Madère de l'Ile*, which in fact were fortified wines from Tarragona or southern France. Eventually, in 1900, the Blandy brothers of Madeira won a lengthy lawsuit against a firm of French shippers who had been caught by one of the brothers unloading a cargo of Spanish wine labelled *vin de Madère* at Le Havre. Thereafter French imitations of Madeira wines ceased.

Readers hitherto unfamiliar, as I was, with the history of Madeira wines will be struck by the formidable list of British and Indian army regimental messes and clubs supplied at one time or another by Mr Cossart's famous ancestral firm of Cossart, Gordon and Co. The list, drawn up during the early years of this century, appears to cover every mess in British India between Madras and the Punjab, every club from Bombay to Calcutta and from Ceylon to Rawalpindi. A special India Market Madeira, of superior quality, paler than the famous English Market London Particular (a catchy name poached by Dickens to describe the kind of pea-souper fog only seen nowadays in Sherlock Holmes films), was evolved by British Madeira shippers to suit the Indian climate. On the whole, though, the heavier after-dinner Madeira such as Bual, inevitably christened 'bull' by the troops, was preferred to the more delicate wines. The loyal toast was drunk in bull and a potent cocktail of half and half gin and bull, with ice, was a popular tipple. Assisting the mess secretary to bottle the pipes of wine – 44 to 45 dozen bottles to a pipe – was even one of the traditional duties of junior subalterns stationed in India.

It was through the eighteenth-century trade in Madeira to the Indies, East and West, that stories about the wines going round the world, and returning to their island of origin worth twice as much as when they set out, first started circulating. Substantially

they were true. Although the original Madeira wines were straightforward unfortified table wines, and remained so until the mid-eighteenth century, they had proved unusually sturdy, retaining their equilibrium even in the cruel summers of India. Often they were found to have improved and mellowed after the long voyage through tropical waters. At a time when so many of the wines of Europe scarcely remained drinkable after a year or two of life, those of Madeira showed rare qualities. All the same, there were times when the wine turned sour. The shippers began to realise that it would be no bad thing if, as one of them put it, they were to add 'a bucket or two of brandy' to every pipe of wine. Two or three gallons per pipe was the quantity advised. It was a method of preservation, to be applied only to those wines judged the most worthwhile. A first stage in the development of Madeira as we know it today had been reached.

The mellowing of wine during long months in vessels making voyages to the East and the West Indies was effected partly by the motion of the ships, partly by the heat engendered in the holds. Noël Cossart mentions that Pliny and later Cervantes both remarked upon the latter phenomenon. Apropos the beneficial effects of motion on the wine, Mr Cossart also relates the endearing story of Leonardo da Vinci pouring his wine into shallow pans, then playing the violin to it. The vibrations set up minute ripples in the wine and the resulting motion, though barely perceptible, was enough to cause an ageing effect. Was there anything that Leonardo didn't find time to experiment with?

Once the Madeira vintners had grasped the reality of the improvement brought about in their wine by the fortification process, backed up by voyages to the Indies, East or West, a substantial commerce in *vinha da roda*, wine which had done the round voyage, was built up. A pipe of West Indian Madeira sold at Christie's in October 1783 fetched £83 16s 0d as against a price of £40 at best for a pipe shipped direct from the island to London. By 1820 a Lot of Curious East India Madeira from the stock of John Grant, wine merchant, fetched £6 7s 0d per dozen bottles. At about the same time a Sercial direct from Madeira could be purchased for as little as 25 shillings per dozen.

The prices and the reputation of the East and West India Madeiras were certainly high, and at the period the wines were at the height of fashion in England, as in America, but the shippers had long since discovered that sending them on those long journeys was a very costly method of ageing them. Normal wasting alone accounted for a loss of five per cent. Pilfering could bring it up to fifteen per cent. Total shipwreck or partial loss of a consignment, due to necessity to lighten a ship's cargo by throwing casks overboard, would also have been ever-present risks. Seizure by enemy or pirate ships was another. Why not devise some method of reproducing the conditions of the voyage through the tropics without ever sending the wine to sea?

The next move in the Madeira wine story came from an observant abbot who had understood that heat from the sun's rays filtering through glass – he must have been a gardener as well as a vintner – would effectively warm the wine during the day and that the sharp drop in night temperature normal in Madeira would counteract the risk of cumulative overheating. Having constructed a suitable glasshouse and moved his pipes of wine into it, he directed his monks to simulate movement by perching astride the casks and stirring their contents with wands cut from laurel saplings inserted through the bungs. The spectacle presented must have been a genial one. How the abbot's system of solar heating in his *estufa* or hothouse persisted in Madeira for many decades, how it was eventually superseded by the use of the *armazen de calor* or hot stores warmed by hot water pipes to a maximum controlled temperature of 50 degrees centigrade, how the system is currently used only for the finest of Madeira's wines, how lesser ones undergo the *estufa* process in vast concrete hot-vats or *cubas de calor*, are details explained in Mr Cossart's admirably clear chapter on wine-making. At what stages, and how different wines are fortified, what are the many processes, from harvesting the grapes to resting the wine following the heating or *estufagem*, how it is racked or fined, are all points made amply clear. They add up to a memorable demonstration of the unique complexity of these wines.

Given these complexities, given in addition the rigorous checks and controls exercised today by officials of the Madeira Wine Institute, not to mention the exacting vigilance demanded of the winemaker himself at every stage of the creation of his product, it is of extraordinary interest to learn from Noël Cossart that he believed Madeira to be akin in many respects (and it is the only wine in the world of which such a claim could be made) to those Falernians drunk by the ancient Romans, beloved of Horace, described by Martial as *immortale* and *firmissima vina*. Those wines too were treated by heat in a way not unlike that evolved for the first *armazen de calor* warmed via flues heated by small open fires. The Romans used *amphorae* as containers for their wine, and warmed it in stores called *apothecae*. Mr Cossart explains that the light volcanic soil on which Madeira vines grow is again similar to that of the Sorrentine hills; that the *verdia* or *verdelho* grape, one of the important ones of the island vineyard, is the descendant of the one which made Falernian; and that the Romans cultivated their vines in terraced vineyards in which they were trained on frames supported by poles. The method was identical to that still used today in Madeira.

How agreeable a thought it is, that by the time of the East India

Company's great prosperity in the early part of the nineteenth century, the Madeira *estufa* system had been in use for several decades and the trade in wine to India such that the Company's warriors and governors, its Lords Auckland, Dalhousie, Wellesley, its chief justices, its civil servants – the young, lofty-minded Thomas Babington Macaulay among them – its eminent churchmen, men such as Bishop Heber of *From Greenland's Icy Mountains* fame, were all accustomed to drinking the loyal toast in Madeira wines which the empire builders, the poets, the law-givers, of ancient Rome's heyday would have appreciated as being related to the noble Falernian of their own world.

Tatler, June 1985

Letter to Gerald Asher

June 6th, 1984

Dearest Gerald

It was a most wonderful treat to see you. Lunch at the café Metro was delicious. Thank you for those *lovely* wines. David Levin is doing a real service with that place, although I could wish there were some way of ensuring that one could enjoy the wine and food without the cigar and cigarette smoke. I must admit that I hadn't experienced it there before, and I think we were unlucky. Anyway, isn't it a pleasure to be able to enjoy good white bur-gundy by the glass, rather than the usual wine bar badly-bought-and-badly-kept-near-but-not-near-enough Sancerre. Also it was a nice surprise to find that they're offering the excellent Beaumes de Venise there. The bad kind has become a plague here. I noted also that the last time I was in S.F. Alice [Waters] was serving grilled pigeon breasts marinated in B. de V. and very good too. I used up half a bottle not so long ago for cooking a piece of pork loin. It made the jelly delicious, whereas the wine was simply not for drinking . . .

Your salted and smoked tunny. Was it called *Tarantella*? That's the name I was trying to remember. I've come across it often in 16th and 17th c Italian books, but so far as I remember I've never encountered either the word (except as a Neapolitan and Caprese dance) or the substance itself in Italy.

Here is what Florio in his Italian-English dictionary, 1611, had to say: 'Tarantella, the utmost part of the belly, that covereth all the entrails, but now used for a kind of salt-fish-meat made of the paunch or belly pieces of the Tunny-fish, and so powdered (salted) and smoak-dryed, used much in Rome and other parts of Italy, to relish a cup of wine; used also for a young Tarantola.' The latter, by the way, was a stinging fly, not the deadly spider. Florio, who seldom fails to come up with some linguistic curiosity says that *tarantolato* and *tarantato* meaning 'stung or bitten with a tarantula' also meant 'pockified, or who hath gotten a clap, by met: a flea-bitten horse'.

A variant of *tarantella* or perhaps just an alternative name, was *sorra* (although maybe this was just salted, not smoked), and Scappi, Pope Pio Quinto's private cook, whose huge *Opera* was published in 1570, gives instructions for cooking both. First they had to be soaked in tepid water, then boiled with meal, *semola*, and when cooked, turned into cold water changed several times. Then it was cut into square mouthfuls, not too large and seasoned with oil, vinegar, boiled must or sugar and served with a *pasta cotta in vino sopra*. I'm not sure what that *pasta* was, perhaps the only edible part of the whole affair – anyway in another chapter Scappi gives a recipe for a *tarantello* pie, and for this it had to be *non rancido* and skinned, soaked for six hours, changing the water, and two more hours in wine, vinegar and boiled must. Then it was put into the crust with spices, sugar, chopped onions, prunes, dried cherries. Half way through cooking you poured in, through a hole in the top crust, some of the wine and must and vinegar marinade. The pie was served hot, but if you should want to keep it, you omitted the sauce.

What a lot of useless information. On the other hand I'm quite glad it *is* useless. I shouldn't want to be doing that tarantello pie very often.

Something about wine I intended to tell you. Sometime in April Richard [Olney] came over and gave a lunch party in a restaurant in Battersea, I think with the object of drinking up some wines he still had in some London cellar. His brother James was over here (I love him) and there were about fourteen people including Mrs T. S. Eliot, Jill [Norman] and her husband, a charming American woman from Time Life and her husband [Kit and Tony van Tulleken] – a couple so good looking, elegant and nice it isn't fair, and a whole lot of good and deserving people. Richard's wines were gorgeous and most especially something he gave us with the foie gras, what else? – a Coteaux du Layon 1928. It was divine. I wish you'd been there to drink it. Foie gras is not my scene, but it was justified with that wine. I do truly think the Coteaux du Layon would have been wrecked with anything sweet. Nothing else in the meal came up to the beginning. We had a fish – brill with a lot of sauce, and more of the Layon, then duck (horribly overcooked. If Richard had been in any other restaurant he would have torn the roof off) with a Pichon-Longueville 62, cheeses with Chateau Rausan Segla 1928. I liked that. Rausan Segla was about the first proper wine I ever drank. In the 30s I had an attic flat in Bloomsbury, and the Editor of the Morning Post, who was called H. A. Gwynne, known to us as Uncle Taffy, although only a remote cousin, used to come to dinner with me. 'I like your friends, and I don't mind climbing your stairs, but don't give me that half crown Chianti' he used to say. 'Here's a fiver. Go and buy something decent at the Army & Navy.' Fiver indeed. I could buy 1928 or perhaps it was 1925 Rausan Segla for 5/- a bottle. I don't know why I chose Rausan Segla but it was a success and of course with all that money it was very profitable having Uncle Taffy to dinner.

Yes, well, back to Richard's lunch. There was a Guiraud 42 with some kind of apple tart. (I haven't got that good a memory. It's just that I've kept the menu. On the cover there's a reproduction of one of those Reynolds children in a mob cap and sausage curls. I couldn't think why. But looking at it again I see it's called Simplicity . . .) Oh well, a simple lunch of ballotine de foie gras with a Layon 28 will do for me any day. But it was all so nice because Richard was really enjoying himself, no outbursts, and the mix worked. I sat next to a very nice American journalist on the Herald Trib. and opposite Mrs T S E, whom I like very much. I was feeling dreadfully ill and almost couldn't go because of the awful sores on my legs, but the good company and the good wine acted like magic.

Who has time to read a screed like this? My apologies and very much love

Elizabeth

Richard Olney's own account of this lunch is in his memoir, *Reflexions*, published by Brick Tower Press, New York, 2000.   JN

Epilogue

by Gerald Asher

In Paris last summer, on a day when there was no fresh basil to be had at the half-dozen or more greengrocers of my local street-market, I eventually found some – grown in England – at the branch of Marks & Spencer opposite the Printemps department store. For that I could thank Elizabeth David, of course, not the Common Market. Without her, Marks & Spencer wouldn't have been in the business of selling basil on Kensington High Street, let alone the Boulevard Haussmann.

It is difficult to exaggerate the part Elizabeth David played in everything and anything to do with food in Britain over the last forty years. Even those not directly concerned (a million or more copies of her books sold in the United Kingdom can hardly have reached every household) have nonetheless been affected by her influence on restaurateurs and other food writers and, most obviously, by the fresh herbs we now take for granted, by the abundance of spices available in any supermarket, by the ease with which we buy vegetables once considered exotic, and by the good cooking-pots and sharp knives in our kitchens. When we travel we are now likely to spend as much time browsing a country's markets and charcuteries as we do in museums and cathedrals. For all this we can thank Elizabeth David.

Born in 1913, Elizabeth David was one of four daughters of Rupert Gwynne, Conservative MP for Eastbourne, and Stella, daughter of the first Viscount Ridley. The Ridleys, at any rate, had long been of the political establishment. Not all of them have been as outspoken as that sixteenth-century Nicholas Ridley who denounced both Elizabeth and Mary as illegitimate, supported Lady Jane Grey, and eventually found himself burned with Cranmer and Latimer opposite Balliol College, Oxford.

But they have included, in our own time, Lord Hailsham, the former Lord Chancellor and Stella Ridley's cousin, and Nicholas Ridley, Mrs Thatcher's sometimes tactless ally, a cousin of Elizabeth David's own generation.

Sent straight from boarding school at sixteen to live with a French family and study at the Sorbonne, she was later to descibe

her hosts, the Robertots, as 'both exceptionally greedy and exceptionally well fed'. She realised, though, once she had returned to England, that they had been only too successful in imbuing her with the essential spirit of French culture.

'Forgotten were the Sorbonne professors and the yards of Racine learnt by heart, the ground-plans of cathedrals I had never seen, and the saga of Napoleon's last days on St Helena,' she wrote in her book *French Provincial Cooking*. 'What had stuck was the taste for a kind of food quite ideally unlike anything I had known before. Ever since, I have been trying to catch up with those lost days when perhaps I should have been more profitably employed watching Léontine [her hosts' cook] in her kitchen rather than trudging conscientiously round every museum and picture gallery in Paris.'

A dazzlingly beautiful young woman, she worked for a while as a *vendeuse* for Worth, and after a spell at the Oxford rep, acted in the Open Air Theatre in Regent's Park. In the late 1930s, by way of Capri and a visit to the writer Norman Douglas, she went to live, not unaccompanied, on a Greek island and was in due course evacuated with a clutch of other British expatriates – it included Lawrence Durrell, Xan Fielding, Patrick Leigh Fermor and Olivia Manning. She escaped to Egypt as Crete fell to the Germans, and spent the war years there as Librarian to the Ministry of Information's Cairo office. In 1944 she married Anthony David, a British Army officer whom she followed to India in 1945. The marriage didn't last, and she returned to a very cold and severely rationed Britain in 1946.

A Book of Mediterranean Food (John Lehmann, the publisher, had wanted to call it *Le Train Bleu* or some such) was as much a reaction, an act of revolt, as anything else. It was published, with evocative woodcuts by John Minton, in 1950 and was followed in rapid succession by *French Country Cooking* (1951), *Italian Food* (1954), *Summer Cooking* (1955), and *French Provincial Cooking* (1960). Together with her articles in *Vogue*, *House & Garden*, *The Sunday Times* and *The Spectator*, those books did more than remind post-war Britain of a world beyond Dover, margarine and a diet originally pulled together to meet siege conditions. In sharpening British appetites for olives and apricots and much else long since forgotten, she succeeded in expanding, indeed reviving, a taste for life itself.

A natural and scrupulous scholar, Elizabeth David also used to good effect the painter's eye with which she was blessed. Capturing the look of a dish or the atmosphere of a town in a few words, she could seize her reader's attention and lead him deep into her subject, a technique reinforced, in any case, by her fresh, informed and irresistibly forthright views. Just one passage, taken from her introduction to Languedoc cooking, shows how she composed what she wrote, much as a shrewd cook builds a menu in tempting steps from *amuse-gueule* to *pièce de résistance*.

'A bottle of cooled white wine is already in front of you,' she begins tantalisingly, 'and from the big table in the centre of the restaurant a waiter brings hors-d'oeuvre to keep you amused and occupied while more serious dishes are being prepared ... quantities of little prawns, freshly boiled, with just the right amount of salt, and a most stimulating smell of the sea into the bargain, heaped up in a big yellow bowl; another bowl filled with green olives; good salty bread; and a positive monolith of butter, towering up from a wooden board.'

From the appeal of the bowls and the confidence she thinks anyone might place in whoever had had the taste to choose them, she moves deftly into a careful review of the dish that followed: langouste in a garlic-scented sauce of tomato and brandy. Her scholarship, enhanced by entertainingly appropriate digressions, is impeccable; her sources are cited elegantly ('these facts are all on record and can be read in M Robert Courtine's book, *Le Plus Doux des Péchés*') and her clarity and wit engage even those with, as yet, no intention of surrending their tin-openers. Then, inevitably and willy-nilly, even they catch her enthusiasm as she pokes around for the origin of the dish, holding its name to the light to unravel its history; they, too, share her curiosity about the restaurant's own version of it; and then, with interest fully piqued, their fingers will fly through the pages to find the actual recipe at the merest mention of where it might be.

Her activities broadened. In 1965 she had opened a kitchen shop in Pimlico – a model for hundreds that have followed, both here and in the United States – and by the time *Spices, Salt and Aromatics in the English Kitchen* (1970) and *English Bread and Yeast Cookery* (1977) were published, the scholar had taken over from the travelling journalist – as, by then, was to be expected. Elizabeth David had severed all connection with the shop by 1973, but she was still there on the day in 1970 when I dropped in to say goodbye, literally on my way to the airport. I was leaving

London to live and work in New York and I knew I would miss her.

Our meetings over the next several years were indeed few and brief, but in 1982, by which time I was living in San Francisco, she came to stay for a while. It was her first visit to California and I took her to Yosemite and the old gold-mining towns of the Sierra, where she was quick to uncover remnants of the nineteenth-century ice trade. She was enchanted by California, and returned again every year – sometimes for a month, sometimes for two – until a badly broken leg last year made travel impossible.

I had known her well in London, but it was in California that I got to know her best. We spent much time together on our own. Her daily routine was to read and write in bed in the mornings while I worked alone in a secluded office hidden behind my kitchen, but we always sat for an hour or two over a late lunch, either at home (usually little more than a slice or two of a local prosciutto, some cheese, a few *gaeta* olives and a bottle of wine) or at one of the two or three San Francisco restaurants she most liked. She appreciated the calm, the light, the views across the city's hills and the bay – and San Francisco bread.

Though she didn't seem much impressed by California's home-grown cheeses, she enjoyed California wines and took a great interest in the young restaurateurs of San Francisco, for whom she had long been a cult figure. (Judy Rogers, the chef at Zuni, one of the city's best and most popular restaurants, asked once in an interview whether her cooking style was more French than Italian, replied, after a second's thought, that it wasn't either really; it was Elizabeth David.) She enjoyed the enormous choice of fruits and vegetables we have on the West Coast and would ask about them often. I remember how amused she was once when we had driven down the coast to lunch at Pescadero, a fishing village between Half Moon Bay and Santa Cruz. It was November, very bright but chilly, and we ordered the hot pumpkin soup-of-the-day. Knowing that the farms around Half Moon Bay were well known for their pumpkins (there is a Pumpkin Festival there every year), she was curious to find out what variety of pumpkin would have been used for the soup. The waitress had no difficulty telling her. 'Oh, that was our Halloween pumpkin,' she said brightly and whisked busily away.

Though Elizabeth David's reputation was bound up with the Mediterranean ('Let's look it up in Braudel' was her answer to most questions) and her favourite dishes, at least in these last few years, were Lebanese, she was just as much an enthusiast for British food. I remember it was she who first introduced me, many years ago, to an Arbroath Smokie; and the treats she most enjoyed recently were good Scotch smoked salmon and farmhouse cheddar. I spent most of last Thursday with her. It was a visit much like any other except that she couldn't move very much. We ate a little together ('I think there's some caviar in the downstairs fridge,' she said); we drank a little ('I need a bottle of good Chablis'); and we laughed quite a lot. She was surprised that I couldn't pick up an allusion she made to Sir Philip Sidney. 'Look it up,' she said, 'I might not have got it right.' I pulled the *Chambers Biographical* off the shelf. 'It doesn't help much,' I told her. 'There's nothing here about a glass of water.' We were both still wondering about Sir Philip Sidney's glass of water when I kissed her before leaving. She knew I would be coming back to London to see her on Tuesday. 'I'll look it up before then,' I promised.

Obituary published in the *Independent*, May 1992

Bibliography

A Book of Mediterranean Food
First published by John Lehmann 1950. Revised editions 1955,
1958, 1965, 1988. New introduction 1991
Copyright © The Estate of Elizabeth David 1950, 1955, 1958,
1965, 1988, 1991

French Country Cooking
First published by John Lehmann 1951. Revised editions 1958,
1966
Copyright © The Estate of Elizabeth David 1951, 1958, 1966

Italian Food
First published by Macdonald and Co 1954. Revised editions
1963, 1969, 1977, 1987
Copyright © The Estate of Elizabeth David 1954, 1963, 1969,
1977, 1987

Summer Cooking
First published by Museum Press 1955. Revised edition 1965
Copyright © The Estate of Elizabeth David 1955, 1965

French Provincial Cooking
First published by Michael Joseph Ltd 1960. Revised editions
1965, 1967, 1970
Copyright © The Estate of Elizabeth David 1960, 1965, 1967,
1970

Spices, Salt and Aromatics in the English Kitchen
First published by Penguin Books 1970. Revised editions 1973,
1975
Copyright © The Estate of Elizabeth David 1970, 1973, 1975

English Bread and Yeast Cookery
First published by Allen Lane 1977
Copyright © The Estate of Elizabeth David 1977

An Omelette and a Glass of Wine
First published by Jill Norman at Robert Hale Ltd 1984
Copyright © The Estate of Elizabeth David 1984

Harvest of the Cold Months
First published by Michael Joseph Ltd 1994
Copyright © The Estate of Elizabeth David 1994

South Wind through the Kitchen: The Best of Elizabeth David
compiled by Jill Norman
First published by Michael Joseph Ltd 1997
Text copyright © The Estate of Elizabeth David

Index